# THE MOTHERS
## OF THE BELIEVERS

## WIVES OF PROPHET MUHAMMAD (SAW)

## HALIME DEMIREŞIK

1. Baskı

**İstanbul, Agust- 2012**

Transleted/Recadtor  : Elif Kapıcı

Editing            : Melek Zeynep Oyludağ/Aslı Tarası
Publishing         : Ömer Faruk Demireşik
Typeset-Cover      : Songrafik Tasarım

İSTANBUL, 2012

## About Halime Demiresik

She was born in Denizli, Turkey in June of 1978. She finished Imam Hatip High School in 1995. While completing Divinity Seminary, she worked as an educator for the the schools sponsored by the Aziz Mahmud Hudayi Wakf (Foundation) for 15 years. During this time, in both Turkey and other countries, she made conferences and seminars about the life of the Prophet Muhammad (saw); increasing affection for him; and the family life in Islam.

In the year 2011, she was given the "Service to the Prophet's Life" Award by the Surayya Anne Foundation in America. She has written many articles and interviews which were printed in the "Altınoluk", "Yuvamız", "Bahçevan" and "Şebnem" Magazines in Turkey.

She has seven books published in Turkey: *"Vakıflara Hayat Veren Vâlide Sultanlar (2003)"*, *"Hanım Gözüyle Mü'minlerin Anneleri" (2008)*, *"Muhabbeti, Hz. Muhammed (s.a.v.)'e Adamak" (2009)*, *"21. yüzyıldan Cennete Koşan Hanımlar" (2009)*, *"Ben, O'nu Sevmeye Muhtacım" (2009)*, *"Dostun Divanına" (2009)*, *"Kalbimiz Aşk Ateşinde" (2012)*. The book "Muhabbeti Hz. Muhammed'e Adamak" has been translated into the Azeri language.

The book **"The Mothers of the Believers"** is her first book translated into English.

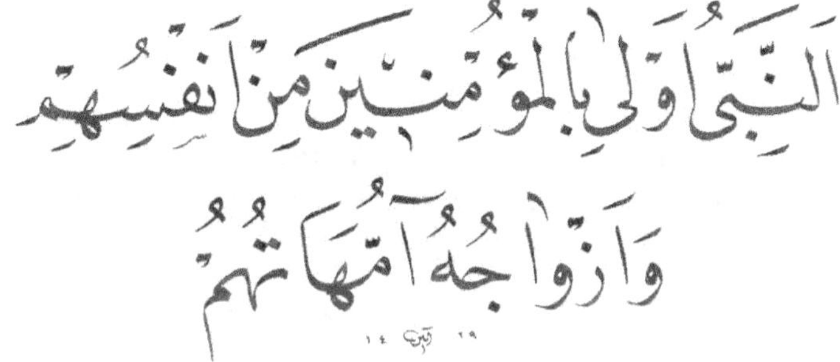



*"The Prophet is closer to the believers than their own selves, and his wives are their mothers."*

(Surah al-Ahzab, 33:6)

# PEACE AND BLESSINGS TO THE "EHL-İ BEYT"

Nakkuş explains:

**"It is not proper for you to annoy the Prophet nor marry his wives after him..."** (Ahzâb, 53) after this ayet was revealed Prophet Muhammad (saw) stood up and said:

"Oh you group of believers! Certainly Allah has put me above you in every way, and He made my wives higher that your wives" (Kadı İyaz, Şifâ-i Şerif, Trans: Naim Erdoğan-Hüseyin S. Erdoğan, Bedir Publishing, pg: 176)

* * *

The Rasûlullâh -sallâllâhu aleyhi ve sellem- said:

*"All of you say this: «Allâhümme salli alâ Muhammedin ve ezvâcihî ve zürriyyâtihî kemâ salleyte alâ ibrâhime. Ve bârik alâ Muhammedin ve ezvâcihî ve zürriyyâtihî kemâ bârekte alâ İbrâhime. İnneke hamîdün mecîd.» (Meaning: Allah!... Send your blessings to the Prophet Muhammad (saw) and his wives and lineage like you sent to Hz. Abraham. Also make the Prophet Muhammad (saw) and he wives and family holy in the same way that you did Hz. Abraham Surely, you are the owner of all the praise and honor.)"* (Buhârî, Kitâbu'l-Enbiyâ, 10; Müslim, Kitâbu's-Salât, 17)

* * *

Abû Hüraira reported that Allah's Prophet said: *"He who wants to be glad by taking the great reward of giving blessings and peace to us; the Ehl-i Bayt; should say this: «Allâhümme salli alâ Muhammedi'n-Nebiyyi ve ezvâcihî ümmehâti'l-mü'minîne ve zürriyyetihî ve ehli beytihî kemâ salleyte alâ İbrâhime. İnneke hamîdün mecîd.»"* (Ebû Dâvud, Kitâbu's-Salât, Bâbu's-Salâti Alâ'n-Nebiyy)

Dedication:

Only for him, the one I love the most, the Beloved!..

* * *

To the one whom Hz. Hatice yearned for through out her years; to the unique pearl which caused Hazret-i Âişe to be jealous of her own eyes; to the love of Hazret-i Ümmü Habîbe; to the Prophet husband of Hz. Mâriye; to Allah's messenger...

* * *

To the greatest masterpiece of Allah's (swt) wonder, who was sent by Allah (swt) to mankind as a "Mercy to the Universe" and to the Believers as the "Greatest Example"; to the Greatest Prophet, to the Perfect Head of the Family, and to the Most Loved Messenger...

to the high souls of his pure wives and the Ehl-i Bayt (his extended family)...

* * *

In spite of all my imperfections and mistakes, I hope this book will be the means to earn his high intercession...

**as**   **:** *'Alaihi as-Salam; peace and blessings be upon him*

         *'Alaiha as-Salaam; peace and blessings be upon her,*

         *'Alaihum as-Salaam; peace and blessings be upon them.*

**saw**  **:** *Salla Allahu 'alaihi wa Sallam"*;
         may the blessing and the peace of Allah be upon him.

**r.ah**  **:** *"Radıy Allahu Anha"*; may Allah be pleased with her

**r.a**   **:** *"Radıyallahu anh"*; may Allah be pleased with him

# INTRODUCTION

*Limitless praises and thanks to our great Protector who bestowed upon us the honor of being in the Ummah (community) of Muhammad Mustafa (saw) who is the crown of the all the Prophets and was given the title Habîbullâh (Allah's Beloved)!*

*Limitless peace and blessings upon our Master, the Honorable Muhammad Mustafa (saw) who was sent as an eternal mercy to all the universe and as a deliverer, healer (of body and soul), guide, messenger of good news, intercessor, and boundless honor of the creation!*

Allah, the "All-Mighty", bestowed Islam, the final and most perfect religion, through the means of the Honorable Muhammad Mustafa (saw) who is the Mercy to the Universe.

That great Prophet, through every behavior and word, is the **"üsve-i hasene"** or the greatest example to all of mankind. About this Allah, the All-Mighty, declared:

**"Indeed you have in the Prophet of Allah a exceelnt exemplar and who remembers Allah much."** (Ahzâb, 21)

Allah, the All-Mighty, made him begin as an orphan, the one who holds the lowest rank in society due to their innate weakness; then he raised him through all of the ranks of life to the level of Commander of State and Prophet, which is the highest point of authority.

The stages in which our Master lived his life show the many ideal models of behavior required for every type of high and low that manifests in a human's life. For this reason his life became an actual, concrete and perfect example to every human who finds themselves in any of these stages and conditions; they can copy him according to their strength and ability. He, with these qualifications, is a unique masterpiece and the greatest favor and gift for humanity from Allah, the All-Mighty.

One of the most important characteristics which form a perfect and concrete example of the Prophet Muhammad (saw) is the way he lived his family life. He established a superior, most virtuous and happiest home with his wives who had different ages, cultures, abilities and characters.

That home that he established was so full of patience and beauty that the scent of happiness covered them even though, for days, they were not able to cook a single hot meal (due to lack of food).  In addition, in that holy home, the room of each wife was merely a place to lay one's head. However, in that home the most delicious provisions were acceptance, patience, and submission.  His education method that he practiced in his family life filled their hearts with a limitless devotion and affection.  No wife can love their husband to the degree that the Holy Mothers loved the Prophet (saw).  No husband can love his wife to the degree of the Messenger's love for his holy wives.  No child can love his or her father to the degree that Hz. Fatima loved her father.  No father can love their child as much as Allah's Messenger loved Hz. Fatima. This is also true for grandchildren...

Our mother Hz. Fatima, the apple of the eye of the Ehl- Bayt, who was one of the rare roses of this exceptional rose garden, means many things to the mothers and fathers these days: her life was short but adorned with taqwa, the awareness of Allah (swt).  She shows them, in a lively way, that raising a child required a big effort and responsibility and that the children's futures where in Allah's hands.

The only purpose in that spiritual home; which had between its members a sense of deep affection, sacrifice, and attachment; was the reaching of Allah's acceptance.  İn that home the biggest worry was about losing Allah's (swt) and His Messenger's (saw) affection and acceptance.

The Prophet's (saw) exceptional wives, were the recipient of the honor of being the "Mothers of the Believers" by Allah's command. They observed the Prophet (saw) as he received the inspirations of Quran, and while he was praying, while he was reading Quran, eating, speaking, and sleeping: shortly, in every point of life, they were cognizant of his spiritual mysteries which were far from all other eyes.

They past their lives with the sensitivity of deserving this big honor and virtue and they became, to the women of the ummah (community), the best guides and teachers. Thousands of hadiths were reported from them which explain the characteristics, attitude and sunnet (actions and sayings) of the Prophet (saw).

The book that is in your hands; which tells the story of the perfect human and family head, and also that of his family life and his wives; is like the summary of this very important and detailed subject.

In society today; where many social and family problems are lived and divorce increases day by day, and the struggling children of these broken homes increase; we need to know the holy and model home of the Prophet (saw) very much: to the degree that we can smell the compassion, mercy, peace and inspiration!

I congratulate my valuable student Halime Demiresik who prepared this book and I hope that it will fill an important emptiness. I pray to Cenab-i Hakk that this book is a means to family happiness and many goodnesses.

**O Allah! Bestow upon us and our families a taqwa life that will be based on service and obedience to you and with which you are pleased!**

**Bestow upon our homes shares from the spiritual matter of the Prophet's (saw) family life and from the Ehl-i Bayt's politeness, elegance, and spiritual depth!**

**Our Lord... Make our Prophet (saw); who made up the color, shape, harmony, feelings, thoughts, delights of the Mu'min; and his exceptional family home, the best guides for us!**

**Fill our homes with the peace, happiness and affection of the home of**

**the Prophet (saw) and grant us a share from that climate of happiness which is from your favor and generousity!**

**Âmîn!..**

**Osman Nûri TOPBAŞ**

August 8, 2008

Üsküdar/İSTANBUL

# PREFACE

Limitless praise and thanks to Allah, the All-Mighty, who created us and made us know his existance, and by giving us the honor of iman (faith) and the blessing of Islam, made us the most honored of creation.

In the amount of all the breaths of creation we send blessings and praise upon the "Habîb-i Edîb" (Well-Mannered, Beloved) and the "Rasûl-i Necîb" (Beloved Messenger of Allah); Hz. Muhammed Mustafa: also to his family, the Ehl-i Bayt and his holy companions.

* * *

I can say as a "tahdis-i nimet" (an admitance of Allah's blessings) the part of my life after 1997 completely passed trying to understand and explain the life of the Prophet (saw).

Surely, this cannot be considered a small amount of time in any human's life. However, when the one who is to be understood and explained is the Beloved of Allah (swt); Muhammad Mustafa (saw); even if thousands of lives are added to this lifetime, it cannot be explained thoroughly. This is because he cannot be understood with only the mind and cannot be described only through words. This is also because in order to be closer to him, and in order to feel him, it is neccesary to live in the same era and breath the same air as him; and absorb the energy of his conversations. For this reason, no one can be equal to the Sahaba (companions) who saw the Prophet (saw) as a Muslim for even one minute and spent with him a little time and took in such an energy from his lessons[1].

As a result of such togetherness, there is a very important position of the "Ehl-i Bayt" and the "ezvac-i tahirat" (Pure Wives) among those distinguished people who reached the level of perfection with Prophet's (saw) oversight and special training. In the same way that that every drop of water from a river that falls over the waterfall keeps the taste of the river, so to when you research the people around the Prophet (saw) you smell and taste the flavor of the river of Jennah. It is as if every child whose head was rubbed by him continues to spread the sweet smells to the human beings until the last day. It is as if every person to whose face he smiled becomes a messenger of peace and happiness to mankind. Every beloved one who in any way found a place in his pure heart, they become like a full moon that lights up the night and thus lights up the lonely and hurt hearts of the believers.

We, in our book, humbly invited the family members of Allah's most Beloved to our pages. In fact, we became guests to their hearts. We tried to make a prescription for our times from their lives full of messages, lessons, and wisdoms.

This is because we are burning in the fire of ignorance like thirsty people who are roasting in the desert. The life-giving water gushed and is still gushing from his holy fingers.

This is because we are like the little girls who were buried under the earth alive. If his heart that is full of compassion and mercy does not pull us from the dirt of the this age, we will cease to exist.

This is because we are like the passengers who lost their way in the darkness. If his nur (holy light) does not light up our way, we will finish our life on a dead end street.

---

1. Of course this general rule doesn't include the prophets to whom Allah choose and gave honor with the duty of being a Prophet and a Messenger. All of the prophets, whether they recieved a Holy book or not, are above all of the other humans. Among these prophets, our Prophet Muhammad (saw), has a different virtue, ascendency and dignity. Prophet Muhammad's (saw) community is more virtuous than the other Prophet's community, and within this community the Sahaba (companions) are more virtuous than the other Muslims.

Thus to not be lost on these dead end streets is only possible by knowing the sun of two worlds (this world and the afterlife) and his exemplary life in every way and following him step by step. However, unfortunately there is a truth that I had seen either in my lessons or in my travels here and abroad: we, the Muslim women, do not know exactly the lives of the Prophet (saw), his wives and his family. How was the Prophet (saw) in his home? How was he behaving toward his wives? Who were his wives? What sort of characteristics; differences and similarities; were there? Were there any conflicts or disagreements between the Prophet (saw) and his wives? And when they disagreed, how did they solve the issues? In short, what sort of lessons and examples for our family and social lives, which are shaky these days, is it possible to take from the Prophet's (saw) exemplary life?

Thus, we tried to prepare our book around questions such as these. Surely, this work is not a perfect work far from every type of exclusion and omission, but we tried our best and tried not to make any conscious mistakes. Our request from our readers who research the book is to share their opinions and evaluations, and help us to minimize any mistakes for the next edition.

With this I consider it a duty to present my most sincere gratitude and thanks to my esteemed teacher, **Osman Nûri Topbaş Hocaefendi,** who taught us about the Prophet (saw),  his distinguished companions and the valuable Ehl-i Bayt, and made us love them and drew us in this direction.  May Allah grant him a long life full of goodness, make him successful in doing many good services, and make us worthy students of him.

In addition, I want to thank my very precious mother Fikriye and father Nuri Cil, who raised me and did their best for my religious education; to the ladies Elif Kapici, Melek Oyludağ and Asli Tarasi who helped the book to be translated from Turkish to English; to my precious life companion and husband, Ömer Faruk Demireşik, who did not begrudge me his support in every stage; and to my daughters, Rukiye Rahmet ve Âmine Meryem Demireşik, who tolerated my being busy with patience.

Lastly, we hope that our book, which reached the publication in the tens of thousands in Turkey and from which benefit was taken, reaches many readers in every age and every nation; woman and men; by being translated into a world language, and to be a means to guidance to Islam. May our Lord give a blessing to our hope and effort with his favor and in his generousity and may our book be a means to a spiritual cure from the Prophet (saw) to the members, families and societies suffering from great crises. The effort is from us, the success is from Allah.

* * *

Oh Allah! Help us to understand and explain your beautiful religion and the last and the highest Prophet (saw)! Make us an ummah worthy of the Prophet's (saw) glory. On the judgement day grant us the right to drink from the Kawther (pool) of the Prophet (saw) and to meet with him under his flag of praise! Amin!

**Halime DEMİREŞİK**
July 14, 2012
24 Şaban 1433
Eyüp/İstanbul

# FOREWORD

*Oh Prophet! Say to thy consorts: "If it be that you desire the life of this world and its glitter; then come! I will provide for your enjoyment and set you free in a handsome manner. But if ye seek Allah and His Messenger (saw), and the home in the Hereafter; verily Allah has prepared for the well-doers amongst you a great reward."* (Ahzab, 33 28-29)

It is with utmost joy that I have read this compilation on the blessed lives of the *Ummahatul Mumineen* (Mothers of the Believers). This book presents to us a glimpse of the character and virtues of the chaste wives of our Holy Prophet (saw), in a straightforward yet comprehensive manner; so that both Muslims as well as non-Muslims will be able to see for themselves the simplicity and the nobility of the Blessed Mothers of Islam. This book likewise seeks to inform us how their marital relations with our Holy Prophet (saw) had produced profound spiritual transformation in each *Ummahatul Mumineen's* inner spirit.

I deeply feel that there is a great need to objectively understand and honestly evaluate the circumstances surrounding Prophet Muhammad's (saw) marriage to each of these blessed souls so that all truth-seekers will, with unprejudiced eyes, see the Divine Wisdom inherent in these matrimonial unions. To a great extent, this book will help remove biased misrepresentations against the person of our Holy Prophet (saw). The facts contained in this book will stop all slanderous attacks against his blessed marriages, by showing the historical contextualities and the divine rationale for each marriage. If the reader is open to the manifestation of the truth, he will see that Almighty Allah arranged these marriages through his Divine Predestination since He himself declared His unequivocal assent of such unions in many passages of the Holy *Qur'ân* and in sacred *hadiths* (*hadith qudsi*).

The Mothers of the Believers were the helpmates of our Holy Prophet (saw) in the propagation of the Islamic way of life; by both their words and examples. Their lives of utter simplicity and sincere spirituality were perfect models of what Islam -as submission and surrender to Allah Almighty- truly stands for. Likewise, their lives effectively exemplify their unconditional love and utmost dedication to the Holy Prophet (saw). The holy wives of our Prophet Muhammad (saw) are potent proofs that women are dignified members of the *Ummah* (Islamic community) and that they are effective partners in the dissemination of Islam to the whole wide world.

I fervently pray that this book will be widely distributed to all honest seekers since by reflecting upon its pages, one will discover the beauty of genuine Islamic conduct. May this book hopefully dispel misconceptions that the uninformed have concerning our Muslim faith. May we, the readers meditate on the spirituality of the mothers of the faithful; thereby adorning our inner souls with godly attributes as manifested in their lives of piety, humility and benevolence. Ameen!

Prof. Henry Francis (Abdil Ghaffar) B. Espiritu

18 Jumada-al-Akhir 1432 AH / 21 May 2011 AD

# FOREWORD

This book gives us a glimpse at the lives of a generation of women who inadvertently found themselves to be the examples, leaders, and mother-figures for an entire community through a period of extremely rapid social change and religious reform. Mother's, home-makers, business owners, teachers, trades-women; they share all of the same roles that women are fulfilling today, and they did it with class and grace. In today's world, where women are finding themselves struggling to maintain their modesty, dignity, and self-esteem, these women can still be held upon a pedestal as pioneers of women's equality and freedom. Much has been said of the "oppression" that Islam places on women, and this book flies in the face of those arguments.

They indeed were all raised to the status of the "Mothers of the Believers" for a reason; and the following book offers a glimpse into their most intimate lives in order to explain why and how this was possible in a patriarchal society which placed no value on women at all. This book is a timely breath of fresh air for women of the Muslim faith, as well as for those who are not, as it teaches and touches on the most intimate details of married life and spousal relationships. It is a recommended read for all women; married, getting married, or getting re-married.

Melek Zeynep Oyludag

5 August 2012

# -I-

# THE MOTHERS
# OF THE BELIEVERS

# BEING THE WIFE OF THE HOLY PROPHET (saw)

If we were to live in the era of the Holy Prophet (*saw*[2]), breathing the same air and walking in the same streets; just what wouldn't we do to be close to him (saw)?

Wouldn't we submit all that we own to him? Wouldn't we say regarding our beloved elders *"O Prophet of Allah[3]! I would forgo my parents for you!";* or for our children *"Here O Prophet of Allah! This is my sole sweetheart, and I dedicate him to you!";* or wouldn't we even submit ourselves, saying *"I too, belong to you along with all my possessions!"*

This was the state of the wives of the Holy Prophet (saw). Before all else, in order to acquire the honour of *imân[4]*, they sacrificed everything that they had; their families, their beloved ones , friends, the countries they were born and bred into, as well as any physical comfort and opulence they had.

Then they married the Prophet of Allah (saw). It wasn't affluence that greeted them. Their home was a tiny room each consisting of four clay walls, and their sustenance was sometimes only a piece of dry bread, sometimes a glass of milk or a handful of dates.

---

2.  These letters are abbreviations for the words *"Salla Allahu 'Alaihi Wa Sallam"*, which means: may the blessing and the peace of Allah be upon him. When the name of Prophet Muhammad is mentioned, a Muslim is to respect him and invoke this statement of peace upon him.
3.  It is a known fact that every language has one or more terms that are used in reference to God and sometimes to lesser deities. This is not the case with *Allah*. *Allah* is the personal name of the One true God. Nothing else can be called *Allah*. The term has no plural or gender. This shows its uniqueness when compared with the word god, which can be made plural; gods, or feminine; goddess.
4.  *Iman* is trust, faith and acceptance. Having faith and belief in Allah according to the *Holy Qur'an*.

They turned their back on all worldly adornments for the sake of the Holy Prophet (saw). They chose Allah and his Prophet (saw).[5]

They saw the Prophet of Allah (saw) as a slave of Allah, as a human being, and as a Prophet; while he prayed, read the *Qur'ân*[6], laughed, shed tears and implored his Lord in the night.

They sensed the verses being revealed to the Holy Prophet (saw). Sometimes they saw *Jibrâ'êl*[7] (as[8]) visit the Prophet (saw) in the form of a man, and their homes brimmed with *nur*[9] -light-.[10]

Sometimes the Holy Prophet (saw) received revelations when they were at home; they witnessed how he perspired and how he became grave during these moments.

They had many co-wives, who were all from different tribes, and even from different nations, with different features and ages. They all had to share their most beloved with the others.

They were obliged to open their doors, even their hearts, to anyone at any moment. They had to share their food and their knowledge; without sending anyone away empty-handed.

---

5. "O Prophet! Say unto thy wives: If ye desire the world's life and its adornment, come! I will content you and will release you with a fair release. But if ye desire Allah and His messenger and the abode of the Hereafter, then lo! Allah hath prepared for the good among you an immense reward." (Surah Al-Ahzab 33: 28-29)

6. The *Quran* is a record of the exact words revealed by God through the Angel *Jibreel* -Gabriel- (AS) to the Prophet Muhammad (saw). It was memorized by Muhammad (saw) and then dictated to his Companions, and written down by scribes, who cross-checked it during his lifetime. Not one word of its 114 chapters, *Suras*, has been changed over the centuries, so that the *Quran* is in every detail the unique and miraculous text which was revealed to Muhammad (saw) fourteen centuries ago.

7. *Jibreel* (Gabriel) (as) is the angel through whom Allah conveyed his words to his prophets. He is also known as *Ar Ruh al-Qudus* (The Holy Spirit).

8. *Alaihi Salaam* - peace be upon him, *Alaiha Salaam* - peace be upon her, *Alaihum Salaam* - peace be upon them. This should always be said whenever mentioning any of the Prophets from Adam through to Jesus, or any of the women regarded as being the most notable women created (e.g. Eve, wife of Adam; Hajar, wife of Ibrahim).

9. *Nur* is the heavenly light or divine radiance bestowed upon all Prophets, and carried on within their families, until the last of the Prophets (saw). *Nur* can also be present in any devout muslim, since *salah* -prayer-, *wudu'*-ablution- and any kind of worship to Allah the Almighty, bestows *nur* on them. *Nur*, "The light", is also one of the ninety-nine attributes of Allah. (Surah An-Nur [24]/35-36).

10. "(O wives of the Prophet!) And recite what is rehearsed to you in your homes, of the Signs of Allah and His Wisdom: for Allah understands the finest mysteries and is well-acquainted (with them). (Surah Al-Ahzab 33:34)"

Being the *Ummuhât al Mu'minîn* -Mothers of the Faithful-[11], they embraced all believers indeed like mothers; they sheltered orphans, they reached out to the poor, the abandoned, and the needy; they educated the illiterate and fostered the children.

In order to preserve themselves, as well as preserving the ones they spoke to; they made it clear that they were out of the ordinary; they also felt this way. They spoke to their male guests from behind a curtain[12]; they remained in their homes[13] and desisted from immodest dressing.[14]

They were steadfast in their *salah[15]* -prayer-; they abided their compulsory fasting, and they fasted voluntarily for a multitude of days; they gave away charity and their *zakah[16]* in abundance.

They dared to stand close to the Holy Prophet (saw) even in the battle fields; fearing the possibility of his death, injury or captivity.

They were aware of the fact that, the reward or punishment they would receive in the hereafter would be doubled, because of their position.[17] Accord-

---

11. *Ummul Mu'mineen* means "the Mother of the Faithful". It is a title given to each of the wives of the Holy Prophet (saw). "The Prophet is closer to the Believers than their own selves, and his wives are their mothers..." (Surah al-Ahzab, 33: 6).

12. "...And when ye ask of them (the wives of the Prophet) anything, ask it of them from behind a curtain. That is purer for your hearts and for their hearts..." (Surah al-Ahzab, 33: 53)

13. "O ye wives of the Prophet! You are not like any other women. If ye keep your duty (to Allah), then be not soft of speech, lest he in whose heart is a disease aspire (to you), but utter customary speech." (Surah al-Ahzab, 33: 32)

14. "And stay in your houses and do not display your finery like the displaying of the ignorance of yore; and keep up prayer, and pay the poor-rate, and obey Allah and His Messenger. Allah only desires to keep away the uncleanness from you, O people of the House! and to purify you a (thorough) purifying." (Surah al-Ahzab, 33: 33)

15. *Salat* is the name for the obligatory prayers which are performed five times a day, and are a direct link between the worshiper and Allah. There is no hierarchical authority in Islam, and no priests, so the prayers are led by a learned person who knows the *Quran*, chosen by the congregation. These five prayers contain verses from the *Quran*, and are said in Arabic, the language of the Revelation. Prayers are said at dawn, noon, mid-afternoon, sunset and nightfall, and thus determine the rhythm of the entire day. Although it is preferable to worship together in a mosque, a Muslim may pray almost anywhere. Prayers are performed towards Makkah.

16. *Zakah* (Purifying Alms) literally means purification, whence it is used to express a portion of property bestowed in alms, as a means of purifying the person concerned and the remainder of his property. It is among the five pillars of Islam and refers to the mandatory amount that a Muslim must pay out of his property. The detailed rules of *zakah* have been laid down in books of *Fiqh*.

17. "O wives of the prophet! Whoever of you commits an open indecency, the punishment shall be

ingly, they enjoyed immaculate lives, full of integrity and righteousness.

They were besides the Holy Prophet (saw) in his last moments; wiping the sweat from his forehead, cooling his fever with water, and trying to soothe his pain, while they shed tears.

They rendered their homes a resting place for the Holy Prophet (saw), until *Qiyâmah*[18] (the Day of Judgement).

They lived a life full of *îmân* (faith), *taqwa*[19] (piety), knowledge, virtue, honour and grace, and they reached their Lord in this state.

May Allah the Almighty be pleased with them, and may they be pleased with us. Amîn.

---

increased to her doubly; and this is easy to Allah. And whoever of you is obedient to Allah and His Messenger and does good, We will give to her her reward doubly, and We have prepared for her an honourable sustenance." (Surah al-Ahzab, 33: 30-31)

18.   *Qiyaamah* (the Day of Resurrection, also referred to as *Yawm al-Qiyaamah* and *Yawm ad-Din* 'the Day of Faith') is the day when all mankind will be brought forth to answer for their deeds. It will consist of a sequence of events, namely; the annihilation of all creatures, resurrection of the body and the judgment of all sentient creatures. Final judgment forms one of the main themes of the Qur'an. *al-Qiyaamah* is also the name of the 75th *surah* of the Qur'an.

19.   *Taqwa* denotes fear of Allah, being careful and knowing one's place in the cosmos. Its proof is the experience of awe, of Allah, which inspires a person to be on guard against wrong action and eager for actions pleasing to Allah. Fearing Allah as He should be feared is one of the major signs of being a faithful Muslim. Piety and restraint (through *Taqwa*) in times of hardship are signs of having achieved the essence and spirit of Islam, and thus Allah's blessing. (Ali Imran, 3: 102-103, al-Hashr, 59: 18-19)

# SAYYIDAH KHADIJAH BINT HUWAYLID (r.ah)

*"The most righteous among the women of the world is Mariam, the daughter of Imran. And the most righteous among the Muslim women is Khadîjah!"*
(Hadith; Bukhârî)


**On the Road to Ka'bah**

Our beloved Kaaba!

The time was one when people are drawn to the Kaaba, wave after wave, and when the advent of Prophet Muhammad (saw) was imminent...

Young Khadîjah, from the Banu Asad branch of the Quraysh tribe, whose ancestry joins that of Prophet Muhammad (saw), was proceeding towards the Kaaba, accompanied by maidens from her tribe. A Jew came from afar, with long and unkempt hair and beard, and approached them. Out of breath, he said:

"Peace be upon you, O, women of the chosen tribe of Mecca! Soon a prophet will come to you. He will possess unparalleled morality and noble features. He will bring *tawhid* (Allah's Unity) to you and will forbid idolatry for you. Strive to be his wife, if you can!"

The women in the caravan ridiculed the Jew. They drove him away; some of them cursing and throwing stones after him, while shouting: "There is no one who can separate us from our idols!"

Yet the words of the Jew left a mark on the heart of Khadîjah, who was only fifteen at this time. Inwardly, she thought: "If there is a person who has such qualities, I should marry him!"[20]

## Sayyidah Khadîjah's Family

Sayyidah Khadîjah's father was Huwaylid bin Asad bin Abdul Uzza bin Qusay bin Kilab[21]. He died in the Battle of Fijar.

Her mother was Fatimah bint Zaidat al-Asam, a descendant of Amer bin Luayya. Khadijah was born in Mecca, in 556.[22]

## *Tahirah*: A Pure Woman

In purity and nobility, Sayyidah Khadîjah woman was the foremost figure amongst her tribe, remaining pure despite the loathsome practices in the Era of Ignorance and the disgraceful treatment displayed towards women at this time. Due to these qualities, she was also known as *tahirah* (pure woman), or *afifah* (chaste woman).[23]

Sayyidah Khadîjah was an esteemed figure in society. She never worshipped idols, even before her marriage to the Prophet of Allah (saw). According to the *Musnad* of Ahmad bin Hanbel, during the Era of Ignorance Prophet Muhammad (saw) had said to Khadijah: "I swear by Allah, that I will never worship al-Lat or al-Uzza!" Sayyidah Khadîjah had replied: "Never mind about al-Lat and al-Uzza! Their names are not even worth mentioning!"

The fact that Sayyidah Khadîjah was known as *tahirah* and led a life worthy of such a name acted as a preparatory period for her to become the beloved wife

---

20. Tahmaz, es-Seyyide Hatice, page: 24 Ziya Kazıcı, Ibid., page: 90.
21. Afzalurrahman, Sîret Ansiklopedisi, v: II, page: 152.
22. M. Yaşar Kandemir, the article of "Hatice", DIA, v: XVI, page: 465.
23. From "Ibnu'l-Esîr" (Usdu'l-Gâbe, I, 434) narrated by H. Kübra Ergin, *"Hz. Muhammed'de Aşk"*, İstanbul, 2005, page: 184.

of Prophet Muhammad (saw), the al-Amin (trustworthy) of Mecca. She had a spiritually and physically pure nature that would be a beautiful accompaniment to the beloved servant of Allah Almighty.

## Before Meeting Prophet Muhammad (saw)

Sayyidah Khadîjah (r.ah) was married twice before she met Prophet Muhammad (saw). She had a son named Hind[24] from her first husband, Abu Halah bin Zurara[25]. For some time, Sayyidah Khadîjah was known by the name of this son, that is, as Ummu Hind (the mother of Hind).

After the death of her husband, she married Ateek bin A'ez (or Abid), and she had a daughter named Hind.

Because of her lineage, beauty and wealth, after the death of her second husband some of the dignitaries of the Quraysh wanted to marry her. However, Sayyidah Khadîjah refused all these offers.[26]

## The Damascene Caravan

Sayyidah Khadîjah took care of her children with the money she earned from trade. Although she was a widower, she was unable to travel with the caravans, and she could not make enough money on her investments. Everyone to whom she entrusted her caravan and assets stole goods from her. She was in desperate need of finding someone to manage her caravans.

A caravan of considerable size was preparing to travel to Damascus. Sayyidah Khadîjah was looking for someone trustworthy to take her merchandise. All the advice she received from her friends centred on the same person: Muhammad al-Amin (saw)!

---

24. According to some reports, she also had had a daughter with Abu Halah. (Celâl Yeniçeri, "Peygamber, Devlet Başkanı ve Âile Reisi Hz. Muhammad, page: 73)
25. M. Yaşar Kandemir, DIA, the article of "Hatice", v: XVI, page: 465.
26. DIA, the article of "Hatice".

Even though Sayyidah Khadîjah met this young man - renowned as a man of his word and for taking special care of whatever was entrusted to him - for the first time, she handed over her entire caravan to him. She also charged her slave Maysara to travel with him and to observe all his actions.

Among the extraordinary events that Maysara witnessed during his journey with Prophet Muhammad (saw) were the words of a Nestorian priest.

While Prophet (saw) and Maysara were travelling with the caravan, they stopped, and Prophet Muhammad (saw) rested in the shade of a tree. A priest came to them and asked Maysara who it was resting under the tree. The priest told Maysara that only a prophet would rest there. He asked Maysara whether the person under the tree had redness in his eyes. When Maysara said "Yes", the priest said: "Then he is the last prophet."

Afterwards someone came to Prophet Muhammad (saw) to buy something. When they disagreed about the price, the man said: "Then swear by Lat and Uzza!" Prophet Muhammad (saw) replied: "I have never sworn an oath on them." The priest turned to Maysara and said: "I swear to Allah that he is the Prophet (saw) whose qualities and features are written in the books of our priests."[27]

While Maysara was closely observing the deeds of Prophet Muhammad (saw), he realized that a cloud was giving them shade. Wherever they went, the cloud moved with them; when they stopped, the cloud stopped, too.

Finally, the caravan that was led by Prophet Muhammad (saw) returned to Mecca. For the first time, this expedition brought back a substantial profit for Khadijah.

Maysara accounted all that he had seen to Sayyidah Khadîjah. As he talked about the nobility, honesty, virtue and other outstanding qualities of Muhammad (saw), the heart of the chaste and modest Khadijah started to feel an attraction towards the young man.

---

27.   Ibn-i Ishak, page: 59; Ibn-i Sa'd, Tabakât, I, 130.

## The Marriage of the Sun and the Moon

After obtaining a good deal of information about him, Sayyidah Khadîjah took a rather unusual step: in contrast to the prevailing customs of Mecca, she proposed marriage to Muhammad (saw), who was then 25 years old, with the help of her friend. Sayyidah Khadîjah was 40 years old; a widow with two children.

One day, Nafisa, a friend of Sayyidah Khadîjah, had the opportunity to talk to Muhammad (saw). She told him that his time had come; that he belonged to a fine and honourable family and was renowned for his good morals, but despite all these factors he had not yet married. She said that if he were willing, she could easily find a suitable candidate.[28] Muhammad (saw) expressed his thoughts, saying that he did not have the financial means to sustain a family, and that no one would marry him under these conditions. When she asked: "What if I were to find someone who is rich and beautiful, as well as belonging to a fine and honourable family?" Muhammad (saw) curiously inquired: "Who might that be?" Nafisa, as if she had been waiting for the question, replied: "Khadîjah!"

Muhammad (saw) replied that he could not imagine this happening, because all the dignitaries of the city had requested to marry Sayyidah Khadîjah, but she had turned down every offer, thus she would not accept his offer either.

Nafisa said that if Muhammad (saw) were to accept her suggestion, he should allow her to handle the situation, and through common friends she would work it out. She must have received approval from Muhammad (saw), because she was soon breaking the good news to Sayyidah Khadîjah. Upon receiving the news Sayyidah Khadîjah, personally this time, spoke to the noble youth. "O my cousin! I am inclined to you, due to your trustworthiness, the way you take care of whatever is entrusted to you, your high morals and your noble position in your tribe."

After consulting with his uncles and receiving their consent, Muhammad (saw) decided to go ahead with this marriage. The wedding ceremony was held in Sayyidah Khadîjah's house. A large wedding was prepared. As Sayyidah Khadîjah's father had died in the Battle of Fijar, her uncle Amr bin Asad was

---

28. Ziya Kazıcı, Ibid., page: 92-93.

expected to perform the marriage ceremony.[29] Although there are a few differing reports[30], according to the generally accepted account, the ceremony in the end was performed by Waraqa bin Nawfal, the cousin of Sayyidah Khadîjah.

The dignitaries of the Quraysh convened in Sayyidah Khadîjah's house. Prophet Muhammad (saw) went there with his uncles Abu Talib and Hamza. Khadijah was represented by her cousin Waraqa bin Nawfal. According to Arab traditions, first Abu Talib, and then Waraka bin Nawfal gave a speech. In his address, Abu Talib said:

"Thanks be to Allah Who has created us from the offspring of Ibrahim, the progeny of Ismail, the essence of Ma'd and the element of Mudar. He ordained us as the guardians of the Ka'bah and thus made us rulers and leaders of men. Coming to the matter in hand; the son of my brother Muhammad bin Abdullah surpasses all the youth of the Quraysh with regard to lineage, wisdom and merits, whomever you compare him to. Although he is not wealthy, this should not be taken into account, because, like a shadow, possession is provisional; it is taken and given. I swear by Allah that in future his fame will be exalted. Now as you see, he has requested to marry your honourable daughter, Sayyidah Khadîjah. I have set aside such and such an amount as mahr (dowry)[31]."

Waraqa bin Nawfal said: "We thank Allah Who created us in the (same) manner as you have described. He made us pre-eminent with more than what you have stated. Hence, we are the nobles and leaders of the Arabs, as are you. The ascendancy of your tribe is undeniable; no one can refuse to acknowledge your righteousness or honour. We, too wish to be related to you! O people! Bear witness that I have married Khadîjah, the daughter of Huwaylid, to Muhammad bin Abdullah."

After the ceremony, Sayyidah Khadîjah said to Muhammad (saw): "Tell your uncle to slaughter one of the camels and feed it to the congregation."

---

29. According to a weak reporting, Khadijah (ra) had an alcoholic uncle anmed Amr bin Asad, and she was afraid that he would not accept the nikah, so she did not tell him. At the wedding ceremony he did drink too much alcohol and she took this chance and named Waraka bin Nawfal to complete her nikah. A little while later, her uncle returned to his sobriety but he could not ruin her nikah.
30. See: Ibn-i Sa'd, I, 131-133; Ziya Kazıcı, Ibid., page: 93.
31. This mahr was from Abu Talib's property was 20 female camels (DİA, entitled "Khadijah"), according to another report it was 12 ukye silver (480 dirham) (Ziya Kazici, pg. 96). This amount was the amount paid in those days to the women of high stature. (Afzalurrahman, II, pg. 154)

Abu Talib slaughtered a camel for the marriage banquet to feed the dignitaries of the tribe. Since Muhammad (saw) was content with this marriage, his guardian and protector Abu Talib was thankful to Allah: "Praise is due to Allah, Who has kept grief away from us!"

Following the wedding ceremony, Muhammad al-Amin (saw) - soon to be the Prophet of Islam - moved into Sayyidah Khadîjah's house. This house became the heart of bliss and tranquillity. So much so, that the marriage of Prophet Muhammad (saw) and Sayyidah Khadîjah has been commemorated as an example for happiness throughout history, and people have prayed for newly wed couples to Allah Almighty, asking Him to bestow on them a state that is similar in attachment, affection and warmth to that which those two shared.[32]

### The Family Life of Sayyidah Khadîjah (r.ah)

Sayyidah Khadîjah (r.ah) led a peaceful and tranquil life with her esteemed spouse, and Muhammad (saw) had received almost no inheritance from his parents: until his marriage he had lived under the protection of first his grandfather 'Abd al-Muttalib, and then his uncle Abû Tâlib. Abû Tâlib had a large family and this meant that the Holy Prophet (saw) in trying to lessen the burden of this family, in which he lived, had to earn a livelihood, though he was still in his youth. It was certainly not an easy period for the young Muhammad. However, with his marriage, he was saved from these difficult straits, and started to live a comfortable life, as described in the Qur'ân:

**"Did He not find you an orphan and give you shelter (and care)? And He found you wandering, and He gave you guidance. And He found you in need, and made you independent."** (Surah ad-Duhâ, 93: 6-8)

He indeed acquired a good deal of wealth in the first years of his marriage, by managing Sayyidah Khadîjah's (r.ah) merchandise[33].

The Holy Prophet (saw) was also considerably fortunate regarding children. His house buzzed with the voices of children. From one side he had his own

---

32.   Celâl Yeniçeri, Ibid., page: 74.
33.   Ziya Kazıcı, Ibid., page: 100.

children from Sayyidah Khadîjah (r.ah) and on the other side the children[34] of Sayyidah Khadîjah (r.ah) from her previous marriages; 'Alî, the son of his uncle Abû Tâlib and Zayd bin Hârithah, his freed slave originally presented to him by Sayyidah Khadîjah (r.ah) were also members of the blessed household.

Sayyidah Khadîjah (r.ah) was very particular about her dear children receiving training under the guardianship of the Holy Prophet (saw). She served all the needs of the Holy Prophet (saw) and the children personally, and disliked employing her servants for this purpose.

Sayyidah Khadîjah (r.ah) was exceedingly cautious not to do anything that would upset the Holy Prophet (saw), and seized any opportunities to please him.

One day, the Holy Prophet's (saw) wet-nurse Halîma came to their house. It was a time when everyone was suffering due to a severe drought and she had come to explain her plight. Sayyidah Khadîjah (r.ah) presented her with forty sheep and a camel. Hence, by pleasing his wet-nurse, she was in fact pleasing the heart of the Prophet of Allah (saw).

**The Source of Bliss in the Family**

In their marriage, the Prophet (saw) and Sayyidah Khadîjah (r.ah) displayed a sincere bond of affection, mutual love and regard for each other. Their married life was filled with peace, happiness, kindness and contentment.

The Holy Prophet (saw) gave glad tidings that Sayyidah Khadîjah (r.ah) will have an outstanding and esteemed position among the women of Heaven. By making her his wife, Allah the Almighty bestowed a generous gift upon His Prophet (saw). Whilst receiving affection and tenderness from Sayyidah Khadî-jah (r.ah), the Holy Prophet (saw) always maintained a state of thankfulness to

---

34. These children probably were under the protection of their father's relatives according to the community's customs. But from time to time they would come to visit their mothers. Especially from these children Hind bin Abi Hâle grew up with the Prophet Muhammad's (saw) training and became Muslim and made the immigration to Madina and joined in the Badr war. He was killed in the "Camel Incident" as he was on Hz. Ali's side (Ziya Kazici, pg. 102). Because he grew up under the protection and training of the Prophet (saw) he described the Prophet (saw) very well when reporting his characteristics and appearance (DİA, entitled "Khadijah").

Allah, as constant as he remained patient and content in the face of hardships which he endured throughout his life and which began at his birth: for this reason alone he is an example to us.[35]

The Holy Prophet (saw) was devoted to Sayyidah Khadîjah (r.ah), though he was much younger. In spite of the fact that the social norms favoured polygamy, and he possessed the means for it, he was content with his wife, and did not seek to marry anyone younger. To the contrary, he had devoted himself to the worship of Allah and to conveying His message: and this whilst he was at the peak of his youth and strength. He and his wife lived as soul mates and confidantes on the same path.[36]

When it comes to the bond of affection among spouses, the Holy Prophet (saw) is an exemplar of love[37] and regard, irrespective of physical and spiritual circumstances.[38] He won the heart of his wife with his high morals and consummate deeds. In this connection he said:

*"The most righteous among you, are the ones who treat their families in the best way!"*[39]

Marriage is essentially a spiritual establishment: by establishing a relationship with a partner through matrimony, love surpasses selfishness and ascends

---

35. *"Really nobody can find everything he hopes for in everything that he loves, but he is not deprived of all of these hopes. In all of our lives there are graces and deficiencies. To be thankful for these graces is a virtue as much as patience is for the deficiencies. In addition, thankfulness increases the blessings and gives them value which is limitless. Our Prophet (saw) never became ungrateful for the love of Khadijah (ra). He never pretended not to notice as we generally tend to do. Most of us, exaggerate the deficiencies and deny the graces, because we think we are entitled to the graces and that the deficiencies are an injustice. Oppositely, the graces are purely a present from Allah, and the deficiencies sometimes come because of people's mistakes, and they are the experiences which are a test and lesson for us."* (H. Kübra Ergin, pg. 189)

36. H. Kübra Ergin, Ibid., page: 189.

37. H. Kübra Ergin, Ibid., page: 191.

38. Allah's Prophet (saw) was behaving with Khadijah (ra) properly for her age and refinement, and with Hz. Aisha (ra) he had the behavior that was necessary to get with her and make her happy; he made runnign races with her and he let her play with toys and her friends; he almost came down to her age (for an example you can look at the chapter on Hz. Aisha (ra)

*"Hz. Aisha (ra), as opposed to Hz. Khadijah, was young and inexperienced. This situation causes her to suffer due to her rawness. The Prophet's (saw) attitude toward these situations was quite calm and mature. He was neither protecting her blindly by becoming frail to this young wife, nor was he denigrating her. He was indulgent but shrewd."* (H. Kübra Ergin, pg. 192)

39. Ibn-i Majah, Nikâh, 50; Dârimî, Nikâh, 55.

to a spiritual quality. This is due to the fact that men are inclined to work and earn their living, and they are content with spending generously on others and enjoy being in control. Women, on the other hand, have a delicate and sentimental nature: they aspire to being with a secure person, loving and protecting them[40]. Families preserving this natural formation become centres of peace and tranquillity.

Although modernism constrained the nature of human beings by almost robotising the spirit, deep in the soul these necessities will always make themselves felt.

## The First Female Muslim

When the Prophet (saw) was approaching his forties and leading a happy life with Sayyidah Khadîjah (r.ah) and their children, he started to experience some extraordinary events. An example is that he witnessed trees and stones greeting him. It was many years later that the Prophet of Allah (saw) said to his Companions:

*"I still know the stone in Mecca, which greeted me before I became a prophet."*[41]

Distressed and troubled by the brutality and oppression which characterised Mecca, the Holy Prophet (saw) frequented the cave of Hira for prayer and seclusion. During these periods, Sayyidah Khadîjah (r.ah) would send him food, sometimes bringing it to him herself.

The Prophet (saw) used to withdraw into solitude in the cave of Hira so often that the women of Quraysh started to come to Sayyidah Khadîjah (r.ah) to make mischief: "You have done so much for Muhammad, you spread your wealth before his feet. Now he forsakes you and goes away!"

Sayyidah Khadîjah (r.ah), who knew the Holy Prophet (saw) intimately and supported him to the end, laughed at such words and said: "I could not even

---

40. H. Kübra Ergin, Ibid., page: 207.
41. Ahmad bin Hanbel, Musned, V, 89; See: Taberî, II, 44-45.

dream about what you are saying. However, there is something that I expect to happen, and you will see that soon!"

One day, when the Prophet (saw) was secluded in Hira, Jibrîl (AS) came in his angelic form and revealed the first five verses of the chapter al-'Alaq, "The Clot". The Holy Prophet (saw), experiencing such an event for the first time, arrived home in great anxiety and while still shivering said to Khadijah (r.ah): "Cover me, cover me!"

When he recovered from his fear and had calmed down, he related what had happened to Sayyidah Khadîjah (r.ah): "I was afraid for myself!"

Sayyidah Khadîjah (r.ah) encouraged him with full devotion and deep insight, and demonstrating that she believed in him under all circumstances she said:

"Don't talk like that! I swear by Allah that He will never humiliate you or forsake you. You take care of your relatives and shoulder the burden of powerless people; you give to the needy; show hospitality to your guests and benefit people like no others can do; and, you help people on the path of righteousness."[42]

Afterwards, Sayyidah Khadîjah (r.ah) went to visit her cousin Waraqa bin Nawfal with the Prophet (saw). Waraqa was an old and sightless man with a good command of the Hebrew language and knowledge of the Torah[43] and the Injîl.[44]

Sayyidah Khadîjah (r.ah) said to Waraqa, "O my cousin! Listen to what the son of your brother has to say." When Waraqa asked, "O the son of my brother, what happened?" the Holy Prophet (saw) narrated all that had happened to him. Then Waraqa said: "What you saw is the *Nâmûs al-Akbar* -Jibrîl- who Allah the Almighty sent to Mûsâ. Oh, how I wish I were young during the days of your

---

42. Bukhârî, Bed'u'l-Vahy, 7, Tefsir, 96/1; Muslim, Iman, 252-254; Ahmad bin Hanbel, VI, 153, 232.
43. The Tawrah (Torah) is the book that was revealed to the Prophet Mûsâ (Moses) (AS), and the Injîl is the book given to Prophet 'Isâ (Jesus) (AS). The Tawrah and Injîl mentioned in the Qur'ân should not be confused with the Old Testament or the four Gospels of the New Testament which are present today. These books have been distorted to a great extent by man, and contain a great deal of additional material. Although, presumably there are still some statements remaining from the original books in them, these are not discernible except for where there is an exact correspondence with the Qur'ân.
44. DIA, the article of "Khadijah."

*da'wah*[45]! Alas! I wish I could be alive and besides you when your tribe is going to banish you!" Then Holy Prophet (saw) asked, "Are they going to banish me from Mecca?" Waraqa said, "Certainly, there is no one who has brought what is revealed to you that has not been met with hostility. If I live to see the days of your *da'wah*, I will help you with all that I can." However, soon after, Waraqa passed away.[46]

As we can see, Khadijah knew her husband very well. By reminding him of his goodness toward others and his good manners, she was saying that the satan and jinn could not even come close to him. Even though she realized this, she went further to take the Prophet (saw) to Waraqa, her cousin, who knew about these things. Waraqa was recounting the future dangers that the Prophet (saw) would face in order to prepare him for these things Waraqa was sad that he would not be able to support him.

Both Sayyidah Khadîjah (r.ah) and Waraqa comforted the Holy Prophet (saw), and he waited for further revelation from Allah the Almighty. However, the will of God was preparing him for this onerous task, and the advent of further revelations would continue but only after an interlude.

An interesting account is related in the books of *sîrah*[47] in which Sayyidah Khadîjah (r.ah) had an idea to dispel the doubt in her and in her husband's heart concerning the source of the revelatory experiences.[48]

One day, Sayyidah Khadîjah (r.ah) requested the Prophet (saw) to let her know when the angel arrives, and after a while the Prophet (saw) said that the angel had come. Sayyidah Khadîjah (r.ah) said: "Come and sit to my left and tell me if you see him." The Holy Prophet (saw) changed his place and confirmed that he could still see the angel. Then Sayyidah Khadîjah (r.ah) said, "Now sit to the right of me and tell me if you still see him." He sat there and confirmed once again. When Sayyidah Khadîjah (r.ah) asked him to sit in front of her there was still no change. Finally, Sayyidah Khadîjah (r.ah)

---

45. *Da'wah* is the propagation of Islam through word and action, calling the people to follow the commandments of Allah and His Messenger, the Prophet Muhammad (saw).
46. Bukhârî, Bed'u'l-Vahy, 3; Muslim, Iman, 252; Tirmîdhî, Menâkıb, 13.
47. *Sirah* is a term used for biographical writings about the conduct and example of the Prophet Muhammad (*saw*).
48. H. Kubra Ergin, Ibid., page: 187.

hugged him and asked, "Do you still see the angel?" This time she received a different answer: "No, I cannot see him anymore." Sayyidah Khadîjah (r.ah) said, "Glad tidings O husband! It is indeed an angel. If it was a devil, it would not have left us."[49]

This test is a fine example, manifesting the intellectual capacity and comprehension of Sayyidah Khadîjah (r.ah). After this event, they were both content that what was coming was "an esteemed being with decorum". The Holy Prophet (saw) was the recipient of a Divine commission and not under a satanic spell.

When the first five verses of the chapter al-Muddathir, "The One Wrapped" were revealed and the Holy Prophet (saw) was fully cognisant of the task that was beginning, he asked his beloved wife: "Who will believe in me?" Sayyidah Khadîjah (r.ah), his supporter throughout his life, shed the first light on this Divine cause by saying "I believe you!" and acquired the honour of becoming the first to believe in him amongst all the many men and women.[50]

It is narrated that the Prophet (saw) performed the first *salât*, prayer, on Monday, and Sayyidah Khadîjah (r.ah) followed suit one day after him.[51] However, in the early stages of his mission, the prayer was not performed five times a day nor was it of the same form and requirements: it was conceivably similar to an invocation. In fact, the Arabic word *salât* literally means invocation.

All sources unanimously agree that Sayyidah Khadîjah (r.ah) was the first person to believe in the Prophet (saw) and attest to the truth of what he was saying. In this connection, Ibn 'Abbâs (ra) said, "Sayyidah Khadîjah, the daughter of Khuwaylid, was the first person to affirm Muhammad (saw), and the first to believe in Allah and His Prophet. When the pagans tormented the Prophet (saw) of Allah and said things which displeased him, Allah would dissipate his distress by Sayyidah Khadîjah. All the suffering and troubles caused by his tribe would subside with the help of Sayyidah Khadîjah."[52]

---

49. Ibn-i Hişam, es-Sîre, I, 174; Ziya Kazıcı, Ibid., page: 106-107.
50. Ibn-i Abdi'l- Berr, el-Istiâb, IV, 274.
51. Ibn-i Abdi'l- Berr, el-Istiâb, IV, 275.
52. Ibn-i Abdi'l- Berr, el-Istiâb, IV, 275; Ziya Kazıcı, Ibid., page: 108.

## Worshipping in the Ka'bah

A man named 'Afîf al-Kindî came to Mecca one time in order to buy some goods for his family. During his visit, while he was besides the Ka'bah in the late morning, a young man came and gazed at the skies, then stood facing Ka'bah. Then a small boy, named 'Alî, came and stood to his right, and a woman stood among them. 'Afîf witnessed all three as they bowed and prostrated. What he was witnessing was the prayer, and it was the first time he had seen such a thing and he looked on with admiration. He asked who they were. The uncle of the Prophet (saw), 'Abbâs, who was there at the time, told him that they were his relatives and informed him about the new religion that was being conveyed: 'Abbâs was not a Muslim at this time. Then the stranger expressed how he wished to become the fourth of them.[53]

In another account, 'Abdullâh bin Mas'ûud said that he saw the three of them—the Prophet (saw), Sayyidah Khadîjah (r.ah) and 'Alî, circumambulating the Ka'bah together, and that Sayyidah Khadîjah (r.ah) had veiled herself.[54]

Here then, we witness Sayyidah Khadîjah (r.ah) praying amidst blasphemy, *kufr*[55] (disbelief), in the same manner taught by Jibrîl (AS). This overt manner of worship is the first *salât* performed in congregation: and it would become, from that specific place and point in time, the most significant observable symbol of Islam which spread, one wave after another, over all the land.

## The Boycott Years

When the Holy Prophet (saw) started to call people to Islam, the pagans of Mecca first responded by ridiculing and insulting him. Day by day they

---

53. Ibn-i Sa'd, VIII, 18; Celâl Yeniçeri, Ibid., page: 75.
54. DIA, the article of "Khadijah."
55. The literal meaning of *kufr* is 'to conceal'. This word has been variously used in the Qur'ân to denote: (1) a state of absolute lack of faith; (2) a rejection or denial of any of the essentials of Islam; (3) an attitude of ingratitude and thanklessness to God; and (4) a non-fulfilment of certain basic requirements of faith. In the accepted technical sense, *kufr* consists of a rejection of the Divine Guidance communicated through the Prophets and Messengers of God. More specifically, ever since the advent of the last of the Prophets and Messengers, Muhammad (saw), rejection of his teaching constitutes *kufr*.

escalated their oppression until they resorted to all sorts of torture. One of the torments they inflicted on the believers was to cluster them together in "Shi'b Abî Tâlib" -the neighbourhood of Banu Hâshim- and to sever all connections with them. During this three year boycott , many believers lost their children due to malnutrition, and they had to satiate their own hunger by chewing the bark of trees. The faithful wife of the Prophet (saw), Sayyidah Khadîjah (r.ah) never left the Holy Prophet (saw) alone[56]; she mobilized all her means and sacrificed her fortune and health in support of his cause.

* * *

The considerable wealth of Sayyidah Khadîjah (r.ah) dissolved day by day, for the sake of Islam. Consequently, during the *hijrah*[57] of the Holy Prophet (saw), only an insignificant amount remained from the substantial wealth he had acquired by marriage.

Sayyidah Khadîjah (r.ah) suffered all the hardships experienced by the Muslims in their early days. The most difficult years of the Holy Prophet (saw) and Islam, coincides with the period of his marriage with Sayyidah Khadîjah (r.ah). This devoted wife of the Holy Prophet (saw) stood beside him and never abandoned him in the face of hardships; when he was repudiated, tormented and offended by his tribe. Throughout the Meccan period of Prophethood, when the Holy Prophet (saw) returned to his home in distress from the oppression and pain inflicted on him by the Quraish, he was solaced and spirited up by this faithful lady. In these difficult times, the peaceful family hearth diligently established by Sayyidah Khadîjah (r.ah) was his greatest comfort and support. All these sacrifices and the affection he received, well explain why the Holy Prophet (saw), who was an exemplar of fidelity, never forgot Sayyidah Khadîjah (r.ah) throughout his life.

Sayyidah Khadîjah (r.ah) also played an important role in the end of the boycott, both by her personal exertion as well as by convincing her relatives and nephews -which hadn't embraced Islam yet- to be mediators.

---

56. DIA, the article of "Khadijah."
57. *Hijrah* signifies migration from a land where a Muslim is unable to live according to the precepts of his faith to a land where it is possible to do so. The *hijrah* par excellence for Muslims is the *hijrah* of the Prophet (saw) from Mecca to Medina, which not only provided him and his followers' refuge from persecution, but also an opportunity to build a society and state according to the ideals of Islam.

As a matter of fact, *Hakîm bin Hizâm* is known to be the first person to take a step in this direction. One night he shouldered provisions as much as he was able to carry, and took them to his aunt. When Abû Jahl came to hear of this he harassed Hakîm and said: "You violated the agreement by providing food to Banu Hashim! I will take you before the Quraish and disgrace you!" When Abû al-Bukhturî bin Hishâm learned about the incident, he opposed Abû Jahl and said to him: "You can't prevent him from providing food to his aunt; you cannot sever the ties of kinship!" This event ignited a heated debate among them, almost ending in a fight.[58] Abû Jahl had disputed with Hakîm on this occasion having become aware of it, but unbeknown to him, Hakîm took every opportunity to by goods and to send them to his aunt.

### Allah Rendered You Most Excellent

It was the tenth year after the advent of the Prophet of Allah (saw). The passing days had carried along many sorrows; tortures, boycott, and after all these, the passing of the Prophet's (saw) protector and uncle, Abû Tâlib at the age of 87, then only a few days later Sayyidah Khadîjah (r.ah) the soul mate of the Holy Prophet (saw) fell ill. The oppression, cruelty and deprivation they suffered during their banishment, and the resulting exhaustion had debilitated Khâdijah (r.ah), who was 65.

After 25 years of a happy and exceptional marriage, she was about to depart from her beloved husband, the Messenger of Allah (saw), and from this transitory world.

The Prophet of Allah (saw) praised her, aware of the fact that the time of separation was drawing near: "O Sayyidah Khadîjah, Allah has rendered you most excellent. He preferred you over Mariam, the daughter of 'Imrân, and 'Âthiya, the wife of Pharoah."

Three days after the demise of Abû Tâlib, Sayyidah Khadîjah (r.ah) passed away, when she was sixty five years old. (in Ramadan, 10 / April 19, 620)

---

58. Ibn-i Hişâm, es-Sîre, I, 240.

The Messenger of Allah (saw) was grief-stricken with these deaths, coming one after another, and he named that year as *'Aam al-Huzn* -the year of grief-.

That year was called the Year of Grief, and what *is* 'grief'? It is when one's heart is wrenched throughout the rest of his life; to perpetually feel that heartache. Despite the other marriages he had, the Holy Prophet (saw) always missed Sayyidah Khadîjah (r.ah) and felt her absence.

The Holy Prophet (saw) took Sayyidah Khadîjah (r.ah) to the *Hajun* cemetery of Mecca,[59] and personally buried her. The *Salat al-Janâzah* -funeral prayer- wasn't compulsory at that time. Later on the Holy Prophet (saw) used to come to the graveyard often to visit her grave.

## The Mother of the Holy Prophet's (saw) Children

Sayyidah Khadîjah (r.ah) had six children from The Holy Prophet (saw); two sons and four daughters. They were; *Qâsim, Zainab, Ruqayyah, Ummu Kulthum, Fatimah* and *Abdullah.*

Since his first son was named "Qâsim", the Holy Prophet (saw) was given the *kunya*[60] of "Abû'l Qâsim", according to the Arabian traditions.[61]

The last child Sayyidah Khadîjah (r.ah) gave birth to was Abdullah. He was also named as *"at Tayyib"* and *"at-Tahir"*[62], the good and pure one, because he came to world after the Prophethood of Muhammad (saw). Some have mistakenly thought that these two epithets belonged to two separate children of the Holy Prophet (saw). However, they both belong to Abdullah.[63]

---

59. "The mausoleum built on top of Khadijah's (ra) grave by Suleiman the Magnificent, was torn down in 1926 along with the others, when Saudi's came to power in Mecca" (DIA, the article of "Hatice/ Khadijah")
60. *Kunya* is a respectful and affectionate way of calling People as *"Abu"* or *"Umm"* (*Abu* = father of, *Umm* = mother of) followed by the name of the eldest son; if there is no male offspring then the *"Abu"* or *"Umm"* is followed by the name of the eldest daughter. It is prohibited to have the same *Kunya* as the Prophet Muhammad (saw), e.g. It is not permitted to call someone *"Abu Qasim"* (Sahih Bukhari, Hadith 205, Vol.8. Sahih Muslim, Kitabul-Adab).
61. Ziya Kazıcı, Ibid., page: 88.
62. DIA, the article of "Khadijah."
63. Ziya Kazıcı, Ibid., page:101.

The boys passed away when they were infants. Qâsim died even smaller, when he was close to two[64], before he was weaned and started to walk.[65]

Among the offspring of the Messenger of Allah (saw), Fatimah (r.ah) was the last to lose her life; she died six months after the Holy Prophet (saw) passed away.[66] All the children of the Holy Prophet (saw), except Fatimah (r.ah), died during his lifetime.

The only child The Holy Prophet (saw) had from his other wives was Ibrahîm. He was born from Mâriya (r.ah), and died when he was two.

Sayyidah Zainab (r.ah), the eldest daughter of the Messenger of Allah (saw) had married her cousin *Abû'l-'As bin Rabî'a*. When her husband remained a pagan after the Prophethood, she divorced him. However, after he embraced Islam, they remarried.

His other daughters Ruqayyah and Umm Kulthum were at first wed to *'Utbah* and *'Utaybah;* sons of *Abû Lahab*[67]. However, after the advent of Islam, Abû Lahab -being a fierce pagan- forced his sons to divorce their wives. Thereupon, first Ruqayyah was married to 'Uthman bin 'Affan (ra) and after she passed away Umm Kulthum was also married to 'Uthman (ra). Because of these marriages, 'Uthman (ra) was named as *"Dhu'l Nurayn"* –Possesor of two lights. The Holy Prophet (saw) married his youngest daughter Fatimah (r.ah) with *'Ali bin Abû Tâlib* (ra).

The progeny of the Holy Prophet (saw), which will carry on until the Last Day, comes from Fatimah (r.ah), and consequently from her mother Sayyidah Khadîjah (r.ah), as the Messenger of Allah (saw) didn't have children from his other wives, except Mâriya (r.ah). *Hasan (ra)* and *Husayn* (ra), the dear grandchildren of the Holy Prophet (saw) were born form Fatimah (ra). He doted on them and gave the glad tidings that they would earn *Jannah*. The *Sayyid's* and *Sherif's;* the progeny of the Holy Prophet (saw) which have spread out throughout the land, all descend from Hasan (ra) and Husayn (ra). These descendants

---

64. Ziya Kazıcı, Ibid., page: 101.
65. DIA, the article of "Khadijah."
66. Ziya Kazıcı, Ibid., page: 101.
67. *Abu Lahab* was the fiercest enemy of Islam and paternal uncle of the Holy Prophet (saw). *Surah al-Masadd* of the Holy Qur'an was revealed about him.

are also named as *Âl Muhammad* (saw), *Âl Rasool, Awlâd ar-Rasûl* and *Ahl al-Bayt*. May Allah not deprive the world from this esteemed family until the Day of Judgement. *Amîn.*

### The High Morals and Virtues of Sayyidah Khadîjah (r.ah)

The life of Sayyidah Khadîjah (r.ah) presents am highly important model for Muslim families, with respect to achieving the acceptance of Allah, peace in the family, and happiness in this world and in the hereafter. The way she led her life and her self-sacrifice earned her an everlasting place in the hearts of believers. She is loved deeply among all Muslims, be they Arab or from other nations, many Muslim families from different *madhab's* -schools of Islamic law- demonstrate this love by naming their daughters after her.[68]

The Holy Prophet (saw) never forgot his blessed wife, and cherished her memory.

Abû al-'As, the husband of Sayyidah Zainab (r.ah) was taken captive by Muslims during the battle of *Badr*[69]. To save her husband from captivity, as a ransom, Sayyidah Zainab (r.ah) sent the necklace which was given to her by her mother Sayyidah Khadîjah (r.ah), when she got married. The Holy Prophet (saw) was moved when he saw the necklace[70], and requested his companions to send it back to Sayyidah Zainab (r.ah).[71]

The author *Muhammad al Ghazâlî wrote*; "Sayyidah Khadîjah (r.ah) held the position of a precious woman, complementing the life of an eminent man. The hearts of the people who are commissioned with Prophethood are remarkably delicate. And these people face grave difficulties in the surroundings they

---

68. DIA, the article of "Khadijah."
69. *Badr* is the site of the first great battle between Prophet Muhammad (saw) and the pagans of the Quraish in 2 A.H. *Badr* is located about 150 kilometers south of Medina (Saudi Arabia). The Muslim army consisted of 313 men and the Quraish had a total of about 1,000 soldiers, archers and horsemen. See Holy Quran, Al-Anfal (8:5-19, 42-48), Al-e Imran (3:13).
70. Khadîjah (ra), in general, wore black garments of good quality. She was also cultured regarding jewellery. She usually wore silver rings, earrings and necklaces with turquoise stones, crafted by skilled artisans.
71. Afzalurrahman, Sîret Ansiklopedisi, II, 160.

aim to transform. Therefore they need someone to comfort and soothe them in their personal lives. In this respect, Sayyidah Khadîjah (r.ah) had surpassed everyone in the life of the Holy Prophet (saw), and had left a pleasant mark on his life."[72]

Certainly such a devoted assistance would not be left unreturned; she became one of the few people who were given glad tidings of Jannah and the acceptance of Allah, during their lifetime.

One day, the Messenger of Allah (saw) retreated to a secluded place for worship. In these times, Sayyidah Khadîjah (r.ah) would prepare food for him and take it to where he was, so that he wouldn't have to interrupt his worship. One day as she brought food for the Prophet (saw) on his retreat, Jibreel (AS) came to the Holy Prophet (saw) and said to him: "O the Messenger of Allah (saw)! Sayyidah Khadîjah is coming to you with a pot of food. When she comes, convey her *salaam* -greeting, salutation- from her Lord and from me! And give her good tidings of a palace composed of pearls in Jannah, where there is no clamour and no fatigue!"

Sayyidah Khadîjah (r.ah) thus responded to this salaam: "He (Allah, with the exalted fame) is the salaam, and His is salaam; and may salaam be upon Jibreel! O the Messenger of Allah (saw), may the salaam, mercy and blessing of Allah be onto you, too."[73]

There is a considerable amount of information regarding the outstanding attributes and praised character of Sayyidah Khadîjah (r.ah). She spent 25 years with the Holy Prophet (saw). She empowered his cause by being the first person to attest the truth of his Prophethood. She spent all her wealth for the sake of the Messenger of Allah (saw) and for the true religion Islam.

Throughout her life, she assisted the Holy Prophet (saw) in all matters. Especially, when he was assigned the duty of proclaiming Islam, and when everyone broke off relations with him, she consoled him and calmed him down with her pleasant counsel. Therefore the Holy Prophet (saw) was content and satisfied with her, and during her lifetime didn't marry again.

---

72. H. Kubra Ergin, Ibid., page: 188.
73. Bukhârî, Menâkıbu'l-Ensar, 20.

Due to her outstanding qualities, in later periods, Sayyidah Khadîjah (r.ah) was named as "al-Kubra" -the greatest woman-.[74]

* * *

The Holy Prophet (saw) was so content with Sayyidah Khadîjah (r.ah) that he used every opportunity to talk about her, and he would often pray for her. So great was his faithfulness and love that even though she had passed away, the Holy Prophet's (saw) young wife Sayyidah Â'ishah (r.ah) was jealous of Sayyidah Khadîjah (r.ah). Indeed one day she asked the Holy Prophet (saw): "O the Messenger of Allah (saw), you always think of Sayyidah Khadîjah. However, she was a widow and an old woman. Allah gave you one (a wife) better than her. Surely you love me more than her?" Thereupon the Holy Prophet (saw) said: "No, I swear by Allah, that I never had such an auspicious woman than her. She confirmed me when no one did. She shared her property with me when others deprived me. I had only one companion in this world, and that was Sayyidah Khadîjah."[75]

* * *

Regarding another event, Sayyidah Â'ishah (r.ah) narrates; "Although I didn't reach her times, I never felt so much jealousy about the other wives of the Holy Prophet (saw), as I felt for Sayyidah Khadîjah. However, the Messenger of Allah (saw) used to mention her often when he was with me. Whenever the Messenger of Allah (saw) slaughtered a sheep, he used to say: "Send some of this to the friends of Sayyidah Khadîjah!".

Again, Sayyidah Â'ishah (r.ah) relates: "One day I was angry and I said 'Sayyidah Khadîjah!?'. Then the Holy Prophet remarked: *"Her love has been bestowed on me as a sustenance."*[76]

As 'Ali (ra) narrates, the Holy Prophet (saw) said: *"The most righteous among the women of the world is Mariam, the daughter of Imran. And the most righteous among the Muslim women is Sayyidah Khadîjah!"*[77]

---

74. DIA, the article of "Khadijah."
75. Ibn-i Hacer, el-İsâbe, IV, 275; Ahmad bin Hanbel, Musned, VI, 117-118.
76. Muslim, Fedâilu's-Sahâbe, 12.
77. Bukhârî, Menâkıbu'l-Ensar, 20; ayrıca bkz: Ibn-i Hacer, el-Isâbe, 8/60; Halebî, es-Sîre, 1/139.

May Allah the Almighty render all Muslim women monuments of virtue and high morals; gracious, chaste and perceptive ladies, such as Sayyidah Khadîjah (r.ah). And mothers, god-fearing and blessed as her!

Amîn!

**Lessons to be Learned From This Exemplary Life**

1- We ought to demonstrate sagacity, as Sayyidah Khadîjah (r.ah) did, and look for high morals and honesty in the person we aim to marry, rather than worldly goods. As a matter of fact, Sayyidah Khadîjah (r.ah) said: "O beloved servant of Allah! I proposed to you, because I admired your high morals."

If we posses more wealth than our spouse, we should abstain from using it in a way which would make him ill at ease. On the contrary, we should seize the opportunity to use our status and find ways to please our companion. Sayyidah Khadîjah (r.ah) conceded the Holy Prophet (saw) "the right to utilize her wealth as he wished", and thus augmented the connection, love and rapport among both (their) souls. Of course, to reap the fruits of this kind of an arrangement, both sides should draw lessons from the attribute of the Messenger of Allah (saw) as al Amîn, the Truthful one.

2- A woman should always support her husband, especially in difficult times. After he received the first revelation, the Holy Prophet (saw) had asked "Oh Sayyidah Khadîjah, who will believe in me?" Sayyidah Khadîjah (r.ah) had reassured him, by reminding him of his outstanding qualities, and expressing her submission she had said: "Even if no one believes in you, O Messenger of Allah (saw), I will!" If she were to say, "Not one soul will believe in you!", she would have abandoned the Holy Prophet (saw) in this consecrated cause.

Also, the tone she used to address the Holy Prophet (saw) when she declared her faith by saying "I will believe in you, O the Messenger of Allah!" denotes the seemly tone to be applied by women in addressing their spouse. At the same time, this reminds them about their responsibility to the addressee.

3- During the period of the oppression and embargo of the pagans, Sayyidah

Khadîjah (r.ah) shared the burden of the Holy Prophet (saw) with all her wealth and strength, and she opened her heart to all Muslims with the compassion of a mother. She used every opportunity to present gifts to the people whom the Holy Prophet (saw) treasured, hence earning his priceless affection and praise. In fact, even years after her demise, whenever he sacrificed an animal, the Holy Prophet (saw) used to remember Sayyidah Khadîjah (r.ah), and set apart a share for her relatives as a token of faithfulness.[78]

4- Sayyidah Khadîjah (r.ah) had won the heart and appreciation of the Holy Prophet (saw) with the sympathy, selflessness, affection and munificence she displayed. Due to this, she attained his approval and blessing. Thus, women approaching their husbands as Sayyidah Khadîjah (r.ah) did, will be able to attain the acceptance of their husband, and consequently of their Lord.

5- We should not forget that the most important support we can provide to our families is love. The Holy Prophet (saw) said to Sayyidah Â'ishah (r.ah), who was jealous of Sayyidah Khadîjah (r.ah): "Allah never gave me such an auspicious woman than her. Her love has been bestowed on me as a sustenance."[79]

We ought to satiate the hearts of our spouses with our immaculate love, so that they may abstain from illegitimate desires.

6- Sayyidah Khadîjah (r.ah) never employed her servants for the personal needs of the Holy Prophet (saw). She herself used to take care of all his needs. Similarly we should strive to provide for the needs of our spouses personally, without employing our children and servants for these matters. This creates an opportunity to let them realize how cherished they are in our estimation. Besides, one feels compassion and kindness towards something, in proportion to one's efforts on it. The more one has dealings with something, the more one feels affection towards it. It is a fact that care fosters love and compassion.

7- Sayyidah Khadîjah (r.ah) is also an example for the working women. Though she was occupied with commerce, she never neglected her family or children. On the contrary, she gave precedence to her family life, and demonstrated that the earliest step of peace and well-being lies in the family. The Holy

---

78.  DIA, the article of "Khadijah."
79.  Muslim, Fedâilu's-Sahâbe, 12.

Prophet (saw) used to support his beloved wife both in the family and business life, shielding her from this heavy weight.

8- "The lover also cherishes the ones whom are dear to their beloved." In compliance with this norm, Sayyidah Khadîjah (r.ah) displayed concern and affection to everyone that the Holy Prophet (saw) used to hold dear; and in this way, earned even more of his love. Just for this reason, she had presented the Holy Prophet's (saw) wet nurse Halîma, forty sheep and a camel, when she visited her. This generosity of Sayyidah Khadîjah (r.ah) exceedingly pleased the Messenger of Allah (saw). *Insha Allah* -God willing-, we will succeed in taking this norm as our model, and earn the hearts of our beloved, by caring for the ones they value.

9- Sayyidah Khadîjah (r.ah) used to take great care in her physical appearance and cleanliness. She used to wear varied garments -as much as possible- and used to show attention to her clothes and body, each day virtually filling the Holy Prophet (saw) with admiration. Due to this merit, she never let go of herself, despite her advancing age, and seized the heart of her spouse. The fact that the Messenger of Allah (saw) didn't want to marry another woman in her lifetime, is also due to these virtues and outstanding qualities of Sayyidah Khadîjah (r.ah), as well as the uprightness and faithfulness of the Holy Prophet (saw). She never let go by saying "In any case I am rich", "I have a righteous husband" or "I have grown old!" Also she never paid insufficient attention to the charm ingrained in the creation of men and women, and wisely employed this to her advantage.

10- It would be useful to mention one last point: In those days of *Jahiliyah*, the society used to ascribe great importance to having a "son", and the traces of this attitude are still present in our society. However, Sayyidah Khadîjah (r.ah) gave birth to two sons and four daughters from the Holy Prophet (saw). Considering that the majority of the children who came into being from this marriage were girls, we can more closely perceive the pressure of the bigoted prejudice applied by that society on this family.

Neither the Messenger of Allah (saw) nor his pure hearted spouse paid attention to this pressure; they considered their daughters as a source of pride, just as their sons; rejoiced with their birth, and made sacrifices for each one of them -*aqîqah*[80]-. In this connection, the fact that the Holy Prophet (saw) named his first daughter Sayyidah Zainab -the adornment of her father- indicates how pleased he was with her birth. This feeling of joy and the urge to embrace their children, which they experienced from the birth of their children continued throughout the lives of this blessed couple.

It is doubtless that this example communicates a significant message to the corrupt perception regarding the gender of children, still prevailing in these days. The virtuous demeanour of Sayyidah Khadîjah (r.ah) regarding her daughters, where not only the fathers, but also the mothers despised bringing a girl into the world, should present a crucial code of conduct for us.

In essence, Sayyidah Khadîjah (r.ah) presents a great example for us with her obedience and submission to her husband; her support and assistance to her husband for the sake of Allah; and later on with the exceptional children she raised.

### She was outstanding, because...

She was the first of the *Umm ul Mu'minîn,*

The first wife of the Holy Prophet (saw),

The first woman to believe,

The first person to the receive good tidings of earning Jannah,

The first person to worship with the Holy Prophet (saw) in a congregation, and the first ascetic,

A rare person to be greeted by Allah the Almighty and Jibreel (AS),

*She was considered ²âhirah,* the immaculate woman who sacrificed all her belongings for Islam,

---

80. *Aqeeqah* refers to the practice of the Holy Prophet (saw) regarding his newborn children. He used to shave off their hair and sacrifice an animal for the sake of Allah, and he used to recommend his companions to follow suit.

*She was considered Kubra,* the great woman who filled the heart of the Holy Prophet (saw).

On the one hand, Sayyidah Khadîjah (r.ah) was a widow and she had children; on the other hand, she was fifteen years older than the Holy Prophet (saw). However, she wiped away these seemingly unfavourable matters with all of the courtesy, elegance, morals, unselfishness and sagacity she possessed, and set forth an exceptional example. She delighted the Messenger of Allah (saw). Together they lead a distinguished life for twenty five years. From all aspects, Sayyidah Khadîjah (r.ah) became the zenith of womanly qualities. She adorned the life of the Holy Prophet (saw) with never fading beauties. She presented a genuine and abiding model for all women aiming to establish a family.

May our Lord enable us to draw lessons from the spiritual world of Sayyidah Khadîjah (r.ah), who was a monument of nobility, elegance and self-sacrifice. Ameen.

# SAYYIDAH SAWDAH BINT ZAM'A (r.ah)

The death of Abû Tâlib, closely followed by the death of Sayyidah Khadîjah (r.ah), had upset The Holy Prophet (saw) and his Companions deeply. As a matter of fact, the year they both passed away was named as "The Year of Grief".

These and the following events brought about profound hardships for the Holy Prophet (saw). On the one hand, there was the absence of Sayyidah Khadîjah (r.ah); she was the mother of his children and his beloved companion in a marriage surpassing 25 years. On the other hand, he was troubled by the lack of a carer who would tend to the needs of the children and maintain the house. The straits of life in Mecca and the cessation of the protection provided by Abû Tâlib all amplified these difficulties.

He was in need of an experienced housewife to restore order to his household, to look after his children and to be a comfort for him.

Muslims were aware of his situation, but were not able to say or do anything. Khawla bint Hakîm, the wife of 'Uthmân bin Maz'ûn broke this silence one day when she said to the Holy Prophet (saw), "O Prophet of Allah, I see you have become very sad after the passing away of Sayyidah Khadîjah." The Holy Prophet (saw) replied, "Yes, she was the mother of my children and the maintainer of my house." Khawla then said, "O Messenger of Allah, you need a woman to take care of you. I can inquire about this if you let me."

The Holy Prophet (saw) asked her whether there was anyone suitable. She said, "O Prophet of Allah, if you want, there are unmarried girls as well as widows." The Messenger of Allah (saw) asked her, "Who are they?" She said, "If you want someone unmarried, there is the daughter of your companion Abû Bakr. If you want a widow, then there is Sayyidah Sawda bint Zam'a."

After this conversation, the Holy Prophet (saw) told Khawla that both of these candidates were suitable. Upon receiving his approval, Khawla went to ask Sayyidah Sawda (r.ah) to marry with the Holy Prophet (saw).

### The Former Life of Sayyidah Sawda (r.ah)

Her father was Zam'a bin Qays bin 'Abdushams and her mother was Shammûs bint Qays bin Zayd.

Sayyidah Sawda (r.ah) was the first in her family to accept Islam. She then convinced her husband Sakrân bin 'Amr to embrace the religion. Sayyidah Sawda (r.ah) had six children from this marriage.[81]

When the torture and oppression levied by the pagans of Mecca had reached an unbearable level, Sayyidah Sawda (r.ah) and her husband joined the second hijrah to Ethiopia, leaving Mecca with the consent of the Holy Prophet (saw). Sayyidah Sawda (r.ah), who abandoned her motherland and the house in which she was born and raised in order to preserve her faith, was eventually left alone in Ethiopia after her husband inclined to Christianity.[82] In spite of her loneliness and many troubles, she held firmly on to her religion.

Sayyidah Sawda did not possess any financial means and after returning to Mecca she had only very scant resources. She had no income to cover her expenses, and she was too old to earn her living by labour. Neither did the prevailing traditions provide a means to take care of this lonely woman.

The Holy Prophet (saw) chose to marry with Sayyidah Sawda (r.ah). He

---

81.  Havva Ergene Işık, Ibid., page: 288.
82.  Some sources report that her husband died in Ethiopia as a Christian (Muhammed Hamidullah, Islam Peygamberi, II, p. 677; Rıza Savaş, *"Hz. Peygamber'in Âile Hayatı ve Evlilikleri"*, Asr-ı Saadette Islam, vol. I, p. 300), there are other reports saying that he returned to Makkah as a Muslim along with his wife, and died in Makkah (Afzalurrahman, II, p. 161) or on the road to Makkah (For more information see: Ziya Kazıcı,p. 123; Âişe Abdurrahman, p. 32).

found the maturity she had gained by the passing years as something necessary for the raising of his children. At the same time, he intended to shelter Sayyidah Sawda (r.ah) and to alleviate the hardships she faced after embracing Islam.

## The Marriage Ceremony

Sayyidah Sawda (r.ah), though delighted with this offer, expressed some uncertainty about accepting the Prophet's proposal. When the Holy Prophet (saw) asked her, "O Sayyidah Sawda, what prevents you from marrying me?" Sayyidah Sawda (r.ah) replied, "There are no plausible reasons keeping me from marrying with you. I only fear that my children will trouble you with all their noise." The Holy Prophet (saw) said to her, "May Allah forgive you! The most outstanding are the ones who overcome the difficulties in raising their young children."[83]

Khawla approached the father of Sayyidah Sawda (r.ah) to ask for his permission for this marriage. Sayyidah Sawda's father, who was not a Muslim, gave his consent by saying, "He is a righteous and beneficent partner for her!.."[84]

With this approval, their marriage took place in AD 620, three years before the hijrah, in either Ramadan or Shawwal. This was to be the second marriage of the Prophet of Allah (saw) after Sayyidah Khadîjah (r.ah). The Holy Prophet (saw) paid 400 dirhams as mahr.[85] At that time he was 50 and Sayyidah Sawda (r.ah) was 55 years old.[86]

'Abd bin Zam'a, the brother of Sayyidah Sawda (r.ah), who had not yet embraced Islam at that time, had strongly opposed the marriage. He even interrupted the hajj which he was performing according to the traditions of Jahiliyah, and came back, demonstrating his disapproval by tearing out his hair. Later in life, when he embraced Islam, he would regret his actions on that day and, ashamed of what he had done, would say: "I do not remember any other occasion

---

83. Havva Ergene Işık, Ibid., page: 289.
84. Âişe Abdurrahman, Ibid., page: 30.
85. Afzalurrahman, Ibid., II, page: 161.
86. There are reports that say that say when Hz. Sauda (ra) got married with the Prophet (saw) she was the same age (50) as him. (Celâl Yeniçeri, pg. 76)

that I fell into such a ridiculous situation than when I tore my hair and scattered dirt on my head and on my face."

Kinship draws people towards each other. The father, brothers, nephews and many other relatives of Sayyidah Sawda (r.ah) were not acquainted with the Holy Prophet (saw) and because of this they treated him with enmity. Shortly after this marriage, they all became Muslims.

The people of Mecca, and especially the tribe of Quraysh, never understood why the Holy Prophet (saw) married such an old widow after Sayyidah Khadî-jah (r.ah) died. Sayyidah Sawda (r.ah) was neither rich, nor young. Neither was she particularly beautiful. Nevertheless, due to the circumstances both he and Sayyidah Sawda (r.ah) were in, he chose cided to marry her.

### Her Second Hijrah

After the Holy Prophet (saw) made hijrah with Abû Bakr (ra), he appointed Zayd bin Hârithah and Abû Râfi' to bring his daughters Fâtimah (r.ah) and Umm Kulthûm (r.ah) along with his wife Sayyidah Sawda (r.ah), from Mecca to Medina. He gave them two camels and 500 dirhams and sent them to Mecca.[87] This was how Sayyidah Sawda (r.ah) emigrated to Medina.

### Sayyidah Sawda (r.ah) and Motherhood

Sayyidah Sawda (r.ah), who cared for and was companion to the Holy Prophet (saw) for 13 years, had no children from him. However, she took care of his children as if she was their real mother.

This blessed woman managed the household of the Holy Prophet (saw) on her own until Sayyidah Â'ishah's (r.ah) arrival. After her arrival, she did her best to comfort the young bride, helping her to settle into her new role. Sayyidah Sawda (r.ah) considered Sayyidah Â'ishah (r.ah) as her daughter because of the love of the Holy Prophet (saw) for her, and also because she was such a young girl. Sayyidah Â'ishah (r.ah) likewise treasured Sayyidah Sawda (r.ah).

---

87.   Ibn-i Sad, I, 237-238.

I would like to draw your attention to a pleasant account, both because of its significance in reflecting the family life of the Holy Prophet (saw), as well as demonstrating the mutual love and affection between Sayyidah Â'ishah and Sayyidah Sawda (r.ah).

Sayyidah Â'ishah (r.ah) narrates that one day she had made soup for the Holy Prophet (saw). Sayyidah Sawda (r.ah) was with them too. Sayyidah Â'ishah (r.ah) invited Sayyidah Sawda (r.ah) to join them. When she held back, Sayyidah Â'ishah (r.ah) cautioned her: "I will smear your face with it if you do not eat!" When 'Sawda (r.ah) insisted on not eating, Â'ishah (r.ah) took some of the soup and smeared it on her face. The Holy Prophet (saw) smiled at the resulting scene and held Sayyidah Sawda's (r.ah) hand, saying: "What are you waiting for; you smear her face, too!" Thereon Sawda (r.ah) smeared Sayyidah Â'ishah's (r.ah) face with the soup, just the same way. The Holy Prophet (saw) smiled at her condition, too.[88]

## The Distinction of this Marriage

As has been alluded to already, this marriage was not based on love in the precise sense; Sayyidah Sawda (r.ah) was aware of this fact. After all, even though he was a Prophet, the Messenger of Allah (saw) was a human being. There were things that his heart desired, as well as things that he disliked. Sayyidah Sawda (r.ah) was quick to grasp this, with the experience she gained with the passing years. In the following years, she was aware of the fact that the Holy Prophet (saw) had other wives which were much younger and more beautiful than her. She was neither in the position to compete with them, nor did she have a desire to do so. She had only one wish: to be among the Ummu'l Mu'mineen, and to be called upon as the wife of the Holy Prophet (saw) in this world and in the hereafter; not as the widow of Sakran (or Sukran)!..

Although the Holy Prophet (saw) was diligent in treating his wives equally, he thought that he wasn't able to display sufficient care and love towards Sayyidah Sawda (r.ah). Out of fear of hurting her feelings and offending her, he decided to talk to her openly. He told her that if she wished so, he could release

---

88. Afzalurrahman, Ibid., II, page: 161.

her from the marriage bond, which he thought did not make her happy; he could divorce her so that she would feel unrestricted.

Sayyidah Sawda (r.ah) had perceived these thoughts beforehand. However, when she heard the word of "divorce" from the lips of the Holy Prophet (saw), she was devastated; as if all the surrounding walls had collapsed onto her. She had a constricted feeling and her face became pale. The Holy Prophet (saw) realized that what he had said saddened her even more, and tried to console her. Sayyidah Sawda (r.ah) explained her decision: "O Messenger of Allah! The feelings that the young brides have for their husbands has passed away from me. My only purpose is to be among your wives in the Day of Resurrection!"[89] This was, of course, a very difficult choice for her; however, in order to be among the wives of the Prophet (saw) in the hereafter, she chose the deprivation of this world.

In addition to this, Sayyidah Sawda (r.ah) stated to the Holy Prophet (saw) that she allotted her day -that she spent with him- to Sayyidah Â'ishah (r.ah), for whom he displayed particular affection.[90]

Sayyidah Sawda (r.ah) was such a selfless woman; noble and anxious regarding her position in the Hereafter. She was an exceptional wife, who found joy in the happiness of the Holy Prophet (saw) and was upset when he was sad.

The Holy Prophet (saw) was always attentive to make Sayyidah Sawda (r.ah) happy, and he never left her without the attention or the means he provided to his other wives.

It is reported that Sayyidah Sawda (r.ah) was hard of hearing in her last years. The other wives of the Holy Prophet (saw) used to joke with her because of this, and she used to respond to them the same way.

---

89. Âişe Abdurrahman, Ibid., page: 34.
90. As it is recorded in Abu Dawud, the reason of the revelation of the 128th verse of the Surah al-Nisa was her decision to give up of her right to be with the Holy Prophet (saw) at night, in favour of Â'isha (ra); thus reaching a settlement among them: **"And if a woman fears ill usage or desertion on the part of her husband, there is no blame on them, if they effect a reconciliation between them, and reconciliation is better, and avarice has been made to be present in the (people's) minds; and if you do good (to others) and guard (against evil), then surely Allah is aware of what you do."** (Abu Dawud, Marriage, 27-28/2125; Celâl Yeniçeri, p. 77)

## The High Moral Virtues of Sayyidah Sawda (r.ah)

After the hijrah from Mecca to Medina, Sayyidah Sawda (r.ah) accompanied the Holy Prophet (saw) in several battles. When describing her, Sayyidah Â'ishah (r.ah) said: "Among all women, Sayyidah Sawda bint Zam'a is the one that I would most love to be like. This is because she possesses a strong temper firm in resolve and unshakeable determination."[91]

The term of 'strong temper' used here denotes perseverance and devotion to religion; not ill temper or peevishness.[92]

Sayyidah Sawda (r.ah) loved to give charity. She used to prepare things with her hands and present them to marriageable girls as dowry.[93] As Sayyidah Â'ishah (r.ah)[94] narrates:

"One day the wives of the Holy Prophet (saw) gathered in his presence and asked him, 'O Messenger of Allah, which one of us will be the first to reunite with you?' The Holy Prophet (saw) said, 'The one with the longest hand!'

Then we found a stick and we all measured our hands. The hand of Zam'a's daughter (Sayyidah Sawda) was the longest. Whereas, by saying 'long hand', the Holy Prophet (saw) had meant 'one who gives a lot of charity[95]; and certainly she loved to give charity.'[96]

When he was the Caliph, Umar (ra) allotted a regular payment to the wives of the Holy Prophet (saw) from the Treasury. He gave them ten thousand dirhams each. Because of the special place of Sayyidah Â'ishah (r.ah) with the Holy Prophet (saw), he made her allocation slightly higher than the others'. Sayyidah Sawda (r.ah) used to give this money which Umar (ra) sent her in charity to the poor and needy, alongside most of the money she earned by embroidering leather...

---

91. Muslim, Redâ, 14.
92. Ziya Kazıcı, Ibid., page: 126.
93. Havva Ergene Işık, Ibid., page. 290.
94. A similar telling was reported from Hz. Sauda (ra).
95. At the time of the death of Zaynab bintu Cahsh, it was understood that in this hadith the **"longest hand"** was the **"most charitable"**, because our mother Zaynab passed away in the 20th year after the Hijra, thus she had won the quality of being the first wife who died after the Prophet (saw). Hz. Umar (ra) made her cenaza (funeral) prayer.
96. Muslim, Fedâilü's-Sahâbe, 101.

One of the reasons for the revelation of the verse of *hijâb*[97] was the following incident which occurred between 'Umar (ra) and Sayyidah Sawda (r.ah) narrated by Sayyidah Â'ishah (r.ah);

"When the wives of the Holy Prophet (saw) went outside at night for their needs, they used to go as far as Manâsi' (the outskirts of Medina). However that place was not well covered. 'Umar (ra) would request the Prophet (saw) to veil his women though he did not do so immediately. One day, Sayyidah Sawda (r.ah) went outside during the *'ishâ* prayer.[98] She was a very tall woman. Umar (ra) was longing for a revelation regarding covering, called out: "O Sawda! Be aware that we have recognised you." After this, Allah the Almighty revealed the verse on hijâb."[99]

In another account, Sayyidah Â'ishah (r.ah) relates:

"Sawda, the wife of the Holy Prophet (saw), went out of the house for some needs. Sawda was a woman with a big frame. Therefore, even though she was completely veiled, people who knew her could recognise her. When 'Umar (ra) saw her, he raised an objection and said: 'O Sawda! I swear by Allah that you are not unknown to us. Why do you leave your home?!' Thereon, Sawda returned home. The Messenger of Allah (saw) was in my room having dinner at the time. He held a bone in his hand, with some meat on it. When he was in this position, Sawda came in and complained: 'O Prophet of Allah, I had left home for some chores. 'Umar (ra) expressed disapproval of this…' "

Sayyidah Â'ishah (r.ah) said: "Just after this, the Messenger of Allah (saw) received a revelation. When the revelation ceased, even before he set down the meat and bone he was holding, he turned to Sawda and said, "You (women) have been allowed to leave your homes (when covered) for your needs.""[100]

You will see more the details of Sayyidah Sawda's relationship in the "honey syrup" event which caused the first verses of Tahrim to be revealed; it

---

97.  *Hijâb* literally denotes any kind of veil, curtain, facial veil, etc. In Islamic terminology *hijâb* refers to the dress code of women. The facial *hijâb* is divided into two types: 1) *Niqâb*: full facial covering. 2) *Khimâr*: partial facial covering; covering the face, but leaving the eyes exposed.
98.  *'Ishâ'* is the fifth and last prayer of the day, offered after the twilight.
99.  Bukhârî, Vudû', 13.
100.  Bukhârî, Tefsîru'l-Kur'ân, 33/8.

is further explained under the subject heading of Hafza.

* * *

There are different reports regarding the date when Sayyidah Sawda (r.ah) passed away. According to some accounts, she died towards the end of 'Umar's (ra) rule (22-23 hijri), and according to other accounts, she passed away at the 54th year of hijrah, in Medina.

Sayyidah Sawda (r.ah) displayed her love for Sayyidah Â'ishah (r.ah) even at the time of her death by leaving her room to her. Therefore, Sayyidah Â'ishah (r.ah) had the chance to widen her room by combining it with Sayyidah Sawda's (r.ah) room. This was the very room which housed the tomb of the Messenger of Allah (saw), a room full of his memories.[101]

Sayyidah Sawda (r.ah) narrated five *hadîth*[102] from the Holy Prophet (saw). Some of these are narrated by Bukhârî in his *Sahîh*. 'Abdullâh bin 'Abbâs or Yahya bin 'Abdullâh bin 'Abdurrahmân narrated *hadîth* from her.

### Lessons to be Taken From Her Exemplary Life

1- Sayyidah Sawda (r.ah) was one of the first believers to make hijrah to Ethiopia. Her first husband died there and she endured many hardships upon her return to Mecca. Her close relatives were pagans, and she was vulnerable for in two respects, firstly that she was a widow and secondly that she had accepted Islam. Despite all of her torment and suffering, she held on to her religion without compromising, even at the most difficult of times. She thus presents us with an excellent model of how we may preserve our belief in the face of hardships.

2- Despite the fact that Sayyidah Sawda (r.ah) did not have any children from the Holy Prophet (saw), she looked after his children as if they were hers; she was almost like a surrogate mother. She did this even though she was well into her fifties when she married the Holy Prophet (saw). Her life is an example

---

101. Celâl Yeniçeri, Ibid., page: 76; Muhammed Hamidullah, İslâm Peygamberi, II, page: 678.
102. The word *hadith* (plural *ahâdîth*) literally means communication or narration. In the Islamic context it has come to denote the record of what the Prophet (saw) said, did, or tacitly approved.

of how we should treat orphans; children, who due to destiny, are in need of someone to play the role of their mother. Sayyidah Sawda (r.ah) used the opportunity to draw closer to Allah the Almighty and to His Messenger (saw). She tried hard to earn a place in the hearts of these orphans, and willingly took care of their upbringing and needs.

3- She chose the Hereafter over the comforts, pleasures and means of this transitory world when she requested to be one of the wives of the Holy Prophet (saw).

4- She deployed all her means for the sake of Allah, and gained the appreciation and compliments of the Messenger of Allah (saw) with her generosity and kindness towards people in need.

5- The Holy Prophet (saw) observed her rights in the finest manner, and while striving to accomplish justice among his wives, he did not neglect her either.

6- Sayyidah Sawda (r.ah) loved the Messenger of Allah (saw) so deeply that, consequently, she loved whoever was beloved to him and displayed a genuine concern towards them. The fact that she displayed a distinctive affection for Sayyidah Â'ishah (r.ah), and for the children of the Holy Prophet (saw) was due to this. Based on this, if we too hold the Holy Prophet (saw) dear, we need to value whatever and whoever he loved; this holds true especially for his family, the *Ahl al-Bayt*. We also need to be fastidiously committed to his *Sunnah*[103] which is the perfect model for us.

---

103.  The *Sunnah* includes the sayings, practices and living habits of the Prophet Muhammad (saw), as recorded in the various *hadîth* collections. Along with the Qur'ân, the *Sunnah* is a source of Islamic law and practice.

# "SAYYIDAH Â'ISHAH BINT ABU BAKR
# HABIBATU HABIBULLAH"[104]

**(A'ishah, the daughter of Abu Bakr and the beloved of the beloved of Allah - *Habibullah*)**

*"If the ones who condemned Zuleikha and cut their
hands upon seeing Joseph (AS) (in their amazement) were
to see the blessed countenance of Allah's Messenger; they
would cut their hearts without knowing it."*

*Sayyidah Â'ishah (r.ah)[105]*

Let our souls, weary in the hands of daily chores, take wings to the age of happiness, to the blessed household; and come to rest at the window of Sayyidah Â'ishah (r.ah), the mother of all believers, the (most) beloved of the Prophet of Prophets, the daughter of Abu Bakr, the peerless pearl whom Muslim women can show to mankind with pride.

This time, let us be enlightened with the vast expanse of the heart of Sayy-

---

104. al-Istiab, IV, p: 1883. As narrated by Ata' bin Abe Rabah, This was expression used by Â'isha (ra) following the "Basmalah" in her letters. Basmalah means "In the Name of Allah" and is a statement, usually made by every Muslim who is about to embark on anything that is Halal (lawful), however trivial that act or deed may seem. ii) First verse of Suratul Fatiha. iii) To be recited before the beginning of every *Surah* except for *Surah at Tawbah* (Surah 9) of the Holy Qur'an).

105. "Ladies said in the City: 'The wife of the (great) 'Aziz is seeking to seduce her slave from his (true) self: Truly hath he inspired her with violent love: we see she is evidently going astray.' When she heard of their malicious talk, she sent for them and prepared a banquet for them: she gave each of them a knife: and she said (to Joseph), "Come out before them." When they saw him, they did extol him, and (in their amazement) cut their hands: they said, 'Allah preserve us! no mortal is this! this is none other than a noble angel!' " (*Surah Yusuf* 12:30-31)

idah Â'ishah (r.ah), a heart brimming with virtue, chastity, generosity, knowledge, sagacity and intellect. She lived the most beautiful days of her life with the inspiration she received from the Prophet of Allah (saw); she acquired manners at which to be marvelled. She wasted not a second of her life uselessly. She was full of love. She tried hard and endeavoured into the unknown with her sharp wits. Under the consummate guidance of the Holy Prophet (saw) she was first a perfect student, and then she became a great teacher. She became a light (inspiration) for future generations and for science. She was as a sun for the science of hadith; a pioneer of *fiqh*,-Islamic law, and an accomplished guide and role model for women. May Allah be pleased with her.

## Sayyidah Â'ishah's (r.ah) Family

The ancestry of Sayyidah Â'ishah (r.ah), who by marrying the Holy Prophet (saw) received the honour of being among the Mothers of the Believer,(*Ummul Mu'mineen*) is famous for its virtue, both on her father's and her mother's side. Her father's tribe Banu Taym, had an outstanding place among other tribes because of their honour, bravery, trustworthiness and veracity.[106]

Abu Bakr (ra), an exceptional member of this tribe, was a man who kept his word at all cost. The men of this tribe were also renowned for their gallent and gentle treatment of their women. Abu Bakr (ra), the father of Sayyidah Â'ishah (r.ah) is known as someone who was easy to get on with; good-natured, with a gentle temperament and who did his best to help others, both as an individual and as the head of state. Because of his knowledge on genealogy, his capacity for relating to people as well as his involvement in trade, initially the Kuraish and in later times the Muslims would ask for his advice in various matters. The Holy Prophet (saw), would also consult him regularly. Because of this, some of the companions used to call him as "the vizier of the Prophet of Allah"[107], even though such a title did not exist in the Muslim world at that time.

Abu Bakr, the companion of the Holy Prophet (saw) during hijrah, who is mentioned in the Quran as the second of two, had an impeccable personality

---

106.   Ziya Kazıcı, Ibid., page: 138.
107.   Ziya Kazıcı, Ibid., page: 139.

and a pre-eminent character. Sayyidah Â'ishah (r.ah) was the daughter of such a man. Abu Bakr, who made immeasurable sacrifices and displayed countless heroic deeds for Allah and for His Prophet, is one of the ten companions who received the good tidings of earning Jannah while they were still on Earth. He is *"As-siddiq"*[108]. This name was given to him by the Prophet of Allah (saw), because of his unhesitant belief and acceptance regarding *Miraj*[109]. Because Sayyidah Â'ishah (r.ah) carried the same noble traits in her personality, she too was named as Â'ishah as -Siddiqah (as-Sadiqah), *Â'isha, the truthfu,-* and also as Â'ishah bint as-Siddiq, *Â'ishah, the daughter of as-Siddiq.*[110]

The mother of Sayyidah Â'ishah (r.ah), *Ummu Ruman bint Aamer ben Uwaymer*, belonged to the Kinana Tribe, and she was amongst the cherished women companions. After the Holy Prophet (saw) and Abu Bakr (ra) made hijrah to Madinah, she followed them. According to one account, when pious Ummu Ruman died in Madinah, six years after the hijrah, the Holy Prophet (saw) personally went down into her grave and said: "Whoever would be pleased by gazing at a *houri* should look at Ummu Ruman".[111]

Being brought up by such parents, Sayyidah Â'ishah (r.ah) learned Islam from childhood. For this reason, it is possible to say that she was raised by the Prophet of Allah (saw): having an exclusive place in his heart and house. Furthermore, she had a charming beauty, a brilliant wit, and a tender youthfulness.[112]

She was born in Mecca, four or five years after the advent of the Holy Prophet (saw) (AD 614 or 615). Both she and her sister Esma had become Muslims, when they were small children, though at that time the number of Muslims was very few.[113]

---

108. "The Truthful". This title was given to Abu Bakr (ra) by the Holy Prophet (saw). When the Prophet Muhammad (saw) related his experience of al-Isra (his night journey to the Masjid al-Aqsa in Jerusalem) wal Mi'raj (and his ascension through the seven heavens) to Abu Bakr (ra) he immediately and without any reservation replied "Sadaqt": "You have spoken the truth". From that time on, Abu Bakr (ra) came to be known as Abu Bakr as-Siddiq.

109. *Miraj* is the Night Journey of the Holy Prophet (saw) from Mecca to Jerusalem and then through the realms of the seven heavens, beyond the limit of forms -the Sidrat al-Muntaha-, to within a bow-span's length or nearer to the presence of Allah. See the Qur'an, Al-Isra (17:1), Bukhari, Hadith 345, Vol. 1, 227, Vol. 5.

110. Mustafa Fayda, DIA, II, 201.

111. Ibn-i Sa'd, VIII, 277.

112. Ziya Kazıcı, Ibid., page:139.

113. Ziya Kazıcı, Ibid., page: 139-140.

## Her Marriage with the Holy Prophet (saw)

After an angel had showed Sayyidah Â'ishah (r.ah) to him in his dream several times and said "This is your wife", the Holy Prophet (saw) became engaged to her in Mecca, and married her in Madinah, two years after hijrah. Hawlah bint Hakeem, the wife of Uthman bin Maz'un, narrated this happy event, in which she took part:

*"After the passing of Khadijah, I went to the Prophet of Allah, and asked him: 'Wouldn't you consider marrying?' Thereupon the Holy Prophet mentioned his intention to get married, but asked me who would be willing to marry him with his children, and under what conditions. I said: 'If you wish, there are unmarried girls, as well as widows'. The Prophet of Allah asked 'Who is there from the girls?' I said: Â'ishah, the daughter of your beloved (companion) Abu Bakr'. Then the Prophet of Allah asked: 'And who is there from widows?' I replied: 'There is Sevdah bint Zem'a, who believes in you'. After this, he told me to ask for both of them, -first Sawda- because he was in need for someone to take care of his children and to manage his household."*

Hawlah accounted the rest of the event in the following way: *"When I reached Abu Bakr's house, I came across Ummu Ruman, the mother of Â'ishah. I said to her: 'Ummu Ruman! Do you know what a blessing and prosperity has Allah bestowed upon you?' Ummu Ruman asked me: 'What is it?' 'Allah's Messenger (saw) sent me to ask for Â'ishah.' 'I wish this would happen, but wait for Abu Bakr, he will be here soon!'"*

When Abu Bakr arrived, this time Hawlah turned to him: *'O Abu Bakr! Do you know what a blessing and prosperity has Allah bestowed upon you? Allah's Messenger (saw) sent me to ask for Â'ishah.'* By pointing to his intimacy with the Holy Prophet (saw), Abu Bakr asked: *'Can Â'ishah be his spouse? She is the daughter of his brother?!'*

Upon this question, Hawlah returned to the Holy Prophet (saw) and told him what Abu Bakr (ra) had said. The Holy Prophet (saw) asked her to go back to Abu Bakr (ra) and instructed her to tell him: *'You are my brother in Allah's religion and His Book, but she (Â'ishah) is lawful for me to marry.'*[114]

---

114.   Bukhari, *Volume 7, Book 62, Number 18.*

Hawlah said: *"Thereon I went back to Abu Bakr, and repeated to him exactly what was told to me. He said, 'Wait until I come back!' After he had left, Ummu Rumman told me: 'Mut'in bin Adey had asked Â'ishah for his son Jubayr. I swear by Allah that Abu Bakr has never gone back on his word.'"*

When Abu Bakr went into Mut'im's house, his wife was there too. His wife, who was a pagan said: *'O the son of Kuhafa! If we marry our son with your daughter, surely you will divert him from his beliefs and attempt to introduce him into your religion!'* Without replying to her, Abu Bakr turned to Mut'im and asked him: *'What is this woman saying?'* Mut'im replied: *'She says something that I hear* (and agree with)!' With this, they made it clear that they didn't want this marriage.

Abu Bakr came back to his home delighted; praising Allah for removing the obstacle posed by his word. He said to Hawlah: *'Let's invite Allah's Messenger (saw) here!'* Hawlah went to the Holy Prophet (saw) and invited him to the house of his companion Abu Bakr. Abu Bakr engaged his daughter Â'ishah (r.ah) to the Holy Prophet (saw).[115]

Only Sayyidah Â'ishah was a virgin out of the women the Holy Prophet (saw) married, This marriage augmented the bond of mutual regard and affection between these friends, even further.[116]

### The Reports Regarding the Age of Â'ishah (r.ah)

When this marriage took place, Makkans did not seem to be alarmed by this occasion. On the contrary, they accepted it as a normal event. None of the adversaries of Islam were able to make a case out of it: and even the fiercest enemies of the Holy Prophet (saw) could not find a reason to criticise him because of this marriage. There was indeed nothing to be said or done. Perhaps someone, who was not familiar with the conditions and circumstances of that time, could only question the age of Sayyidah Â'ishah (r.ah). Nevertheless, previously Mut'im bin Adiy had asked for her for his son Jubayr. If the age of Â'ishah (r.ah) was

---

115. Taberî, Tarih, II, 412.
116. Muhammed Hamidullah, İslâm Peygamberi, II, 678.

so young that she would be considered unfit for marriage in that period and society, the family who had asked for her before the Holy Prophet (saw) would have been condemned. However, no one said anything, neither about Jubayr nor about the Holy Prophet (saw).[117]

The conclusion we can draw from thisis that in that day and age the customs and the common law held no objections to the marriageof teenagers. The two conditions for a girl to be marriageable in practical terms are: to be psychologically and biologically fit for marriage.

When we study Sayyidah Â'ishah (r.ah) from the psychological aspect, we see that she was engaged to someone else before the Holy Prophet (saw). If she was not ready for it, she would not have accepted such an offer and become engaged. The socio-cultural conditions of those times psychologically prepared girls for marriage at very early ages: even as early as 10. In her day and age there were many such examples. Obviously,these conditions can vary according to the time, customs and society.

On the other hand, biological preparedness refers specifically to pubescence. Because of the climatic conditions in the Arabian Peninsula, girls reached puberty around the age of eight or nine, which we may consider quite early.[118] This shows that Sayyidah Â'ishah (r.ah) was also biologically prepared for marriage.

Nowadays, because of the hormones used in the growing of vegetables that are then consumed by people, and because of excessive sexual stimulants in the social environment, the age for the onset of puberty has started to reduce to the age of around nine or ten.

It is reported regarding this, that an unprejudiced orientalist who journeyed around the Arabian Peninsula said: *"Â'ishah must have reached the maturity peculiar to the Arabian women, despite her small age. This rapid growth of the Arabian people causes women to grow old very quickly in the years following their twentieth."*[119]

---

117.  Afzalurrahman, Ibid., II, 162.
118.  It is clear that as one moves towards the polar regions, the age of puberty moves to higher ages; to 15 and even to 17 and beyond. In this respect, the age of 9-10 in the Arabian Peninsula corresponds to 15, and in some cases, higher ages, in northern regions. (Celal Yeniceri, p.78)
119.  See: Ayşe Abdurrahman, Ibid., page. 257-258; See: Ayşe Abdurrahman, Ibid., page: 40-42.

Setting these facts aside, the historical sources contain different accounts regarding the age of Sayyidah Â'ishah (r.ah) when she got married. For instance, Zakai Konrapa writes that she made hijrah when she was 17, and married Allah's Messenger (saw) at the age of 18.[120] Although there are other contemporary researchers[121] sharing the same point of view, there are also differing views, saying that she was younger.[122]

Setting the uncertainty of her birth date aside, we can say that she married with Allah's Messenger (saw) after the death of Khadijah (r.ah), three years before the hijrah. This corresponds to the month of Shawwal, on the tenth year of his advent. And they entered the nuptial chamber in Madinah in the first year of hijrah, again in the month of Shawwal.[123]

---

120.   Zekâî Konrapa, Peygamberimiz, 434.

121.   Regarding the age of Â'isha (ra), Ramazan Balci, who wrote a book on her, says: "Considering that Â'isha (ra) remembered her parents (only) as Muslims, then her age is either the same as Islam's, or two to three years more; since to remember her parents which were among the first Muslims, she had to be at least three or four years old. As an inevitable conclusion of this analysis, we have to accept that when Â'isha (ra) was engaged to the Holy Prophet (saw), she was around 9 or 10, and when she got married with him in Madinah, she was 14 or 15 years old.

There are also some accounts narrated by Â'isha (ra), which support this inference. She said: "Allah's Messenger prayed: 'O Lord! Honour Umar with Islam'."

This account from Â'isha (ra) opposes some other reports which narrate this hadith as: "O Lord! Honour Islam with Umar." This is because Islam itself is honourable, and it gives honour; nothing else can honour Islam. It is important to consider the age which would permit such an intellect which can decipher such subtle meanings. Â'isha (ra) must have heard this prayer personally, which was made in the fourth or fifth year of the Prophethood. If not, she wouldn't have attempted to correct a hadith based on her personal judgement. According to this, at that time -the fifth year of Prophethood- it is not possible for Â'isha (ra) to be smaller than 6 or 7.

Also, the events narrated by Â'isha (ra) regarding the hijrah of her parents, represent mindful observations of a mature personality." (Ramazan Balci, En Sevgilinin Sevgilisi Hz. Aişe, İstanbul, 2005, p: 28-29)

122.   Muhammad Hamidullah says that she was 7 years old, when she got married [was engaged?] with the Holy Prophet (saw), two years before the hijrah. (M. Hamidullah, *Islam Peygamberi*, II, 678)

Afzalurrahman, the author of the *Encyclopaedia of Sirah*, claims that Â'isha (ra) was engaged with the Holy Prophet (saw) in the 10th year of the Prophethood, when she was six; and that the marriage was completed when she was nine years old (Afzalurrahman, II, p.161).

After assessing all these reports, Mustafa Fayda doesn't find the accounts strong, which say that Â'isha (ra) married with the Holy Prophet (saw) at the ages of 14 or 18. (The article on "Â'isha", *Diyanet Islamic Encyclopaedia* -DIA-, II, 201). He bases this view on a word of Â'isha (ra): "My parents were Muslims, as long as I knew them" (Bukhari). This word clearly shows that Â'isha (ra) was born after the advent of the Holy Prophet (saw).

123.   See: DIA, the article of **"Âişe"** , v: II, page: 201; Prof. Dr. Ziya Kazıcı, Ibid., page: 136-187.

## The Dreams of the Holy Prophet (saw)

Allah the Almighty also prepared the Holy Prophet (saw) for marriage with Sayyidah Â'ishah (r.ah), by dreams. Sayyidah Â'ishah (r.ah) narrated this event as follows: "*Allah's Apostle said (to me), 'You were shown to me in a dream. An angel brought you to me in a piece of silken cloth and said to me, 'This is your wife, open it.' I opened the cloth and the one inside was you. I said to myself, 'If it is from Allah, then it will surely be.'*"[124]

The Holy Prophet (saw) saw this dream for three nights. This means that it was a true,*sadiq,* dream: a divine inspiration by Allah. This fact shows that the marriage of the Holy Prophet (saw) and Sayyidah Â'ishah (r.ah) took place with the command and permission of Allah the Almighty. If this was an improper marriage, Allah the Almighty would not have permitted it. Beyond this, there is no authority to judge this event. Since this event took place under the commandment of Allah, it is a blessed and exemplary marriage, both for them, as well as for us.

Regarding this matter, Â'isha Abdurrahman says:

"When the news of kinship among these two esteemed and loyal friends was spread, Meccans were not taken by surprise: they received this news as natural and as a resolved matter. Even the adversaries of Allah's Messenger (saw) were not able to say a word about this kinship. Moreover, it did not occur even to his fiercest enemies, who in their attempts to debase him often resorted to any means including lies and slander, to use his engagement with Sayyidah Â'ishah (r.ah) as a matter to criticise him.

What could have they said; would they criticise the engagement of a child like Sayyidah Â'ishah, at the age of seven or eight? This engagement has, however, preoccupied several of the historians who have written about Prophet Muhammad (saw): but they have looked at this event only from the perspective of the modern society in which we live. They could not appreciate the fact that similar engagements are still the custom in Asia, and that this custom is still present in Eastern Europe, Spain, Portugal and in some regions of the United States."[125]

---

124. Bukhârî, Nikâh, 9, 35, Tâbir, 20-21; Muslim, Fedâilü's-Sahâbe, 79; Tirmîdhî, Menâkıb, 3875.
125. Balley, page: 129, narrated by Ayşe Abdurrahman, Ibid., page: 40.

As it is reported from Sayyidah Â'ishah (r.ah), the Prophet (saw) married her when she was six years old and he consummated his marriage when she was nine years old, and then she remained with him for nine years.[126]

## The Hijrah

The pagans, who initially scorned and ridiculed the *da'wah*, (call to Islam), of the Holy Prophet (saw), decided to take some measures when the number of Muslims started to increase. These measures consisted of brutal torture, oppression, physical and social boycotting, and murder attempts. In time, the scope of the violence, torment and torture expanded, which at the outset had only applied to the weak and solitary Muslims, so that none of the Muslims were safe. It was then that Allah the Almighty permitted Muslims to make hijrah to countries safer than Mecca. The Holy Prophet (saw) had sent two Muslim groups to Ethiopia. However, when the majority of these migrants came back to Mecca, after believing a rumour claiming that the Meccans had converted to Islam, the intended objective was not accomplished.

Allah's Messenger (saw) was left alone after the deaths of his blessed wife Khadijah (r.ah) and his uncle Abu Talib, who had protected him since his childhood, and he had started to seek out other safe places in order emigrate. He first turned to Taif. The people of Taif first invited the Holy Prophet (saw) to their city, later they had their children and slaves attack him by throwing stones. After these afflictions, Allah the Almighty gave His Prophet consolation with Miraj; then He placed the love of Islam into the hearts of the people of Madinah, and brought them to the presence of His Prophet. The people of Madinah pledged allegiance to him at two meetings in the Aqaba Hills[127]. With these events, the new location for hijrah was determined: Madinah.

Allah's Messenger (saw) advised his companions to travel to Medina gradually and under concealment. However, he had not yet received permission for his own hijrah. All of the Muslims, who were able to travel had set off and settled in

---

126. Al-İstiâb, IV, page: 1882; See: Bukhârî, Nikâh, 38-39; Abû Dâvud, Nikâh, 34.
127. *Aqabah* is a place just outside of Mecca, in Mina where the first Muslims from Yathrib (Madinah) pledged allegiance to the Holy Prophet (saw) in the year 621 AD. A similar meeting took place the next year when more Muslims from Yathrib pledged their allegiance to the Holy Prophet (saw).

Madinah, apart from the Holy Prophet (saw), Abu Bakr (ra), Ali (ra) and a few elderly and isolated people: no other Muslims remained in Mecca.

One time, the pagans conspired to kill the Holy Prophet (saw) in his bed in the dark of night. They gathered the selected fighters from each tribe and surrounded the house of the Holy Prophet (saw). When Jibreel (AS) informed him of their plan, Allah's Messenger (saw) let Ali (ra) lie in his bed (as a trick). Then, while reading verses from the *Surah al-Yasin*, he passed amongst the assassins who had come there to kill him. His first stop was the house of his devoted companion Abu Bakr. Let's listen to the rest of the event from Sayyidah Â'ishah (r.ah), the daughter of Abu Bakr (ra):

*"(My father Abu Bakr) asked for permission from the Holy Prophet to travel to Madinah from Mecca, when the torment he suffered from the Quraish became too violent. The Holy Prophet said to him: 'Wait and remain in your place.' Then Abu Bakr asked him: 'O Allah's Messenger (saw)! Do you also want to receive permission to travelto Medina?' Allah's Messenger replied: 'I am waiting for this'."*

*Abu Bakr waited a long time for this permission to be given. Then, one day around noon, the Holy Prophet (saw) came to Abu Bakr and called out to him: 'O Abu Bakr!' And when he came inside he said: 'Send outside whoever is with you'. Abu Bakr said 'I have my two daughters with me'. The Holy Prophet said: 'Did you sense that I have received permission to leave Mecca?' When Abu Bakr asked: 'Am I going to be with you?' The Holy Prophet replied: 'Yes, you will be with me, as you had wished'. Thereon Abu Bakr said: 'I have two female camels for riding. I had prepared them to leave Mecca for hijrah.'*

*He gave one of the camels to the Holy Prophet. This camel was named as 'al-Jadwa.*[128] *The Holy Prophet and Abu Bakr mounted the camels and departed. Eventually they reached the cave in Mount Sawr and hid there..."*

When we examine the *hijrah* from the point of Sayyidah Â'ishah (r.ah), we see it as a more subtle event, filled with longing. On the one hand her father was leaving her, but on the other hand, her future husband, who she would share her life with, and who she loved and believed in was separating from her. They

---

128.  It is also reported that this camel was 'Quswa' (See: Ziya Kazici, p:146).

were being left in this pagan society on their own, without money and without a guardian, and as well as the many dangers that could be awaiting them on the road; naturally, Sayyidah Â'ishah (r.ah) was thinking about these, and she could not keep herself from being concerned and worried.[129]

The manner in which Abu Kuhafa the father of Abu Bakr (ra) reacted, sets forth an interesting illustration of the financial straits they would undergo after the Holy Prophet (saw) and Abu Bakr (ra) had left. The historians narrate this event as follows:

That day the Holy Prophet (saw) and Abu Bakr sat together at home the whole day. When nightime set in they departed. Abu Bakr, who had sold many of his belongings, had approximately five thousand dirhams. He took them with him, to use on their journey. Asma, the daughter of Abu Bakr narrates: "My grandfather Abu Kuhafa was blind. He said to us: 'By God, Abu Bakr left nothing for you. He left you in destitution and shortage.' In response to this, I said: 'Grandpa, he left us plenty' and I reached with my hand to the place Abu Bakr kept his money where I had placed pebbles. And then I said: 'This is the money he left for us'. Abu Kuhafa said: 'Then don't worry, this amount of money will be sufficient for you.' Esma said: 'I swear by Allah that he had left us nothing. I did this only to calm the old man down'.[130]

The Holy Prophet (saw) used to come to the house of Abu Bakr (ra) either early in the morning, or towards evening. However, this time, it was late morning, when the sun was high in the sky and the heat was scorching, while Abu Bakr (ra) was sitting at his home with the members of his family someone came and announced that the Holy Prophet (saw) had come wearing a turban on his head.

Sayyidah Â'ishah (r.ah) says: "It wasn't his habit to come at that time. My father had said: 'Something important must have happened. Otherwise why should he come at this time?'

Then Allah's Messenger (saw) came in, and without looking around, directly went to his place and sat down. It was apparent that his mind was

---

129.   Ziya Kazıcı, Ibid., page: 146.
130.   Ziya Kazıcı, Ibid., page: 146-147.

preoccupied with something important. There was only Sayyidina Abu Bakr, Sayyidah Â'ishah and Esma at home. Attentively they looked at him.

The Holy Prophet (saw) turned directly towards Abu Bakr, and without looking to the others in the room, he said: 'Send everyone in the room outside'. Then Abu Bakr (ra) said: 'O Allah's Messenger! These are my daughters', and to understand the matter he asked: 'I would forgo my parents for you, what is this about?' When Allah's Messenger (saw) replied: 'I have been permitted to leave Mecca for hijrah', Abu Bakr excitedly asked: 'Will I be able to accompany (you)?' The Holy Prophet said: 'Yes, you will'."

Sayyidah Â'ishah (r.ah), who narrates this, said: "I had never seen anyone crying from happiness until that day I saw Abu Bakr crying for joy."

Presumably due to her youth, until that day Sayyidah Â'ishah (r.ah) had not thought someone could cry out of happiness, and now she saw those tears of her father's. Then, preparations for the journey started and Abu Bakr (ra) sent for Abdullah bin Urayqit. He had placed the camels in the care of Abdullah bin Urayqit, who was a trustworthy man and knew the desert roads well. The Holy Prophet (saw) called Ali (ra) and informed him about the developments. He also handed the goods entrusted to him for safekeeping to Ali (ra) to be returned to their owners.

Before he left, Allah's Messenger (saw) gazed at the Ka'bah for the last time. Then he must have smiled at Sayyidah Â'ishah (r.ah) as a farewell to console her, since he had seen her in his dream and it was said, 'This is your wife'.[131] Eventually when darkness fell, they gave some orders regarding the strategy to be followed in their absence, and they left. They went directly to the cave in the Mount Thawr.

According to the instructions given, Abdullah, the son of Abu Bakr (ra) and the brother of Sayyidah Â'ishah, would stroll about near the Quraish in the daytime to catch any news regarding them, and he would then report back as to what he had heard. Abdullah's sister Esma would prepare food and carry it to the cave in the evenings. Abu Bakr's slave Amir bin Fuhayrah would graze his sheep among the shepherd of Mecca, and then, in the evening, would bring the sheep to the front of the cave.

---

131. Ziya Kazıcı, Ibid., page: 148.

As can be seen, when these tasks were distributed, Sayyidah Â'ishah (r.ah) was not given any responsibility, and this is because she was not mature enough to assume such a responsibilities. At that time, she was spending her days grinding wheat. The days seemed to be interminable to Sayyidah Â'ishah (r.ah): as if each day was as long as a month or even a year. She listened attentively to all the news. She impatiently waited for the return of her sister Asma, from taking food to the two faithful companions. When Asma returned, Sayyidah Â'ishah used to ask her to tell what she had seen. Then Esma told her about the difficulties of living in a cave, how narrow and dangerous the cave was, and how their father was sad about these conditions. Asma also told her that during the second day, when the pagans had come upon the entrance of the cave, a pigeon's nest and a spider's web had appeared at the entrance and that this had saved their lives of her father and the Holy Prophet's.

On the third night, following an anxious day, Sayyidah Â'ishah (r.ah) climbed to her usual spot and started to watch the road. However, this watch took longer than the previous ones. She waited for her sister for a long time without moving from her position. At last she felt relieved when she saw her approaching from a distance. When Esma finally arrived, she was pale and breathing heavily.

Asma told her that the travellers had left the cave safely. She had torn her sash into two parts, so that they could tie their provisions and water.[132] Then Asma realised that Sayyidah Â'ishah was looking at her rather worriedly, as if asking: 'Did something happen to you?'

To calm her down she explained why she was so late: the small company had left the cave and departed from Mecca. Asma had waited until they disappeared from sight and had come back to her home silently to avoid raising suspicion.

Just when she had finished explaining what had happened to Sayyidah Â'ishah, there was a pounding at their door. It was midnight. Asma opened the door, to see that it was Quraishis, and Abu Jahil bin Hisham from the Manzum Tribe was among them. He barked at her: "Daughter of Abu Bakr, where is your father!" When she said that she did not know where her father was, Abu Jahil fiercely smacked her

---

132.   For this reason Asma, the daughter of Abu Bakr (ra) was called as *Zatu'n-Nitakayn* (owner of two sashes). This name was given to her by the Holy Prophet (saw).

face. He hit her so hard, that it tore her earring off. Asma indeed did not know the whereabouts of the convoy. They had already left the cave and were on their road. Asma was not lying. She did not know where they were.

Days and nights followed each other. Allah's Messenger (saw) reached Madinah with his companion, safe and sound. The Quraish could not deal with one man who was protected by Allah, and could not prevent him from leaving Mecca. Up to that point, they had regarded all kinds of torments as befitting for the Muslims, however, those same Muslims were now out of their reach, living in safety and comfort, and since Allah's Messenger (saw) had also gone to Medina it was time for the Quraish to be afraid, because Madinah was on the road to Damascus, which Meccans used for their trade route. What would happen if the Muslims obstructed their trade? In a city which was hundreds of kilometres away, they did not have a chance to apply any kind of torment as they were used to doing.

After the Holy Prophet (saw) settled in Medina, he sent Zayd bin Harithah to Mecca, to bring his daughters to Medina. Zayd also took a letter from Abu Bakr (ra) to his son Abdullah. Abu Bakr asked his son Abdullah to bring his wife Ummu Ruman and his daughters Esma and Sayyidah Â'ishah to Medina. Abu Rafi, the manumitted slave of the Holy Prophet (saw) was also travelling with Zayd.

We do not have much information about how Sayyidah Â'ishah (r.ah) spent her days in Mecca and what she did whilst waiting. However, it is certain that they experienced great difficulties among the pagans. Upon receiving news from Madinah, both families immediately started to prepare for travel. With great joy, they set off towards the city of Allah's Messenger (saw), and in this delight the first days of travel passed quickly. As Ibn Sa'd narrates, when Sayyidah Â'ishah (r.ah) was asked about this journey, she recounts as follows:

*"When the Holy Prophet (saw) arrived at Madinah, he sent Zayd bin Harithah and Abu Rafi' with two camels and five hundred dirhams, they would use this money to buy necessities. Abu Bakr had sent Abdullah bir Uraykit with two or three camels. He wrote to his son Abdullah, to bring my mother Ummu Ruman, my sister Esma and me. Then Zayd bin Harithah bought three camels with the money he had been given. We started our journey from Mecca together.*

*On the road we came across Talha bin Ubaidullah, who wanted to accompany the family of Abu Bakr. Then Zayd bin Harithah and Abu Rafi' took the Holy Prophet's family and daughters, Abdullah bin Abu Bakr took us, and we set off. At one point on the road, my camel started with fear. Thereon Ummu Ruman cried out for help: 'My God, my little daughter! My little bride!' "*

*"She was frantic until the men reached us and got hold of my camel. Then Allah conveyed us to safety, and we reached Madinah. I settled near the family of Abu Bakr, I was staying with my father. The Holy Prophet settled his family (Sawda -r.ah- and his children) in the houses which were built around the masjid on that day. After that, I stayed at the house of Abu Bakr for some days."*

*"One day my father Abu Bakr asked the Holy Prophet (saw): 'What keeps you from taking your family?' He said: 'It is the mahr.' Thereupon Abu Bakr lent him twelve and a half ukiyyah (five hundred dirhams).[133] When he gave this to me, the marriage was completed and he entered the nuptial chambers, with me in my room. Later, the Holy Prophet (saw) was to die in this room."*

As can be seen from this event, Sayyidah Â'ishah (r.ah) entered the nuptial chamber with the Holy Prophet (saw) after making hijrah to Madinah. Since she was small, they had waited until she reached puberty. However this time the 'mahr' situation had appeared. When this was solved, the marriage was completed. It would be useful to note that the Holy Prophet (saw) did not approach any of his wives without having paid their mahr.

### The Days After the Marriage

When Sayyidah Â'ishah (r.ah) had made hijrah, the houses near the Masjid, which would belong to the family of Abu Bakr (ra), were not yet built. The family temporarily settled in the house of Harith bin al-Hazraj from Ansar. At this time the Muslims who had migrated from Mecca had difficult days. Many people from the *Muhajireen*[134] could not get used to the weather and water of Medina and fell ill.

---

133. DIA, the article of **"Âişe"** II, 201.
134. *Muhajir* is a Muslim who emigrated from Mecca to Madinah during the time of the great repression of the Muslims by the pagan Quraish up until the conquest of Mecca in 8AH by the Prophet Muhammad (saw). Plural: *Muhajireen*.

Sayyidah Â'ishah (r.ah) narrates: *"When Abu Bakr and Bilal reached Medina, they became ill. I would go to them and ask: 'O Father, How do you feel? Ey Bilal! How are you? 'When Abu Bakr's fever got worse, he would say: 'To every person it is normally said "Good Morning" however Death is nearer to him than His shoelaces.' And Bilal, when his fever deserted him, would recite: 'Would that I could stay overnight in a valley wherein I would be Surrounded by Idhkhir and Jalil (kinds of good-smelling grass). Would that one day I could drink the water of the Majanna, and would that (the two mountains) Shama and Tafil would appear to me!' Bilal said, 'O Allah! Curse Shaiba bin Rabi'a and 'Utba bin Rabi'a and Umaiya bin Khalaf as they turned us out of our land to the land of epidemics.' I went an reported to the Messenger (saw) how they missed Mecca with all their hearts. Allah's Apostle then said, 'O Allah! Make us love Medina as we love Mecca or even more than that. O Allah! Give blessings in our Sa and our Mudd (measures symbolizing food) and make the climate of Medina suitable for us, and divert its fever towards Al-Juhfa.'*[135]

*"When we were staying at the house which belonged to Bani Harith Tribe from Hazraj, I became ill, too: I lost my hair and I lost a lot of weight."*

*"My mother intended to make me fat to send me to the house of Allah's Messenger (saw), but nothing benefited me till she gave me cucumber with fresh dates to eat. Then I became as she wanted for me."*[136]

*"I was on the swing, playing with my friends when Ummu Ruman came. She called me. I didn't know what she wanted from me. She held my hand. By the time we reached the door of the house, I was short of breath. We rested for a while until I caught my breath. At the door, Ummu Ruman brought some water, washed my face and wiped my hair. Then we entered the house. There were the women of Ansar. They told me: 'May you prosper and have blessings and have good omen!' Ummu Ruman left me with them. I wasn't afraid of them until I saw Allah's Messenger (saw). The women of Ansar handed me over to him. On that day I was a girl nine years old."*[137]

---

135. Bukhârî, Fedâilu'l-Medina, 11; Muslim, Hajj, 480; Muwatta, Jâmi', 14.
136. Abû Dâvud, Tıbb, 20; Ibn-i Majah, At'ime, 37.
137. Al-Bidâye ve'n-Nihâya, III, 132; See: Bukhârî, Nikâh, 38,39; Muslim, Nikâh, 69; Abû Dâvud, Nikâh, 34; Nesâî, Nikâh, 29. *Bukhari, Volume 7, Book 62, Number 86:* Narrated Â'isha: "When the Prophet married me, my mother came to me and made me enter the house where I saw some women from the Ansar who said, 'May you prosper and have blessings and have good omen'."

*"On the day of my wedding, there was no meal to celebrate, we didn't have the means for it. Neither a camel nor a sheep was slaughtered. There was only one bowl of milk which Sa'd bin Ubadah had sent. He drank some, and then I drank the rest of it."[138]*

When the people of Medina realised that Allah's Messenger (saw) could not afford a meal for the celebration, they set into action: they asked for the permission of the Holy Prophet (saw) to prepare a meal with presents brought by Ansar. Dishes of meat braised in fat and dates were brought from many houses with these, a banquet was given to the people who gathered in the mosque before noon.

## The House of the Holy Prophet (saw)

The most beautiful example of love and affection between spouses took place in this small plain house, made of mud-bricks. Perhaps, just by witnessing the way he treated his wife was sufficient to understand that he was Allah's Messenger (saw).

He used to say: *"The most righteous among you are the ones who are righteous to their wives. I am the most righteous to my wife ."[139]*

He would not hold any of his wives above the others, and he would always visit them in proper order.). He would perform the *asr*[140] prayer in one of the rooms of his wives, and then he would leave and inquire about his other wives. In the evening, he would go to the room of his wife whose turn it was, and he would spend the night there. When he was going on a journey, he would draw a lot among his wives, and he would set off with whoever had won the lot.

On a normal day, after performing the isha prayer, the Holy Prophet (saw) would go to his room, use his *siwak*[141] and then go to sleep. Towards midnight,

---

138.  Ramazan Balcı, Ibid., page: 27.
139.  Tirmizi, Menakib 85, (3892).
140.  *Asr* is the late afternoon Prayer, the third compulsory Prayer of the day. It can be prayed between midafternoon and a short time before sunset.
141.  *Siwak* is a piece of branch or root of a tree called al-Arak used as a toothbrush.

he would wake Sayyidah Â'ishah (r.ah), and they would perform the *witr*[142] prayer together. Sometimes the Holy Prophet (saw) and Sayyidah Â'ishah (r.ah) would occupy themselves with prayer until the morning. Sayyidah Â'ishah (r.ah) would follow him in prayers. When daybreak approached, Allah's Messenger (saw) would perform the *sunnah*[143] of the *fajr* prayer. Then he would lie down for a while, and after speaking with Sayyidah Â'ishah (r.ah) for a while, he would go out to the mosque to perform the *fajr*[144] prayer.

* * *

Sayyidah Â'ishah (r.ah) used to take care of her husband's daily chores; she would wash his hair and comb it, put apply his perfume, and wash his laundry. When the Holy Prophet (saw) went to bed, she would put water and *siwaq* beside his bed. When he had guests, she would serve them.

* * *

Sayyidah Â'ishah (r.ah) narrates: *"I would prepare nebiz for him in the evening; he used to drink this in the morning. I also used to prepare three covered bowls at night: one for making wudu[145], one for his siwaq, and one for drinking."*

*"When Allah's Messenger (saw) was going on a journey, I would make preparations for him. These included oil, comb, mirror, scissors, kohl and siwaq."*

* * *

More often than not, there would be no food at the home of the Holy Prophet (saw). Sayyidah Â'ishah (r.ah) said: *"Sometimes, one month would pass, but*

---

142. *Witr* is a prayer which is performed last thing at night before one goes to sleep, or else delayed and prayed at the end of the night prayer by those who rise in the night, seeking the pleasure and the face of Allah the Almighty.

143. *Sunnah Prayers* are prayers which are considered recommended in view of the fact that the Holy Prophet (saw) either performed them often and/or made statements about their meritorious character.

144. *Fajr* literally denotes "The Dawn". It is the time of the first obligatory prayer. It can be prayed at any time between the first light of dawn and just before sunrise. Also called *Subh* (morning). See Surah 89 of the Holy Qur'an.

145. *Wudu* refers to the ablution made before performing the prescribed Prayers. It requires washing (1) the face from the top of the forehead to the chin and as far as each ear; (2) the hands and arms up to the elbow; (3) wiping with wet hands a part of the head; and (4) washing the feet to the ankle.

*none of the stoves would be lit in any of the rooms of Muhammad (saw)'s family."* She was asked: *"Then what would they eat in those days?"* She said: *"Two things: dates and water! However, our true neighbours from Ansar had milk animals, and they used to send the Holy Prophet (saw) the milk of these animals, and he would have us drink it."*

* * *

*"Whoever says that we ate dates until we were full, would be lying to you. When Quraiza was conquered, we received some dates and animal fat. When Khaibar was conquered we said: 'Now we will eat our fill of dates!' However, when we had dates aplenty, Allah's Messenger (saw) passed away."*

* * *

There was abundant happiness and love in the household of the Holy Prophet (saw), where worldly assets did not matter. When Sayyidah Â'ishah (r.ah) drank something from a cup; he used to take the cup, place his lips on the same place where she had drank from, and he would drink like that. When she ate from a bone with meat on it, he used to take it from her hand, and eat from the same place where she ate. In her room, he used to rest his head on her, and read Qur'an. When he was performing *i'tikaf*[146], he used to reach his head out of his tent, and even if she was in her period, he would let her comb his hair. He would kiss her even when he was fasting. Such was his kindness, and high morals. He would provide her opportunities for entertainment. He had her watch the Ethiopian company performing in the mosque, as long as she wanted. Once, Sayyidah Â'ishah (r.ah) was leaning on his shoulder watching the performers. They had raced twice when they went on campaigns; and once they had pushed one another to be first through the door.

* * *

As a beloved husband, he would always do things to make his family feel good.

---

146. *I'tikaf* refers to the religious practice of spending the last ten days of Ramadan (either wholly or partly) in a masjid so as to devote oneself exclusively to worship. In this state one may go out of the masjid only for absolutely necessary requirements.

*"In my time of the month[147], Allah's Messenger (saw) used to invite me to eat with him. Then he would take a bone with meat on it and he would offer it to me, insisting that I start first. I would take it, bite some and then pass it over to Allah's Messenger (saw). Then he would start to eat from the same place where I had bitten. Sometimes he would ask for something to drink, and then he would insist that I drank first. I would take the cup, drink some and then leave the rest to him. He used to take the cup and drink from it, by placing his lips on the same place where I had drunk from."*

* * *

*"Sometimes, Allah's Messenger (saw) would take a bath. And then he would be cold, and he would snuggle up to me and ask me to warm him. I would embrace him and keep him warm.*

* * *

*"One night he entered my chamber. I was on my period. He went to the spot where he used to pray. He stayed there for a long time, and I drifted off. Then he came to me, he was cold. He said: 'Come closer'. I replied: 'I am in my time of the month'. He said: 'Still, open your arms!' I opened my arms. He rested his head and chest on my lap and I embraced him. We fell asleep like that."*

* * *

His life was like a window open towards the hereafter. No worldly goods could find a place in these chambers, to cloud this fact:

*"One day when Allah's Messenger (saw) entered my chamber, he saw two large rings without collets on my hand and he asked: 'What is this, O Â'ishah?' 'O Allah's Messenger (saw)! I am wearing these to adorn myself for you. He asked, 'Did you pay the zakah of these?' 'No.' 'Then these are as fire for you'."*

* * *

Sayyidah Â'ishah (r.ah) narrated: *"I bought a cushion with pictures, and when Allah's Messenger (saw) saw it he stood at the door and did not enter. I*

---

147.   Monthly regl period, menstruation.

*noticed the sign of disapproval on his face and said, 'O Allah's Messenger (saw)! I repent to Allah and His Messenger (saw). What sin have I committed?' Allah's Messenger (saw) said. 'What is this cushion?' I said, 'I have bought it for you so that you may sit on it and recline on it.' Allah's Apostle said, 'The makers of these pictures will be punished on the Day of Resurrection, and it will be said to them, 'Give life to what you have created.' The Prophet added, 'The Angels of Mercy do not enter a house in which there are pictures of animals'."[148]*

* * *

*"On another occasion, I acquired two beds, stuffed with fiber and izhir (grass). Allah's Messenger (saw) saw them, and he asked: 'O Â'ishah! Do you want the world? I said: 'I acquired them for you. They are stuffed with fiber and izhir (grass)...' Thereupon he said: 'O Â'ishah! What would I need the world for? I and the world are like a man who takes rest in the shade of a tree. When he gets up and leaves that place, eternally he won't return again'."*

* * *

That blessed household was even plainer than a temporary encampment which a traveller would set up for three days:

*"We had one mat, and we used to cover ourselves with that in the night, and in the daytime we used to spread it on the floor of our room. We used to sit on that with our guests, and pray on that. We both would sleep under the same mat. When one side of the mat was on me, he would say his prayer on the other side of it. At home, he used to do as anyone of you does in their household. He would sew his clothes and mend his shoes."*

* * *

The Holy Prophet (saw) used to look for any excuse to please Sayyidah Â'ishah (r.ah), who was a young woman, and to meet her need for entertainment, which is a requisite of human nature. He never feigned the care he displayed for her. This care came like the natural flow of life, displayed when and where it was fit in the form of a most pleasant forbearance.

---

148.   Bukhari, Volume 7, Book 62, Number 110; Afzalurrahman, II, 165.

*"Allah's Messenger (saw) returned from either the Tabuk or the Khaibar Ghazwa[149]. There was a cover on the sofa. The wind blew and lifted the cover partly. At this moment, Allah's Messenger (saw) saw Â'ishah's dolls, and asked: 'O Â'ishah, what are these?' She said: 'They are my dolls.' Then he saw a horse with wings and asked: 'What about this, Â'ishah?' 'It is a horse.' 'And what are these on it?' 'Two wings.' 'Do horses have wings?' 'Didn't you hear that the horses of Prophet Sulaiman had wings?' Upon hearing this, the Holy Prophet (saw) laughed until his molar teeth could be seen."*

* * *

*"When I was with Allah's Messenger (saw), I used to play with my dolls. He used to leave the room and send my girlfriends, and we used to play together."*

* * *

*"It was a festival day, and while two female slaves were singing songs about the bravery regarding the Buas Battle, Allah's Messenger (saw) came in. He went to his bed, lay on his side and turned his back to us. Then my father came in and reprimanded me, saying: 'The devils instruments in the house of Allah's Messenger (saw)!' Allah's Messenger (saw) admonished him: 'Leave them O Abu Bakr, it's a festival day.' When they were deep in conversation, I glanced at the slaves, and they left."*

* * *

*"It was another festival (Eid). Black men were performing with their shields and swords in the mosque. I don't remember whether I asked for permission, or he called me. He asked me: 'Would you like to watch?' I said: 'Yes'. He stood up and screened me behind him; I stood with my cheek on his cheek. He was saying: 'O the sons of Arfidah, show me what you can do!' I watched until I was bored. Just imagine how inclined to entertainment a girl at my age would be. When he realised that I was bored, he asked: 'Is it enough?' I said: 'Yes!' Then he sent me off."[150]*

---

149. *Ghazwa* is a holy battle for the cause of Allah the Almighty in which the Prophet Muhammad himself, may Allah bless him and grant him peace, took part. Plural: *al-Maghazi* or *Ghazawat.*
150. Bukhari, Volume 7, Book 62, Number 118: Narrated 'Ursa: "Â'isha said, 'While the Ethiopians were playing with their small spears, Allah's Apostle screened me behind him and I watched (that

*"In another festival a Sudanese came besides the Holy Prophet (saw) dancing. The Holy Prophet (saw) sent for me. I was watching them from over the shoulder of Allah's Messenger (saw), and I continued watching them until I wanted to leave."*

A'isha (r.ah) narrates that she prepared a lady for a man from the Ansar as his bride and the Prophet (saw) said, *"O Â'ishah! Haven't you got any amusement (during the marriage ceremony) as the Ansar like amusement?"*[151]

* * *

*"We had gone on a Ghazwa together with Allah's Messenger (saw). We came to a region covered with thorny plants and siwaq trees. I left them and went into the shrubs to relieve my self. Allah's Messenger (saw) came and said to me: 'Come on, let's have a race.' I collected my skirts around my waist; we came into line and then started to run. He passed me, and then said: 'This is in response to Zimajaz"*

*(He had come to see us when we were in Zimajaz. At that time I was a small girl, and we hadn't married yet. My father sent me with something for him. He had said 'Give that to me', but I didn't want to give it and I ran away. He had run after me but wasn't able to catch me.")*

* * *

The Holy Prophet (saw) used to call Sayyidah Â'ishah (r.ah) "Uwaysh", which meant "Little Â'ishah". When he asked for something, he would say: "O Little Â'ishah, water!"

* * *

*"Often he would ask: Â'ishah, what did you do with the poems?' I would say: 'Which poems O Allah's Messenger (saw)! I have many poems.' Then he would reply: 'The ones about thankfulness'."*

---

display) and kept on watching till I left on my own.' So you may estimate of what age a little girl may listen to amusement."

151. Bukhari, Volume 7, Book 62, Number 92.

Any unpleasant event which took place in the family would turn into sweet jests in his tolerant heart. One day Abu Bakr (ra) asked for permission and then entered the room of the Holy Prophet (saw). He saw that Sayyidah Â'ishah (r.ah) was yelling at the Holy Prophet (saw). Abu Bakr (ra) held her collar and scolded her: '*O the daughter of Ummu Ruman, are you yelling at Allah's Messenger (saw)?*' The Holy Prophet (saw) separated them. Abu Bakr (ra) left angrily. To propitiate Sayyidah Â'ishah (r.ah), Allah's Messenger (saw) said to her: '*See how I separated you, and your father?*' After he calmed down, Abu Bakr asked for permission and came back into their room to find them laughing together. He said: '*O Allah's Messenger (saw)! Make me a partner of your peace, just as you made me a partner in your war*'.

* * *

The Holy Prophet (saw) could not bear Abu Bakr (ra) and Ummu Ruman treating their daughter Sayyidah Â'ishah's (r.ah) harshly, and he would be uncomfortable with such action. Once Abu Bakr (ra) raised his hand to Sayyidah Â'ishah (r.ah) and hit her on the chest. When the Holy Prophet (saw) saw them in this situation, he said to Abu Bakr: "*I want you to apologize for what you have done.*"

* * *

One day, a captive was brought to Sayyidah Â'ishah's (r.ah) room. Sayyidah Â'ishah (r.ah) was busy with other women, and taking advantage of this, the captive ran away. Allah's Messenger (saw) came to see the captive. He was upset to learn that he had run away, and when he was going outside to search for the captive he said: "*May Â'ishah's hand be broken!*" When Allah's Messenger (saw) came back, Sayyidah Â'ishah (r.ah) was turning her hands over and over. Looking at her, the Holy Prophet (saw) said: "*Are you crazy?*" Â'ishah (r.ah) replied: "*You cursed me. I am trying to figure out which one of my hands will be broken.*" Thereupon the Holy Prophet (saw) made this prayer: "*O my Lord! I am a human being, and I become enraged like human beings. O my Lord! Whoever I curse from the Muslims, be it a man or a woman, turn my curse to goodness for them.*"[152]

---

152.  Bukhari.

*"I asked Allah's Messenger (saw) to pray to Allah for me. He said: 'O my Lord! Forgive the open and hidden, past and future sins of Â'ishah.' I started to laugh. I laughed so much that I was nearly going to fall back. Allah's Messenger (saw) asked: 'Did my prayer make you happy?' I said: 'Is there something wrong with me that your prayer would not make me happy?' Then the Holy Prophet said: 'This prayer was for my entire ummah'."*

* * *

Allah's Apostle said to her, *"I know when you are pleased with me or angry with me."* I said, *"Whence do you know that?"* He said, *"When you are pleased with me, you say, 'No, by the Lord of Muhammad!' but when you are angry with me, then you say, 'No, by the Lord of Abraham!' "Thereupon I said, 'Yes (you are right), but by Allah, O Allah's Messenger (saw), I leave nothing but your name, your love lives in my heart'."*[153]

* * *

Sometimes, the Holy Prophet (saw) used to take her with him, when he was invited somewhere.

Anas reported that Allah's Messenger (saw) had a neighbour who was Persian, and he was an expert in the making of soup. He prepared soup for Allah's Messenger (saw) and then came to invite him. He (Allah's Messenger) said: *'Is she invited as well?'*. The Persian said: 'No'. Thereupon Allah's Messenger (saw) said: 'No'. The Persian returned inviting him again, and Allah's Messenger (saw) said: *'Her also?'*. Again the Persian said: 'No'. Thereupon Allah's Messenger (saw) also said: 'No' (and declined his offer). The Persian returned once more and again invited him, and Allah's Messenger (saw) again said: *'Her also?'* He (the host) said: 'Yes' after the third time. Then the Prophet accepted his invitation, and both of them set out for his house.[154]

* * *

Sayyidah Â'ishah (r.ah) displayed complete submission towards the Holy Prophet (saw), and never asked him to repeat anything. She would throw out

---

153. Bukhari, Volume 7, Book 62, Number 155; Afzalurrahman, II, 163.
154. Bukhari, Book 023, Number 5054; Muslim, Eşribe, 139; Afzalurrahman, II, 167.

anything that the Holy Prophet (saw) disliked without waiting for a second warning. She strove to take care of both the personal needs of Allah's Messenger (saw), and to treat his visitors hospitably and generously, as far as possible.[155]

* * *

Since the people of Medina knew the affection of Allah's Messenger (saw) for Sayyidah Â'ishah (r.ah), they would offer their presents to him when he was in her room. This situation bothered some other wives of the Holy Prophet (saw). Several of them had voiced these feelings on different occasions. However, Allah's Messenger (saw) had not responded to their complaints. Thereupon, they made Fatimah (r.ah), the beloved daughter of the Holy Prophet (saw), a mediator. When Fatimah (r.ah) conveyed his blessed wives' appeal to the Holy Prophet, he asked her: *'O Fatimah! Don't you love whom I love?'* She said: *'Of course I do!'* Then the Holy Prophet said to her *'Then love Â'ishah, too!'* and reminded her of Â'ishah's place in his heart.[156]

* * *

The love, pain, patience, grief and sadness of great people becomes manifest behind a curtain woven with indescribable manifestations of destiny. They experience grave sorrows in their most joyful moments, and see the lofty escarpments of peace out of a scene of anguish; just as the Holy Prophet (saw) foresaw *Karbala* when he was enjoying the scent of his grandson Husayn (like a fresh rose). Or as on another occasion he said: *'The palaces of Kisra and Byzantium have been presented to me'* during a fearful day of the Trench Battle. The deeds of exalted hearts are grand in proportion to their grandeur.[157]

One day Sayyidah Â'ishah (r.ah) became ill. She was feigning, saying: *"O my head, I am dying! O my head, I am dying!"* The Holy Prophet (saw) teased her: *"If only that happened when I am alive; I would pray for your forgiveness!"* Thereupon Sayyidah Â'ishah (r.ah) suddenly flared up: *"Woe is me! I swear to God that you want me to die. So I will die and you will stay alone with another of your wives in the evening!"* However, at that time the

---

155. Afzalurrahman, Ibid., II, 167-168.
156. Afzalurrahman,Ibid.,II,page:164.
157. Ramazan Balcı, Ibid., page: 41.

passing of Allah's Messenger (saw) was quite close. He said: *"To the contrary, I am dying, Woe is me!"*

## The Beloved of the Most Cherished (One)

The most dear among the wives of the Holy Prophet (saw) were Khadijah (r.ah), and then Sayyidah Â'ishah (r.ah). Sayyidah Â'ishah (r.ah) was the object of the love of the Holy Prophet (saw), after Khadijah (r.ah). She was different from his other wives as regards her physical and spiritual attributes. A scholar of hadith, *Zahabi*, recounts these characteristics:

*"She was a beautiful fair woman. Because of this she was called Humeyra. She was the only virgin among the wives of Allah's Messenger (saw). He didn't love any woman more than her. I have never seen a more knowledgeable woman than her. She is the wife of Allah's Messenger (saw) both in this world and in the hereafter. Can there be a greater reason to be proud?"*[158]

The new bride moved to the house of Allah's Messenger (saw), following the wedding ceremony. Her house was one of the rooms around the mosque, which was built from mud-bricks and date branches. There was a mat on the floor of the room, and on this mat was a leather mattress which was stuffed with date fibres. A curtain made of goat hair cloth was used as a door. Sayyidah Â'ishah (r.ah) started her matrimonial life in this simple and plain house.

The future of Islam was not clear during the first years of their marriage, and even the Holy Prophet (saw) worried about the times lying ahead for his ummah. There was a need for an intelligent, willing and sedulous woman to explain this new religion to women; to correct their mistakes and to complement their deficiencies: Sayyidah Â'ishah (r.ah) met these conditions exceedingly well. For nine years she was the closest person to Allah's Messenger (saw). The knowledge she gained from the Holy Prophet (saw), meant that in a short time she was trained as a great scholar of hadith and *fiqh*[159]. Especially, women would refer special questions and issues concerning themselves to Sayyidah Â'ishah (r.ah). She also had a refined cultural and literary taste.

---

158.  Zehebî, II, 140.
159.  Islamic jurisprudence

**Her Names and Kunyas**[160]

Sayyidah Â'ishah (r.ah) never had a child. The Arabian people had the custom of naming mothers and fathers after their eldest son's name (kunya). She felt sorry for not having such a kunya. When she told the Holy Prophet (saw) about her feelings, he gave her the kunya of "Ummu Abdullah, The Mother of Abdullah" by referring to her sister Esma's son Abdullah bir Zubayr.

The Holy Prophet (saw) doted on Sayyidah Â'ishah (r.ah) and sometimes called her names such as "Uwaysh" or "Aish".

She was also named as "Humeyra" because of her white skin, and from time to time Allah's Messenger (saw) called her with this name, too.[161]

While narrating a hadith, Ali (ra) mentioned her as *"Khalilatu Rasulillah -The Beloved of Allah's Messenger (saw)"*. In another hadith narrated from Sayyidah Â'ishah (r.ah), Masruk from the *tabiun* said, regarding her: "The beloved of the most cherished one of Allah; the one who was exonerated with a verse from heaven."[162]

**How Should I Not Be Jealous?**

The transition of Sayyidah Â'ishah (r.ah) from adolescence to maturity was completed in the house of the Holy Prophet (saw). As it was mentioned before, when she came into this house, she was still playing with the young girls of the neighbourhood and with her playthings. The Holy Prophet (saw) received this with tolerance and affection. Sometimes he would take her to watch the folkloric plays of the Ethiopians in the mosque, and sometimes he raced with her.

Allah's Messenger (saw) regarded her as a precious and beloved wife. Nevertheless, this did not stay her from doing things dictated by her temperament. Maybe the considerable affection and tolerance displayed by the Holy Prophet (saw) played some part in this too. Above all the others of his wives, Sayyidah

---

160. Epithets or offspring titles.
161. DIA, the article of **"Âişe"** II, 202.
162. DIA, the article of **"Âişe"** II, 202.

Â'ishah (r.ah) used to display jealousy the most. Her jealousy even lead to the revelation of some verses form the Qur'an. For instance, the verses regarding the "Honey syrup"[163] were revealed as a result of an incident caused by jealousy, in which Sayyidah Â'ishah (r.ah) had played a key role.

Among the wives of the Holy Prophet (saw), Sayyidah Â'ishah (r.ah) was without doubt most jealous[164] concerning him, and also the one who exerted the greatest effort to win his love. The main reason for this was the fact that she was the only virgin Allah's Messenger (saw) married. All the other wives of the Holy Prophet (saw), except Sayyidah Â'ishah (r.ah), had married previously, and even some of them had children from their first marriages. However, the first and only love to occupy Sayyidah Â'ishah's (r.ah) heart was the Holy Prophet's (saw), and she had experienced the happiness of marriage in its most delightful form with him, for the first and last time.

On several occasions, Sayyidah Â'ishah (r.ah) had stressed her distinction from her fellow wivesin that she was a virgin when she married Allah's Messenger (saw). To illustrate this, we can quote a conversation which took place between Allah's Messenger (saw) and her:

Sayyidah Â'ishah (r.ah) narrated:

*"I said, 'O Allah's Messenger (saw)! Suppose you landed in a valley where there is a tree of which something has been eaten and then you found trees of which nothing has been eaten. Of which tree would you let your camel graze?' He said: 'Of the one of which nothing has been eaten before.' I said, ' I am this tree'* [165]

* * *

Furthermore, Sayyidah Â'ishah (r.ah) was the youngest among the wives of the Holy Prophet (saw), as well as being the daughter of his most beloved friend Abu Bakr (ra).

We can listen to the feelings of jealousy, from her own words:

*"One night Allah's Messenger (saw) went out, whilst he was staying with me (in my home). I felt jealous, thinking that he might have gone to another one*

---

163. See the section of Sayyidah Hafsa in this book.
164. DIA, the article of **"Âişe"** II, 201.
165. Bukhari, Volume 7, Book 62, Number 14; Afzalurrahman, Ibid., II, 163-164.

*of his wives (during my turn). When he came back, he realised my condition and asked me: 'Did you feel jealous?' I said: 'How can it be that a woman like me should not feel jealous about a husband like you?'"*[166]

* * *

On another night, she woke up and could not see the Holy Prophet (saw) beside her. She started to feel around the room in the darkness. When she touched the feet of Allah's Messenger (saw) who was prostrating, she was relieved.

Another time she could not find the Holy Prophet (saw) in the bed at night. She thought that he had left her alone and had gone to one of his other wives. Just at that moment, she saw the Holy Prophet (saw) praying while bowing and prostrating. This time she muttered to herself: *"I would forego my parents for you O Allah's Messenger (saw)! What are you doing, and what am I thinking of!"*[167]

### On the Battle Fields

Although there are a few narratives which mention that Sayyidah Â'ishah (r.ah) participated in the Ghazwa, the military campaign, of Badr, it is not possible to reconcile these with the reports relating that her marriage with the Holy Prophet (saw) took place after Badr. On the other hand, during the *Ghazwa* of Uhud, she worked behind the front; carrying water, gathering information and attending to the wounded.

During the Battle of Handak she stayed in the castle of the Banu Haaritha Tribe with the mother of Sa'd bin Muaz.

---

166. *Muslim, Book 39, Chapter 14, Number 6759.* Â'isha the wife of Allah's Apostle (may peace be upon him), reported that one day Allah's Messenger (may peace be upon him) came out of her (apartment) during the night and she felt jealous. Then he came and he saw me (in what agitated state of mind) I was. He said: A'isha, what has happened to you? Do you feel jealous? Thereupon she said: How can it he (that a woman like me) should not feel jealous in regard to a husband like you. Thereupon Allah's Messenger (may peace be upon him) said: It was your devil who had come to you, and she said: Allah's Mes- senger, is there along with me a devil? He said: Yes. I said: Is devil attached to everyone? He said: Yes. I (Â'isha) again said: Allah's Messenger, is it with you also? He said: Yes, but my Lord has helped me against him and as such I am ab solutely safe from his mischief.

167. Afzalurrahman, Ibid., II, 163.

She was also present during the Hudaybeya Treaty. After the conquest of Khaibar, Allah's Messenger (saw) allotted a portion to her along with his other wives. When Umar (ra) exiled the Jews of Khaibar to Palestine, he gave the wives of the Holy Prophet (saw) the options of receiving their allotted portion in Khaibar either as yield or as land; Sayyidah Â'ishah (r.ah) opted for land.

When he started the preparations for the conquest of Mecca, the Holy Prophet (saw), kept the target of the campaign as a secret from everyone, and had told it only to Sayyidah Â'ishah (r.ah); so that, even Abu Bakr (ra) learned the direction of the campaign from her.

She joined the Last Hajj along with the other *ummuhat al-mumineen*, on the tenth year of hijrah.[168]

One of the most important campaigns Sayyidah Â'ishah (r.ah) joined was the Ghazwa of Banu al-Mustalik, which took place on the sixth year of hijrah. Due to its importance, let's narrate this battle in some detail.

## The Slander Incident: A Malicious Scandal

There is an incident which had a profound effect on Sayyidah Â'ishah (r.ah) and constituted a turning point in her life, which is entitled "The Slander Incident" in the books of Islamic history. Upon this incident, Sayyidah Â'ishah (r.ah) shed tears for days and secluded herself in her house. The event, which was conspired by Abdullah ibn Ubayy bin Salul, chief of the hypocrites, took place as follows:

"In the sixth year of Hijra. The Prophet (saw) was preparing for the battle to Beni Mustalik. As was his custom, he drew lots to choose which wife would journey with him, and Sayyidah Â'ishah was selected. The battle ended with the Muslim victory. The soldiers started back for Medina and they stopped for a rest close to Medina. At that time, in order to relieve herself, Sayyidah Â'ishah came down from her place on her camel and went a distance away from the others. As she was returning she realized she had lost her necklace. She started

---

168.   DIA, the article of **"Âişe"** II, 202.

searching for it in the places she ahd been. At the same time the group left without realizing they had left her behind. This was because she was so slight, and since her camel-litter was covered, no one realized that she was not inside. When the group reached Medina in the early hours of the morning, her camel was lowered in front of her house and her camel-litter was gentle brought down. It was a big shock to see she was not in it!

The Messenger of Allah (saw) andhis companions worried, and after a short while and some set out to look for her. Finally, far away they saw her on a camel and Safwan bin Muattal As-Sulemi. Safwan was a companion who had a duty to clean up the rest areas. The chief of the polytheists, Abdullah bin Ubey bin Selul saw them and he began the slander.[169]

Let's listen to the rest of the incident from Sayyidah Â'ishah (r.ah):

*"After that we returned to Medina, and I became ill for one month while the accusers from the people were spreading false statements. I was feeling, during my ailment, as if I were not receiving the usual kindness from the Prophet which I used to receive from him when I was sick. But he would come, greet me and say, 'How is our sick one?' I did not know anything of what was going on till I recovered from my ailment and went out with Um Mistah to the Manasi where we used to answer the call of nature, and we used not to go to answer the call of nature except from night to night and that was before we had lavatories near to our houses. And this habit of ours was similar to the habit of the old Arabs in open country. Thus, I and Um Mistah bint Ruhm went out walking. Um Mistah stumbled because of her long dress and she said, 'Let Mistah be ruined!' I said, 'You are saying a bad word. Why are you abusing a man who took part in Badr?' She said, 'O Hanata (you there) didn't you hear what they said?' Then she told me the rumors of the false accusers."*

*"My sickness was aggravated, and when I returned home, Allah's Messenger (saw) came to me, and after greeting me he said, 'How is our sick one?' I requested him to allow me to go to my parents. I wanted to be sure of the news through them. Allah's Messenger (saw) allowed me, and I went to my parents and asked my mother, 'What are the people talking about?' She said, 'O my daughter! Don't worry much about this matter. By Allah, A woman as charm-*

---

169.   DIA, the article of **"Âişe"** II, 201.

*ing as you, and one so loved by her husband and shares him with so many; it is very rare not see slander about her.' I said, 'Glorified be Allah! Are the people really taking of this matter?' That night I kept on weeping and could not sleep till morning."*

*"In the morning Allah's Messenger (saw) called Ali bin Abu Talib and Usama bin Zaid when he saw the Divine Inspiration delayed, to consul them about divorcing his wife (i.e. Â'ishah).*[170]

*Usama bin Zaid said what he knew of the good reputation of his wives and added, 'O Allah's Messenger (saw)! Keep you wife, for, by Allah, we know nothing of her but good.' Ali bin Abu Talib said, 'O Allah's Messenger (saw)! Allah has not imposed restrictions on you, and there are many women other than she, yet you may ask the woman-servant who will tell you the truth.' On that Allah's Apostle called Buraira and said, 'O Buraira. Did you ever see anything which roused your suspicions about her?' Buraira said, 'No, by Allah Who has sent you with the Truth, I have never seen in her anything faulty except that she is a girl of immature age, who sometimes sleeps and leaves the dough for the goats to eat'."*

*"On that day Allah's Messenger (saw) ascended the pulpit and requested that somebody support him against the slander of Abdullah bin Ubai bin Salul. Allah's Messenger (saw) said, 'Who will support me against that person (Abdullah bin Ubai bin Salul) who has hurt me by slandering the reputation of my family? By Allah, I know nothing about my family but good, and they have accused a person about whom I know nothing except good, and he never entered my house except in my company'."*

*"On that day I kept on weeping so much so that neither did my tears stop, nor could I sleep. In the morning my parents were with me and I had wept for two nights and a day, till I thought my liver would burst from weeping. While they were sitting with me and I was weeping, an Ansari woman asked my permission to enter, and I allowed her to come in. She sat down and started weeping with*

---

170.  "We see that although Allah's Messenger (saw) had complete confidence in Â'isha (ra), he didn't automatically reject the imputation. If he were to take such a course, most probably some would doubt that he was trying to "cover up" an incident. The pshychological condition of the society was in such a state. He preferred stillness. He was most probably expecting a divine intervention. The fact that the decision in this case -which he was a side- came from above, saved not just Â'isha (ra), but also Allah's Messenger (saw) from accusation." (Celal Yeniceri, page, 81)

*me. While we were in this state, Allah's Messenger (saw) came and sat down and he had never sat with me since the day they forged the accusation. No revelation regarding my case came to him for a month."* In fact, he insisted on waiting for a revelation regarding this situation.[171]

*"He recited Tashahhud (None has the right to be worshipped but Allah and Muhammad is His Messenger) and then said, 'O Â'ishah! I have been informed such-and-such about you; if you are innocent, then Allah will soon reveal your innocence, and if you have committed a sin, then repent to Allah and ask Him to forgive you, for when a person confesses his sin and asks Allah for forgiveness, Allah accepts his repentance'."*

*"When Allah's Messenger (saw) finished his speech my tears ceased completely and there remained not even a single drop of it. I requested my father to reply to Allah's Messenger (saw) on my behalf. My father said, 'By Allah, I do not know what to say to Allah's Messenger (saw).'[172] I said to my mother, 'Talk to Allah's Messenger (saw) on my behalf.' She said, 'By Allah, I do not know what to say to Allah's Messenger (saw)'."*

---

171.   This incident manifests that Allah's Messenger (saw) did not always possess information regarding incidents that he had not personally seen. For the knowledge of human beings, even of a prophet, solely consists of what Allah has revealed to them. Allah's Messenger (saw) did not possess information pertaining to the hidden things either, other than what Allah had revealed to him through divine inspiration or through Jibreel (as).

On the other hand, this incident displays another fact: that the Qur'an has not been written by Allah's Messenger (saw), but it solely consists of divine inspiration revealed to him by Allah. If the Qur'an was concocted by the Holy Prophet (saw), as some pagans and orientalists claim, he would not have waited for one month regarding such a sensitive issue concerning his own family life, but he would have clarified the issue immediately with a few verses, as it would please him. To the contrary, this incident had been spread mouth to mouth, and was regarded as an golden opportunity by the pagans of Mecca and the hypocrites of Madinah, who were on the lookout for any sign of the slightest weakness in Allah's Messenger (saw). Even some credible Muslims were brought into this gossip, and for a long time this topic was muttered in nearly every neighborhood, and in the every house of every street.

The delay in the divine revelation for such a long time on such a sensitive issue and on such a fragile period had placed Allah's Messenger (saw) in a desperate situation. Allah's Messenger (saw) had deeply felt himself helpless in the face of these events and regarding the delay of a revelation.

172.   This state of Abu Bakr (ra) carries many lessons, too. It was very easy and almost a natural tendency for a father to be carried away by his feelings and pronounce his daughter good and righteous. However, this was regarding an issue about which the Holy Prophet (saw) could not arrive at a decision and remained silent, and so he left the final judgement to Allah and His Prophet and refrained from making a statement about his daughter whose innocence he had complete faith in. This devotion and submission of Abu Bakr (ra) displays the exalted position he had attained and how worthy is he of the title *"Siddiq"*.

She continued:

*"I was a young girl and did not have much knowledge of the Qur'an, and I said. 'I know, by Allah, that you have listened to what people are saying and that what has been planted in your minds you have taken as truth. Now, if I told you that I am innocent, and Allah knows that I am innocent, you would not believe me; and if I confessed to you falsely that I am guilty, and Allah knows that I am innocent, you would believe me. By Allah, I don't compare my situation with you except to the situation of Joseph's father; «(Jacob)* **who said, 'So (for me) patience is most fitting against that which you assert and it is Allah (Alone) whose help can be sought.'»**[173] *Then I turned to the other side of my bed hoping that Allah would prove my innocence. By Allah I never thought that Allah would reveal Divine Inspiration in my case, as I considered myself too inferior to be talked of in the Holy Qur'an. I had hoped that Allah's Messenger (saw) might have a dream in which Allah would prove my innocence. By Allah, Allah's Messenger (saw) had not got up and nobody had left the house before the Divine Inspiration came to Allah's Messenger (saw). So, there overtook him the same state which used to overtake him. He was sweating so much so that the drops of the sweat were dropping like pearls though it was a wintry day: When that state of Allah's Messenger (saw) was over, he was smiling and the first word he said, Â'ishah! Thank Allah, for Allah has declared your innocence.' My father told me to go to and thank Allah's Messenger (saw). I was so broken-hearted that I reproached sweetly: 'By Allah I will not thank (anyone) but Allah.'[174] So Allah revealed: "Verily! They who spread the slander are a gang among you..." (Surah an-Noor 24/11)"*[175]


**The Verses of Surah an-Nur**

There are many lessons to be derived from the verses of the Surah an-Nur which were revealed regarding this incident. These are as follows:

Verse 11: *"Lo! they who spread the slander are a gang among you. Deem*

---

173. Surah al-Yusuf, 12/18
174. Bukhârî, Shahâdah, 15; "DIA, Article of **"Âişe"** II, 202. See: "İfk", DIA.
175. Bukhari, Volume 3, Book 48, Number 829.

*it not a bad thing for you; nay, it is good for you. Unto every man of them (will be paid) that which he hath earned of the sin; and as for him among them who had the greater share therein, his will be an awful doom."*

This means that there will always be groups like this who desire to spread evil among us, and who will attempt to slander the pure family of Allah's Messenger (saw). Even though this appears to us as a bad thing, it carries goodness for us, as it is proclaimed in the verse. Because hypocrites disclose themselves by way of such incidents and we have the opportunity to identify them.

Verse 12: *"Why did not the believers, men and women, when ye heard it, think good of their own folk, and say: It is a manifest untruth?"*

This verse explains how the men and women believers should react when they hear such a slander. According to this, when we face a slander, we should prevent it from spreading by saying "If a similar calumny were to be said about me I would have liked people to think good of me…" Because testifying to something we did not witness and spreading such words is an evident slander. On this issue even the thought of "Maybe they committed it" is condemned. The verse commands us to hold a good opinion regarding such incidents.

Verse 13: *"Why did they not produce four witnesses? Since they produce not witnesses, they verily are liars in the sight of Allah."*

While Allah demands two witnesses to prove wrongdoings of people, He calls for four witnesses regarding adultery and states how severe a felony in the presence of Allah is the calumny of adultery. If the party who claims adultery cannot produce four witnesses they will face a major punishment. The punishment for calumny is stated as to be flogged eighty times in the fourth verse of Surah an-Nur.

Verse 14: *"Had it not been for the grace of Allah and His mercy unto you in the world and the Hereafter an awful doom had overtaken you for that whereof ye murmured."*

The calumny of adultery is a grave felony which leads to the punishment of Allah the Almighty. Yet the blessing and mercy of Allah in the world and in the Hereafter comes to the aid of his servants and he does not destroy them. Therefore we need to be extremely catious regarding slander.

Verse 15: *"When you received it with your tongues and spoke with your mouths what you had no knowledge of, and you deemed it an easy matter while with Allah it was grievous."*

In this verse, listening to a calumny, believing it and spreading it from mouth to mouth without any knowledge, is stated as a grave felony in the presence of Allah. It does not suffice to say "We did not commit it; whoever did it should be ashamed." Even the mentioning of a slander without proof is against the rights of that person and causes injury.

Verse 16: *"Wherefor, when ye heard it, said ye not: It is not for us to speak of this. Glory be to Thee (O Allah)! This is awful calumny."*

Here we are all taught a lesson of good manners, in the admonishing of the companions: Allah the Almighty declares how the behaviour of His servants should be in such cases. What is best for a Muslim is to think good of his brothers and sisters.

Verse 17: *"Allah admonishes you that you should not return to the like of it ever again if you are believers."*

Allah the Almighty sets out the example of the slander incident in front of us and warns us to avoid becoming an instrument of similar incidents. The rest of the verses continue as follows:

*"And Allah makes clear to you the communications; and Allah is all Knowing, Wise."*

*"Surely (as for) those who love that scandal should circulate respecting those who believe, they shall have a grievous chastisement in this world and the hereafter; and Allah knows, while you do not know."*

*"And were it not for Allah's grace on you and His mercy, and that Allah is Compassionate, Merciful."*

*"O you who believe! do not follow the footsteps of the Shaitan, and whoever*

*follows the footsteps of the Shaitan, then surely he bids the doing of indecency and evil; and were it not for Allah's grace upon you and His mercy, not one of you would have ever been pure, but Allah purifies whom He pleases; and Allah is all Hearing, all Knowing."[176]*

### Mistah and Abu Bakr (ra)

Sayyidah Â'ishah (r.ah) narrates:

*"…When Allah gave the declaration of my Innocence, Abu Bakr, who used to provide for Mistah bin Uthatha, for he was his poor relative, said: 'By Allah, I will never provide Mistah with anything because of what he said about Â'ishah.' But Allah later revealed: "And let not those who are good and wealthy among you swear not to help their kinsmen, those in need and those who left their homes in Allah's Cause. Let them forgive and overlook. Do you not wish that Allah should forgive you? Verily! Allah is Oft-forgiving, Most Merciful."[177]*

*After that Abu Bakr said, 'Yes! By Allah! I like that Allah should forgive me'; he paid the penalty fort he oath he swore and resumed helping Mistah whom he used to help before."[178]*

* * *

*"Allah's Messenger (saw) also asked Zainab bint Jahsh (another of the Prophet's wives) about me, saying, 'What do you know and what did you see?' She replied, 'O Allah's Apostle! I refrain to claim hearing or seeing what I have not heard or seen. By Allah, I know nothing except goodness about Â'ishah'."[179]*

Sayyidah Â'ishah further added *"Zainab was competing with me (in her*

---

176. Surah an-Nur, (24) 18-21
177. Surah an-Nur 24:22.
178. Bukhari, Volume 3, Book 48, Number 829
179. Although there was a light-hearted competition among them, Zainab bint Jahsh had not become a slave to her feelings and had not abandoned truthfulness and justice. We can learn a lesson from this: we need to remain silent regarding an inciden or event which we have not seen or heard personally, and we should only think good of our Muslim brothers and sisters, resisting the enticement of the devil and men.

*beauty and the Prophet's love), yet Allah protected her (from being malicious), for she had piety.*"[180]

After this, the slanderers were punished according to the fourth verse of Surah an-Noor: *"And those who accuse free women then do not bring four witnesses, flog them eighty stripes, and do not admit any evidence from them ever; and these it is that are the transgressors."*

## Her Father's Daughter

Allah's Messenger (saw) said:

*"On the Day of Judgement, Allah will punish the ones who slandered Â'ishah by flogging them eighty times in front of all the people of that Day. We will pray our Lord to forgive the ones among them who had made hijrah. And for this, O Â'ishah, we will ask for your permission."* Upon hearing this, Sayyidah Â'ishah cried and said: *"O Allah's Messenger (saw)! By the One who sent you with truth, I cherish and hold dear your happiness over mine."* Allah's Messenger (saw) smiled and said: *"She is her father's daughter!"*[181]

## An Honour Which will Prevail Until the Day of Judgement

The delay of divine revelation regarding the slander incident, all but brought down the curtains concealing the real truth about people, and their true identities. Faithful believers held on to justice and truthfulness and kept on an upright path and this incident reinforced their belief, supplemented their devotion, faith and love to Allah, His Messenger (saw) and the people of the House, the Ahl-al-Bayt. As a matter of fact, upon hearing about this, the leading chiefs of the companions such as Usama and Abu Ayyub said: *"Subhanallah! What a grave slander is this!"*

When it comes to the hypocrites, their sins swelled up because of the dis-

---

180. Bukhari, Volume 3, Book 48, Number 829. (Bukhârî, Shahâdah, 15).
181. Jam'u'l-Fawâid, IV, page: 105; Ramazan Balcı, Ibid., page: 52.

cord they sowed and the calumny they spread. The rancor, enmity, hatred and evil intentions they carried within their hearts against Allah's Messenger (saw), his Ahl-al-Bayt and the Muslims were revealed.

The prayers of Sayyidah Â'ishah (r.ah) and her esteemed parents were answered, and their nobility, purity and eminence was registered with divine revelation.

Urwah says: *"If Â'ishah had no other virtue other than the one in the slander incident, this alone would suffice her as goodness. For a chapter of Qur'an which will be recited until the Day of Judgement was revealed regarding her."*

About the verses on the slander incident, Zamahshari says: *"Such grave expressions have not been used for any other sin in the Qur'an. Various literary methods have been used regarding this incident which display the ugliness of slander, such as: harsh warning, befitting chastisement, severe reproof and aggrandisement, along with laconic and persuasive expressions. As in the warnings directed to pagans, the reason of this was to display the ugliness of this event as well as to manifest the eminence and righteousness of His Prophet in the presence of Allah."*[182]

Qadi Abu Bakr Bakillani says: *"In the Qur'an, Allah the Almighty absolves His Exalted Self from the maliciously false imputations the pagans allege about Him. For example he says:* ***"And they say: The Beneficent Allah has taken to Himself a son. Glory be to Him (Subhanallah)!.."***[183]. *Like this, after expressing the slander which the pagans spread about Â'ishah, He said:* ***"It is not right of us to speak of this: Glory be to Thee!.."***[184], *thus absolving Himself on behalf of the innocence of Â'ishah, the same way as he exonerated Himself from the calumny of the pagans."*[185]

She is such an esteemed woman that her case was drawn to the heavens and her acquittal came from there.[186]

---

182. Ramazan Balcı, Ibid., page: 53.
183. Surah al-Anbiya 21:26
184. Surah an-Nur 24:16
185. Ramazan Balcı, Ibid., page: 54.
186. Celal Yeniçeri, Ibid., page: 80.

On the other hand, this incident is an example of trust in people, displayed in the person of Allah's Messenger (saw). Indeed, freedom from guilt is a fundemantal principle of Law, and all men are innocent unless proved otherwise. Spreading rumours about people and libelling someone based on pure doubt without seeing anything, and even relating all that one hears, has been prohibited in our religion.

The fact that this verse has been revealed after an event in the Holy Prophet's (saw) life, as the majority of verses of judgment were, provides an example of conduct in such situations to future generations.

Unfortunately, many innocent women have fallen victim to doubts and calumny under the influence of customs and usage contradicting Islam. In such cases men who believe in the innocence of their wives are also placed under pressure by society. However, this event establishes a general rule: no one can blame or accuse another without witnesses, proof should be provided by whoever makes the allegation.[187]

As a last word, we can say that whilst we can believe in the innocence of Mariam (AS) in having a child without getting married, we should question in whose ranks our heart places us if we have difficulty in believing the explicit verses of the same Qur'an regarding the innocence of Sayyidah Â'ishah (r.ah).[188]


## A Sweet Memory

The chamber of Fatimah (r.ah) was adjacent to the chamber of Sayyidah Â'ishah (r.ah). There was a window in the wall separating these chambers, and Sayyidah Â'ishah and Fatimah (r.ah) used to talk to eachother through this window.[189]

On one occasion, Sayyidah Â'ishah (r.ah) and Fatimah (r.ah) were debating over who was the more virtuous. Fatimah (r.ah) said: *"I am more virtuous than you, since I am a piece from Allah's Messenger (saw)."* Sayyidah Â'ishah (r.ah)

---

187.   H. Kübra Ergin, Ibid., page: 196.
188.   Celal Yeniçeri, Ibid., page: 82.
189.   Kütüb-i Sitte, Murshid, no: 6554.

replied: *"In the world, matters are as you have stated; however, in the Hereafter I will be along with Allah's Messenger (saw) and on his level, and on the other hand, you will be with Ali and on his level. You compare the difference between the two levels yourself!"* Fatimah could not find an answer and started to weep. Upon seeing this, Sayyidah Â'ishah (r.ah) stood up and kissed Fatimah (r.ah) on her head and said to her: *"I wish I could be a single hair on your head!"*[190]

## The Holy Prophet (saw) from the Mouth of Â'ishah (r.ah)

The Holy Prophet (saw) who illuminates both this world and the Hereafter, was seen off by more than one hundred thousand of his companions when he left this world. He left behind a distinct hue, a different memory and an exceptional beauty to each one of his companions. Amongst the people whom he left behind; the ones who introduce him to us are doubtlessly the ones who had the most chances to be acquainted with him. Let's lend our ears to Sayyidah Â'ishah, the most beloved wife of Allah's Messenger (saw):

*"Allah's Messenger (saw) was extremely charming and good-looking. His blessed countenance used to glow like the full moon. He was slightly taller than average, with a slightly big head and wavy hair. If his hair parted by itself, he wouldn't straighten it and he would leave it as it was; if it fell to one side, he would again leave it like that. When he grew his hair long, it would be below his earlobes. He was fair with a wide forehead. There was a vein between his lush eyebrows which used to swell when he was angry. He had a beautiful nose, slightly higher close to his eyebrows, with a glowing nur, light. One who didn't pay attention would think that his nose was slightly slanted. He had a thick beard, large eyes, flat cheeks, a wide mouth and teeth which would shine like pearls when he smiled. His neck was like a beam of silver. His figure and limbs were proportionate and his flesh wasn't loose by any means. His stomach and chest were flat. His shoulders were large and his shoulder bones were stout. He was generally hairless and had a fair complexion. He had a thin line of fine hairs extending from his throat to his navel. The hairs on his abdomen were also fine. His stomach was hairless, and his arms, shoulders and chest were slightly hairy. He had long wrists, wide palms, and thick fingers and toes. The*

---

190. Asr-ı Saâdet, III, page: 310.

*soles of his feet were arched, the upper sides were flat. They would slightly spread when he stood on them. He had a measured and balanced walk. He used to walk quickly but unhurriedly, in a dignified manner and comfortably as if he was walking downhill."*

*"When he turned, he used to turn with his whole body. He used to cast his looks down. His downcast looks would be longer than his looks towards the sky. He had an expressive look." While walking, he used to give prefer- ence to his companions, and he would be the first to give salam[191] to whoever he met."*

*"He had a pensive mood; he was always thoughtful, and he would remain silent for a long time and wouldn't speak unnecessarily. The words would fill his mouth when he spoke. There would be no excess or deficiency in his utterance. He would speak pithily and tersely. He wasn't stern and he wouldn't look down on anyone. We used to cherish blessings, even a small amount."[192]*

* * *

*"I was spinning whilst I was standing, and Allah's Messenger (saw) was trying to sew his patten. I looked and saw that sweat had formed on his blessed forehead; and it was flowing down from his cheeks, and light was radiating from the drops of sweat. I was stunned at the beauty of his countenance. He looked at me and asked: "What's up with you?" I said: "Your forehead is sweating and the sweat drops are radiating. If Abu Kabir al-Huzali were to see you, he would grasp that you are more worthy of the couplet:*

**'When I gazed upon the traces of light appearing on the smiles of his luminous countenance,**

**It was evident that whoever nursed him was remote from all kinds of blemishes of monthlies, troubles and nursing flaws'."**

*The Holy Prophet (saw) left what was in his hands, he rose to his feet and came towards me. He kissed me in between my eyes and said: "May Allah rec-*

---

191.   *Salam* is the greeting one should give to fellow Muslims: "*Assalamu alaikum*" (Peace be upon you). The reply to this is "*Waalaikum Salaam*" (And upon you be peace).
192.   Jam'u'l-Fawâid, no: 8425.

*ompense you with goodness, O Â'ishah! I don't remember feeling happier for any other thing, than I felt happy with these words of yours."*[193]

* * *

*"I never saw him laughing loudly: when he liked something, he used to smile. When he got angry, he usually used to stroke his beard."*

* * *

*"When the Holy Prophet (saw) was going to attend a congregation he used to comb his hair and beard. I asked: 'O Allah's Messenger (saw)! Why are you doing this?' He said: 'Allah loves who makes himself comely before appearing to his brothers'."*

* * *

When Sayyidah Â'ishah (r.ah) was asked: "O the mother of the faithful, how were the morals of Allah's Messenger (saw)?", she responded: *"His morals were the Qur'an. Don't you read the Surah al-Mu'minun?"*[194]

* * *

*"When he had two options, he would opt for the easier one, unless it was unlawful. If that task was unlawful, he would be the farthest from it, among men. He would not take revenge for himself; however, in a case where the boundaries drawn by Allah were violated, he would avenge for Allah."*

* * *

*"Allah's Messenger (saw) didn't like to attend his companions with an unpleasant smell. Even at the end of the night, he would use a pleasant odor, and he would go like that."*[195]

* * *

---

193.   Ramazan Balcı, Ibid., page: 88-89.
194.   Ramazan Balcı,Ibid., page: 90.
195.   Ramazan Balcı Ibid.,page: 91.

*"He used to sleep in the beginning of the night and be awake in the final hours of it."*[196]

* * *

*"He had two sets of clothes. He would wear one of these on Fridays. When he took it off we used to fold it up together."*[197]

* * *

*"I have never seen a more severe pain than he suffered from his illness."*[198]

* * *

*"I saw him frozen rigid, with sweat pouring from his forehead whilst a divine inspiration was revealed; and it was as if his head was going to split under the weight of the revelation."*[199]

* * *

*"O Allah's Messenger (saw)! May I be sacrificed for you! Why don't you eat by leaning against something?" After bowing his head until his forehead almost touched the ground, he said: "No, I will eat like a slave and sit like a slave."*[200]

* * *

*"When something he liked was harmed, he used to say: 'Praise be to Allah, who completes beauties with his blessings'."*[201]

* * *

*"When he wanted to sleep, he used to read the Muawudthatain[202] surahs, breathe into his palms and then sweep his hands over his body".*

---

196. Ramazan Balcı,Ibid., page: 92.
197. Ramazan Balcı, Ibid., page: 92.
198. Ramazan Balcı, Ibid., page: 92.
199. Ramazan Balcı, Ibid., page: 92.
200. Ramazan Balcı, Ibid., page: 93.
201. Ramazan Balcı, Ibid., page: 93.
202. The two Surahs of seeking protection; *Surah Al-Falaq* (113) and *Surah An-Nas* (114).

*He loved to look at the bright side of things.*

* * *

*"He liked to start everything from the right, even when he was taking a step and going somewhere."*

* * *

*"When Allah's Messenger (saw) visited a sick person, he would place his hand over the aching place and he would say: "Bismillah, it is all right!""*

* * *

*"He would accept gifts and return the favour (respond to them)."*

* * *

Sayyidah Â'ishah (r.ah) witnessed many exceptional events regarding the Holy Prophet (saw). For example:

*"It was on a night when Allah's Messenger (saw) was staying with me. I woke up, and felt that he wasn't near me. I listened to the room; he was perform-ing a prayer. I made ablution at once and stood behind him in prayer. He prayed through a portion of the night as long as Allah wished. Then a light appeared. The ceiling of the room was illuminated. It stayed as long as Allah wished, then disappeared.*

*The Messenger of Allah (saw) continued to make dua (supplication) for the duration which Allah wished. Then another light, which was brighter than the previous one appeared. It was as if you could find a grain of mustard thrown into the room. Then that disappeared, too. After the prayer, I asked: 'O Allah's Messenger (saw). What was that light that I saw?' 'Did you really see it, O Â'ishah!' 'Yes, I did.' Then he said:*

*'I implored Allah for my ummah. One third of them were given to me. I praised and glorified Allah, and I pleaded for the rest of them. The second third was given too. After praising Allah, I asked for the last third. They were also given to me. I praised and glorified Allah'."*

*"One night I approached him; he was prostrated like a garment thrown onto the floor. I listened, he was saying: 'My complete being has prostrated to You. My heart believes in You. My Lord, here are my hands: they are not protectors over my self. O the Exalted, to whom appeals for all big things are made, forgive my major sins!' After raising his head, he said to me: 'Jibreel came and enjoined me to pray with these words when I prostrated. It is such that whoever recites these words while prostrating, his sins will be forgiven before he raises his head'."*

* * *

Said bin Hisham asked Sayyidah Â'ishah (r.ah): *"Can you inform about the prayer Allah's Messenger (saw) made at night?" "Haven't you read the Surah Muzzammil? Prior to this surah, Allah the Almighty had made the night prayer compulsory. Allah's Messenger (saw) and his companions rose at night for this prayer for one year. Allah the Almighty revealed the last section of that surah twelve months later. The night prayer was extenuated and it was changed from being compulsory to voluntary."*

* * *

*"For his night prayer, his siwaq and water for ablution would be prepared in advance; he would be roused at a time Allah willed; then he would use his siwaq and after making ablution he used to pray two or nine rak'ahs[203] on foot. In his old age, he started to perform these prayers whilst he was sitting. He wasn't able to get up at nights during his illness, so he performed twelve rak'ahs in the day time. If he started performing a prayer, he used to perform it regularly. He would say the prayers which he wasn't able to perform at night, during day time."*

* * *

*"He used to pray at nights until blood set at his feet. I asked him: 'O Allah's Messenger (saw)! Why are you doing this, when Allah the Almighty has forgiven your past and future sins?' He replied: 'Shouldn't I be a thankful servant?'"*[204]

---

203. *Rak'ah* denotes units of prayers consisting of a series of standing, bowing, sitting and prostrating positions.
204. Ramazan Balcı, Ibid., page: 93-96.

Abdullah bin Umar came to Sayyidah Â'ishah (r.ah) and asked her: *"Inform me about the most curious thing you saw of Allah's Messenger (saw)."* After crying for a long time, Sayyidah Â'ishah narrated: *"All of his deeds were curious. One night he came to me, joined me under my quilt and came so close that his body touched mine. Then he asked me: 'O Â'ishah! Would you release me tonight, to pray to my Lord?' I said: 'O Allah's Messenger (saw)! I love both your closeness and the desires in your heart: I assent'*

*He rose, and he went to the water-skin in the room, made ablution with a little water, then he started praying. He was crying whilst reciting Qur'an; then he raised his hands and he was still crying: I even saw that his tears were falling and moistening the floor. When Bilal came to wake him for the morning prayer, he saw him crying and he asked: 'O Allah's Messenger (saw)! Are you crying even though Allah has forgiven your past and coming sins!'*

*'O Bilal! Shouldn't I be a thankful servant? Tonight Allah revealed the verses:* **'To Allah belongeth the dominion of the heavens and the earth; and Allah hath power over all things. Men who celebrate the praises of Allah, standing, sitting, and lying down on their sides, and contemplate the (wonders of) creation in the heavens and the earth…'**[205] *How can I not cry?' Then he said: 'Woe to the ones who recite these verses but don't think!'"*[206]

* * *

*"A woman came along with her two daughters. I gave the poor woman three dry dates. The woman gave one date to each one of her children. And then she divided the third date between her children, too. Soon the Holy Prophet (saw) came. I related the event to him. He said: "Were you amazed by this? The woman earned the Jannah because of this deed."*[207]

* * *

*"I had seen in my dream three moons falling into my chamber. I told my dream to my father Abu Bakr. He remained silent and didn't answer. Whenever Allah's Messenger (saw) passed away and was buried in my room, my father*

---

205. Surah Al-i Imran, 3:190-191
206. Hak Dini, Kur'ân Dili, v: II, page:1256.
207. Abû Dâvud, Sunen, 28 (4755).

*came and said: 'This is one of the three moons (you had seen in your dream) and the most blessed one!' "*[208]

With the passing time, it became evident that the other two moons were Abu Bakr and Umar (ra): they were both buried in the chamber of Sayyidah Â'ishah (r.ah), near the Holy Prophet (saw).

## Sayyidah Â'ishah (r.ah) and Islamic Knowledge

Another characteristic of Sayyidah Â'ishah (r.ah), which distinguishes her among the wives of the Holy Prophet (saw), is her vast knowledge in the field of Islamic knowledge. She was a scholar who was often referred to in many different fields, due to her intelligence and competence, the fact that she had been in knowledge circles both before and after her marriage, and that she was married to the Holy Prophet (saw) in her youth.

Now let's delve into these three points and examine her place in the Islamic knowledge.

She was a very bright woman, who possessed a sharp wit and profound thoughts. We can easily discern this from the questions she asked Allah's Messenger (saw) during his life; as well as from the position she held in the events taking place after his death.

Furthermore, she was raised by distinguished parents, Abu Bakr (ra) and Ummu Ruman. Abu Bakr was very close to the Holy Prophet (saw); he was acquainted with the poetry, literature, history and culture of the jahiliya period, and he was also well informed in accounting. Due to his involvement in commerce he was: a good judge of men; had been in contact with many different cultures; had acquired vast experiences, and a broad world view. This eminent companion had transferred these qualities he possessed to his offspring.[209] We can easily understand this from Sayyidah Â'ishah's (r.ah) profound knowledge, the way she spoke, the poems[210] she recited at appropriate times, and the vast information she possessed on history.[211]

---

208.  Abû Dâvud, Janâiz, 32 (3141).
209.  DIA, the article of **"Âişe"** II, 204.
210.  She had memorized hundreds of poems. She could recite a poem as lon as 160 couplets at once and by heart. Afzalurrahman, II, p: 166.
211.  Additional to her stong command of the Arab language, she was well versed in Arabian poetry. She

In addition to these qualities, Abu Bakr and his blessed wife were among the fortunate people who were the first to believe in Allah's Messenger (saw). The Holy Prophet (saw) used to visit their homes nearly every day. Consequently, they were aware of each verse of the *Qur'an*, starting from its first revelation.

Thus, Sayyidah Â'ishah (r.ah) came into the world in very cultured environment. She obtained a lot of information regarding the poetry and literature of the jahiliya period, and learned Islam from her first days by living it. And in fact her marriage to the Holy Prophet (saw) in her youth brought her right to the source of knowledge. Conscious of this core of knowledge, she never abstained[212] from asking whatever came to her mind, and she immediately shared whatever she learned with the companions, and especially with Muslim women. With time, this sharing made her a scholar whom people turned to in all matters. Especially following the passing of Allah's Messenger (saw); the four caliphs, Abu Hurayra, Ibn Abbas and many other companions turned to her to solve their problems, because she was the closest, most beloved and most knowledgeable wife of the Holy Prophet (saw). Particularly, Umar (ra) held her above all others; and referred all matters concerning women or the family life of Allah's Messenger (saw) to her.[213] Due to the large number of these appeals, Sayyidah Â'ishah (r.ah) related more than two thousand[214] *ahadith*[215], joining the *muksirun,* the seven companions who related the largest number of hadiths[216].

---

knew many of Lebid's couplets, almost all of Ka'b bin Malik's *kasidas,* and the poems of Hassan bin Sabit and Abdullah bir Rawaha by heart. She used to point out to the importance of poetry in understanding the Qur'an and hadith, as well as in using the Arabian language, by saying: *"Teach your children poetry, so that their speech may become sweet."* (Article on Â'isha, DIA, II, 203)

212. DIA, the article of **"Âişe"** II, 202.

213. Müslim, 2493; Ebû Dâvud, 3655; Tirmîzî, 3643; Buhârî, 322/6.

214. The exact number is 2,210. Bukhari and Muslim related 174 of these unanimously. Besides these, Bukhari relates 54 and Muslim 69 additional hadiths. Based on these figures, Bukhari has narrated 228 and Muslim 243 hadiths from Â'isha (ra). (The article on 'Â'isha', DIA, II, 204) Other hadiths narrated from her take place in different hadith collections. For example, Ahman bin Hanbal compiled the hadiths narrated from Â'isha (ra) in his Musnad, which is one of the six famous hadith collections -*Kutub as-Sittah-,* and this collection amounted to 253 pages; a single volume on its own.

215. *Ahadith* is the plural of *hadith.*

216. Muksirun; the companions who related the largest number of hadiths are: 1-Abu Hurairah (5374 hadith), 2-Abdullah bin Umar (2630 hadith), 3-Anas bin Malik (2286 hadith), 4-Â'isha (2210 hadith), 5-Abdullah bin Abbas (1660 hadith), 6-Jabir bin Abdullah (1640 hadith), 7- Abu Said al-Hudri (1170 hadith).

As narrated from Sayyidah Â'ishah (r.ah), the wives of the Holy Prophet (saw) used to take children into their homes in order to enliven the month of Ramadan with religious exercises.[217] They would teach them Qur'an, acquaint them with prayers and occupy themselves with their education.

Likewise, for girls who reached puberty a tent, called *hidr,* would be set up in a corner of the Holy Prophet's (saw) house. When one of the girls completed her education and reached pubescence she would be placed in this tent, then the name of the man who would like to marry her would be pronounced by saying: *"Such and such (man) wants to marry such and such (woman)"*. If the prospective bride remained silent, that would mean she consented to the marriage. On the other hand, if she did not want to marry this person, she would let it be known by hitting the tent with her hand.

Sayyidah Â'ishah (r.ah) took a girl under her protection from among the Ansar, after she grew up Â'ishah prepared for her wedding. The wedding was very plain. The Prophet (saw) came to the wedding and asked: *"O Â'ishah, Do you have any entertainment? The Ansar like entertainment."*[218]

These services which Sayyidah Â'ishah (r.ah) rendered in the lifetime of the Holy Prophet (saw) increased and expanded after he passed away: she virtually devoted herself to knowledge. Wherever Sayyidah Â'ishah (r.ah) settled, at home or away, was turned into a knowledge centre; especially Madinah, in the first sixty years following the *hijrah.*[219] It is reported that many women stayed with her in order to learn *hadith.* These women, whose number varied between 40 and 70, used to stay in either her chambers or in other chambers adjacent to hers.[220] This college of Islamic instruction educated many esteemed women scholars. To illustrate this, when Imam Zuhri, who is considered an authority in recording the *ahadith,* started his training in the field of *hadith,* one of his teachers told him: *"If you are after knowledge, I recommend Amra, who is a treasure trove of knowledge. Go before her, and take your lessons from her. She was trained by Â'ishah (r.ah)."*

---

217.   Bukhârî, Niqâh, 63.
218.   Muwatta, Zakât, 10 (1, 250).
219.   DIA, the article of **"Âişe"** II, 204.
220.   Ramazan Balcı, Ibid., page: 164.

Imam Zuhri says: *"When I went to her, I saw that she was a boundless sea as regards knowledge and comprehension."*[221]

Sayyidah Â'ishah (r.ah) raised more than two hundred select scholars such as Amra. One of her students, Sayyidah Â'ishah the daughter of Talha (ra), described what she gained from being raised under her guardianship as follows:

*"Many people would come to see her from all around. Because of my position near Â'ishah (r.ah), the old people would treat me with respect, and the young ones would see me as an elder sister. After they returned to their countries, they used to write letters and send presents. I would show the letters I received from them to Â'ishah (r.ah) saying: "Aunty! This is the letter and present of such and such!" Â'ishah (r.ah) would say: "My daughter! Answer her and respond to her present!"*[222]

There were many close relatives of Sayyidah Â'ishah (r.ah), among the women she trained; her sister, Ummu Kulthum; Sayyidah Hafsa and Esma, the daughters of Abdurrahman; and, Sayyidah Â'ishah, the daughter of Talha, are just a few of these.

In addition to this private training circle she established from among the women she selected, Sayyidah Â'ishah (r.ah) would go to *hajj*[223] each year and in her tent, which she established there, she would answer everyone's questions. She would also reply to questions which came by letter from far away regions.[224] With all these efforts, she fulfilled the duty of communicating Islam to the highest degree. She followed the example of the life of the Holy Prophet (saw) in every aspect and especially in his private life so carefully that the knowledge she passed on to us regarding all these areas are beyond praise. It can be said that without Sayyidah Â'ishah (r.ah) it would be extremely difficult to understand the Islamic family.

Sayyidah Â'ishah (r.ah) used to scrutinize the ahadith which were either submitted to her, or related by other companions, taking into account aspects

---

221. Ramazan Balcı, Ibid., page: 164-165.
222. Ramazan Balcı,Ibid.,page: 165.
223. *Hajj* is the fifth pillar of Islam. It is the pilgrimage to Mecca which every Muslim must take once in their lifetime, but only if they are healthy enough and able to afford it.
224. DIA, the article of **"Âişe"** II, 204.

of the narrators, with regards to: their reasoning, language, history and experience; as well as using well-known sunnahs, and the aspects of the *Qur'an*.[225] She would then give her opinion, and make a critique of some relatings. She had a single objective: to convey the religion taught by Allah's Messenger (saw) to the future generations, in its purest and most accurate form.

Regarding this issue, let's refer to a hadith which displays the attentiveness of the companions in relating hadith:

When Amr bin Umayya was bargaining for a shawl in the market, Umar (ra) turned up.

Umar asked: *"What is this, O Amr?"*

Amr replied: *"I am going to buy a shawl, and then I will give it away as alms."*

Umar (ra) said: *"Go on with your business"* After a while he called in on Amr and asked what he did with the shawl.

Amr said: *"I gave it away as alms."*

*"To whom?"*

*"To one of my wives."*

*"Hadn't you said that you would give it as alms?"*

*"Yes I had, but I heard Allah's Messenger (saw) saying: 'Whatever you give to your wives is charity for you'."*

*"O Amr! Don't lie on behalf of Allah's Messenger (saw)!"*

*"By Allah, I will not leave you, unless we go to the mother of the faithful together!"*

*"O Amr! Don't lie on behalf of Allah's Messenger (saw)!"*

---

225.   Muslim, 2493; DIA, Article of **"Âişe"** II, 204.

After the discussion, they both came before Sayyidah Â'ishah (r.ah) and asked her permission.

Amr said: *"Would you swear in the name of Allah: did you hear Allah's Messenger (saw) saying: 'Whatever you give to your wives is charity for you'?* Sayyidah Â'ishah said: *"O Allah, be my witness, yes! O Allah, be my witness, yes!"* Thereupon Umar (ra) said: *"Where was I that I didn't hear this? Probably shopping chores detained me."*[226]

There are a few issues in this account which attract attention, which we cannot refrain from pointing out: The first is the sensitivity displayed by Umar (ra) regarding the accounts which are narrated as hadith, even if they are related to ordinary matters; and the fact that he did not give up until he established the authenticity of the account, showed his intolerance regarding making up hadith and alleging it to be from Allah's Messenger (saw). This sensitivity is an indicator of the strength of his faith; and the way he acknowledged his mistake when he saw the truth, displays his moral virtues.

However, the main issue which should be pointed out here, is the position Sayyidah Â'ishah (r.ah) holds as "an expert and arbiter" among the companions, regarding scholarly disagreements on issues such as reporting of hadith. This is sufficient to display her authority regarding knowledge, during her era.

Furthermore, this and similar incidents clearly display the position of women in Islam: that two men, one of them the Head of the State, go before a woman and resort to her arbitration, and submit to her decision. Considering the attempts to label Islam as a religion which *"considers women as second rate beings"*, how contradictory is the aforementioned event and many others. Of course, for people who acknowledge truth sincerely, without false preconceptions or conditioning!

Sayyidah Â'ishah (r.ah) holds a distinctive position, whether in narrating and interpreting *ahadith*, or in resolving conflicting opinions regarding these. Occasionally, she intervened in the accounts related by Umar (ra), Abdullah bin Umar (ra), Abu Hurairah (ra), Ibn Abbas (ra), Uthman (ra) and many others from the companions; critically reviewing and correcting their accounts, either

---

226. Bukhârî, Salât, 22; Muslim, Salât, 267; Muwatta, Salâtu'l-Leyl, 2.

partially or in its entirety.[227] She had a pre-eminent position due to the volume of the accounts she related, her interpretations and her vigor in setting forth proof.[228] She had an outstanding knowledge not only in the field of hadith and *sunnah*, but also in other fields such as: *tafsir*,[229] *fiqh*,[230] history, genealogy, poetry, literature and medicine. She was all but a *madrasah*[231] on her own. Abu Musa al-Ash'ari, who is among the scholars of the companions, says: "*When the companions of Allah's Messenger (saw) faced a difficulty, they would refer it to Â'ishah; and by all means, she would have some knowledge about that matter.*"[232]

Urwah bin Zubayr remarks that he had not seen anyone so cognizant of the Islamic knowledge related to *halal*,[233]*haram*, poetry, medicine, history and genealogy, as much as Sayyidah Â'ishah.[234]

Ata bin Abi Rabah says: "*Among all people, Â'ishah had the most knowledge and comprehension regarding fiqh.*"

All of these accounts show that Allah the Almighty had chosen Sayyidah Â'ishah for training both the women, who constitute half of the ummah, and the companions of her day; equipping her with outstanding capabilities and attributes, and preparing the environment necessary for her to fulfil these services.

Just as the blossoming and fading of a tiny flower is not useless, meaningless, needless and without importance, the merits, virtues, competences and attributes which all eminent companions, the wives of the Holy Prophet (saw) and especially Sayyidah Â'ishah (r.ah) possessed, are not coincidental. Allah the Almighty created all the conditions which are necessary to preserve the last book He revealed, from being distorted, until the Day of Judgement. This manifests the wisdom and augustness of the Divine predestination. Sayyidah

---

227. Recounting from "Asr-i Saadet, III, p: 379", Ramazan Balcı, p: 171.
Some self-contained works have been published, displaying her percipience regarding the mistakes she rectified from her contemporaries, which included many eminent Companions, and displaying the reasons of these mistakes. (Tha article on "Â'isha", DIA, II, 204)
228. DIA, the article of "**Âişe**" II, 204.
229. A commentary, usually referring to the commentary of the Holy Qur'an.
230. Islamic jurisprudence.
231. A college for Islamic instruction.
232. Ramazan Balcı, Ibid., page: 174.
233. Lawful, or permissible as defined by Allah the Almighty.
234. Afzalurrahman, Ibid., II, 166.

Â'ishah (r.ah) fulfilled her significant duty within this Divine predestination with perception, comprehension, recollection, intelligence, decorum, eloquence and affection.

Regarding her knowledge, Imam Zuhri said: *"If the knowledge of the other wives of Allah's Messenger (saw) were to be added up with the knowledge of all other women, and then compared to the knowledge of Â'ishah (r.ah), her knowledge would surpass all of them. This ummah hasn't witnessed any other woman, who even came close to her knowledge. Allah's Messenger (saw) didn't love any of his wives, as he loved her. Many of her attributes have been related in Qur'an and Sunnah."*[235]

## Her Later Years

Allah's Messenger (saw) had returned to Madinah from his first and last hajj, on the tenth year after hijrah. After a short while, on the last week of the month of Safar in the eleventh year after hijri, he fell ill. He moved to Sayyidah Â'ishah's (r.ah) chamber with the consent of his other wives.[236] All of them willingly agreed to his wish to spend the days of his sickness where he wanted. They all conceded their days to Sayyidah Â'ishah (r.ah). Thereupon Allah's Messenger (saw) moved into the chamber of Sayyidah Â'ishah (r.ah). He passed away in her chamber, while his blessed head was resting on her lap. Then he was buried in that chamber.[237]

Sayyidah Â'ishah (r.ah) depicts the moment of his passing, which she personally witnessed, as follows: *"One of the blessings Allah granted me is the fact that Allah's Messenger (saw) passed away in my room, on my watch, while his blessed head was between my neck and bosom. And the way Allah mixed my saliva with his when he was passing away: Abdurrahman came into the room with a siwaq in his hand, as Allah's Messenger (saw) leaned against me,and I saw that he was looking intently at the siwaq. Since I knew that he loved siwaq, I asked him: 'Shall I take the siwaq for you?' He nodded with his head, mean-*

---

235. Bünyamin Erul, Hazret-i Âişe'nin Sahâbe'ye Yönelttiği Eleştiriler, page: 54; Afzalurrahman, Ibid., II, page: 166.
236. DIA, the article of **"Âişe"** II, 202.
237. DIA, the article of **"Âişe"** II, 202.

*ing 'Yes, take it.' I took it and offered it to him. However, it was hard for him. I asked: 'O Allah's Messenger (saw)!. Shall I soften it?' He nodded his head. After I softened the siwaq (in my mouth) and gave it to him, he brushed his teeth with it. There was a small water container made of leather besides Allah's Messenger (saw). Every so often he dipped both of his hands into the water, and he wiped his face with his wet hands, saying: 'La ilaha illa Allah!" Then he raised his hands. He continued praying as 'O Allah, render me among the community of the highest companions!', until he died. And with this prayer, the hands of the Last Prophet fell down."*[238]

Sayyidah Â'ishah (r.ah), who became a widow when she was very young (around 18) along with the other wives of the Holy Prophet (saw), did not marry again, observing the decree revealed in the Qur'an, as, the wives of Allah's Messenger (saw) were honoured as being **"the mothers of the believers"**[239] and they were forbidden to marry with someone else after Allah's Messenger (saw) passed away.

Sayyidah Â'ishah (r.ah) led a very simple life after the Holy Prophet (saw) passed away, as she had during his lifetime. The Holy Prophet (saw) had made provision for Sayyidah Â'ishah, along with his other wives, the equivalent of 480 gallons (80 *vesk*) of dates and 120 gallons (20 *vesk*) of barley (or wheat) each year, from the income of Khaibar.

She spent most of her time fasting, whether during the lifetime of Allah's Messenger (saw), or after it. She was never involved in any incident during the Khilafat of either her father Abu Bakr, or Umar (ra): the relationship between them was built on mutual respect and understanding.

When Umar (ra) was apportioning money for the wives of Allah's Messenger (saw) during his reign, he had allocated Sayyidah Â'ishah (r.ah) more than the others (twelve thousand dirhams), considering the special affection Allah's Messenger (saw) showed to her.[240]

Although Sayyidah Â'ishah (r.ah) was financially in a better position than

---

238. Afzalurrahman, Ibid., II, 174.
239. "The Prophet is closer to the Believers than their own selves, and his wives are their mothers." (Surah al-Ahzab, 33: 6)
240. DIA, the article of **"Âişe"** II, 203.

the other wives of the Holy Prophet (saw), she used to love to give out the money and the precious goods she possessed as alms. She was so open-handed that she would not leave anything for herself even when she was fasting.

Khalifah Umar (ra) used to consult her regarding legal matters concerning women. When he was heavily wounded after an assassination attempt, through his daughter Sayyidah Hafsa he asked Sayyidah Â'ishah's (r.ah) permission to be buried at the foot of the grave of Allah's Messenger (saw). Sayyidah Â'ishah (r.ah) allowed him to be buried in that place, which she had thought for herself, saying: *"I prefer Umar to myself."*[241]

Sayyidah Â'ishah (r.ah), who had been married to the most auspicious of men, used to visit the graves of Allah's Messenger (saw) and her father Abu Bakr. Throughout these visits, she would be engrossed; deep in thought, such that she would not care much for her veil during these visits, because it was her spouse and her father, who were laid to rest there. However, when Umar (ra) was buried there, her habit changed: she was now saying: *"I would be ashamed of going there withou a veil since Umar is there."*

## The Jamal Incident

Sayyidah Â'ishah (r.ah) found herself amidst some political developments, towards the end of the Khilafah of Uthman (ra) and during the time of Ali (ra), even though they were against her wish. It is reported that she was remorseful about what had happened for a long time[242], and that she used to cry until her veil was soaked. Toward the Muslims she did not hold any anger nor kept any bad feelings.

Toward the end of Hz. Uthman's (ra) khalifaship, from the new countries that had been conquered, there was controversial news was coming to the capitol, Medina. The people who did not like the governor, the judge, or the people in charge of the treasury, or if they did not like their performance, would come and complain making appeals to the Khalifah.

241. DIA, the article of **"Âişe"** II, 203.
242. DIA, the article of **"Âişe"** II, 203.

Khalifah Hz. Uthman (ra) would listen to the committees one by one, but he would not accept their suggestions to take his own family members out of their jobs. Just as he was soft with the creation, he was also one to soft toward his family. Some of Hz. Uthman's (ra) family took advantage of his nature and used that softness to abuse the power and started to oppress the people.

There were some groups already making these problems bigger and turning this into a reason for rebellion. They were working with all of their strength to rip Islam apart and turn the Muslims against each other. This organized group of provacateur, led by Abdullah bin Sebe and his supporters, gathered around Medina from other areas. They literally turned the city into a roofless prison. The Khalifah was a prisoner in his own home. No one could easily leave their house. A short while later, while Hz. Uthman (ra) was in his house reading Quran, they brutally murdered him.

* * *

Hz. Aisha (ra) has opposed some of the decisions that Hz. Uthman (ra) had made and as a result of this had found herself inside a political life. When the rebels came to Madina, she was on her way to Mecca for Hajj. On her way back to Medina she learned that Hz. Uthman (ra) had been murdered and that Ali (ra) had become Khalifah, so she returned back to Mecca.

While in Mecca, a group of Muslims gathered around her; they asked for her help to end the controversy between the Muslims and they wanted to get the "blood money" for Hz. Uthman's (ra) death from the rebels who murdered him. She (ra) did not have any animosity or diappointment with the new Khalifah, Hz. Ali.[243] All she wanted to do was to punish the people who killed Hz. Uthman (ra) and to reunite the Muslims. That was the only goal of the big group that left Mecca heading toward Basra.

When their trail passed through the area of Hav'eb, the dogs started to bark. Hz. Aisha (ra) asked where they were and the guide said: "We are near the waters of Hav'eb."

At that point Hz. Aisha (ra) remembered a thing that the Prophet had said

---

243.     [243] DIA, the article of "Âişe" II, 203.

to his wives: "I wonder for which one of you the dogs of Hav'eb will bark!" [244] And then she said: "Apparently I was the owner of the waters of Hav'eb! Turn me around, turn me around!" while having the people lower her camel.

She wanted to turn back to Mecca but Zubeyr bin Awwam and Talha bin Ubaydullah thought they would lose their main source of strength, so they convinced her to stay by saying: "Perhaps because of you Allah will grant the Muslims peace and comfort!" [245]

One reason that kept her on the journey was the ayat that said fix the controvery and keep the peace between the Muslims: **"And if two factions among the believers should fight, then make settlement between the two. But if one of them oppresses the other, then fight against the one that oppresses until it returns to the ordinance of Allah . And if it returns, then make settlement between them in justice and act justly. Indeed, Allah loves those who act justly."** (al-Hucurat, 9)

Instead of waiting around to see what would happen, she decided to follow the rule of this ayat and fix the chaos that started among the Muslims of Medina because of Hz. Uthman's death.

Hz. Aisha (ra) and the people with her arrived at Basra.  At that time Hz. Ali (ra) was preparing an army to go against Mu'awiya, Hz. Uthman's (ra) cousin, who was the governor of Syria because he made a case regarding Hz. Uthman's (ra) death.  When Hz. Ali (ra) learned that Hz. Aisha and those with her had arrived in Basra, the first thing he did was head toward Iraq.  He knew that they had no intentions of rebellion.  Therefore he was going to persuade this sincere group and face Mu'awiya.

Both sides faced each other at Zakar; at a place near Basra.  They passed notes and letters between each other and found terms on which they could both agree.  Hz. Aisha (ra) and the people with her prepared to turn back, but the rebellious people within Hz. Ali's (ra) army they were unhappy and uncomfortable with the terms of the agreement.  This provocative group started shooting arrows toward the people with Hz. Aisha even before the sun came up.  Before

---

244.   Ahmed b. Hanbel, VI, 52-92.
245.   Ahmed b. Hanbel, Müsned, 6/92.

they could realize where the arrows were coming from, or from who, the two armies came together in battle. Hz. Ali (ra) had about 20,000 soldiers and Hz. Aisha had about 30,000 soldiers.

Because of the fact that during this war Hz. Aisha (ra) managed and administered her army from atop a camal, it was named the "Jamal (Camel) Incident". In the end Hz. Aisha's (ra) army lost the war. Talha bin Ubeydullah and Zubeyr bin Awwam, the companions who were among the Aşere-i Mübeşşere (the people promised Heaven even before they died) and who were on Hz. Aisha's (ra) side, were martyred, even though Hz.Ali (ra) had told his soldiers absolutely not to touch Hz. Aisha (ra) or these two great Sahaba.

Hz. Ali (ra) did not allow either side to take captives. He helped Hz. Aisha and her brother, Muhammad bin Abu Bakr, to return first to Basra and then to Madina in a very a comfortable way. However, because she had made the intention for Hajj, she first went to Mecca and then on to Madina.

In spite of joining solely for the sake of completing Allah's command, her political life, which started at the end of Hz. Uthman's (ra) time and end with the "Jemal Incident", saddened her a lot in her later life.

While praying or reading Quran in private, everytime she came to the ayat sent down especially for the Prophet's wives **"abide in your houses"** (el-Ahzâb, 33), she would cry until all of her clothes were wet.[246]

And sometime when she got very sad she would say: "I wish I would have died long ago so I would not have joined this event (which had killed so many Muslims)."[247]

* * *

In conclusion, this event that the Prophet had refered to in his health was going to happen sooner or later. The part that falls to us is to not put the Sahaba, who are all valuable to us, into a race which ranks them higher or better than the others. It is not possible for us to know the intention or reasons that they had to do the things that they did. So the best thing to do is to leave it to Allah

---

246. İbn-i Sa'd, Tabakât, VIII, 80.
247. DIA, c: II, sh: 203.

(swt) who knows everything which is hidden and open. He is able to make the right choice because he is "Al-Adl"; The Just.

The scholars of Islam say "we should try not to do with our tongues what the sahaba did with their swords." We should try to look at this incident with a future perspective: and Allah knows best.


## Her Death

This blessed woman who had been married to our beloved Prophet, whose morals consisted of Qur'an, fell ill towards the end of her life: she had an acute illness. She used to smile at people who would console her by saying that she would be reunited with Allah's Messenger (saw). She was sixty-six years old when she passed away on a Tuesday night, on the 17th or 19th of the month of Ramadan. There are different accounts regarding the year she passed away: according to some it was the 57th year of hijrah, and according to the others, it was the 58th.[248]

Sayyidah Â'ishah (r.ah) was buried at the Baqi' cemetery, in Madinah, and her funeral prayer was led by Abu Hurairah (ra) who was the deputy mayor of Madinah. In accordance with her wishes: her body was carried to the Baqi' cemetery at midnight, under the light of torches made of cloth and tied onto wooden sticks and dipped in oil. An unparalleled number of people attended the funeral. Her body was placed into the grave by her nephews.[249] Her grave was besides the graves of the other wives of the Holy Prophet (saw).


## The Virtues of Sayyidah Â'ishah (r.ah)

Sayyidah Â'ishah (r.ah) earned an exceptional position beside Allah's Messenger (saw) with her attributes such as; intellect, strong memory, comprehension, eloquence, and striving to understand the Qur'an and the Holy Prophet (saw) in the best possible way.

---

248.   DIA, the article of "Âişe" II, 202.
249.   DIA, the article of "Âişe" II, 202.

When the Holy Prophet (saw) fostered the betterment of her competencies, the skills she had acquired in her family home flourished and matured under the guidance of Divine revelation. Sayyidah Â'ishah (r.ah) never held back from asking about whatever matter bothered her, of the Holy Prophet (saw). She would not refrain from deliberating with him, either.

* * *

Sayyidah Â'ishah (r.ah) led a very plain life. She spent her nights with supererogatory prayers, and her days by fasting, as far as possible. Sayyidah Â'ishah (r.ah) disliked talking about anyone. She was content with what she had. She was also generous and moderate. She used to take orphans and poor children under her protection, and she would take great care in their nurturing and training. It is reported that she emancipated many slaves, and that the number of these reached sixty two.[250]

* * *

She is a distinguished mother of the faithful, who received good tidings of being one of the wives of the Holy Prophet (saw) in Paradise.[251]

She is the one who has been acquitted by Allah, the Beloved of the beloved of Allah, and Siddiqah, the truthful, the daughter of Siddiq.

* * *

In several accounts, it is related that Allah's Messenger (saw) used to receive the divine revelation mostly when he was in Sayyidah Â'ishah's (r.ah) chamber. Apart from a few instances, he did not receive it in his other wives' chambers.[252] This account alone is sufficient to display the position of Sayyidah Â'ishah (r.ah) among the wives of the Holy Prophet (saw).

Sayyidah Â'ishah (r.ah) sets out the distinction between herself and the other wives of Allah's Messenger (saw) as follows:

---

250.  DIA, the article of **"Âişe"** II, 202.
251.  Ibn-i Sa'd, VII, 65.
252.  Bukhârî, Hibe, 8.

*"I have been rendered above other women in several points:*

*Allah's Messenger (saw) didn't marry any other virgin, except me;*

*None of the women who Allah's Messenger (saw) married had both parents from the muhajireen;*

*My acquittal was brought down from heaven by Allah;*

*The divine revelation used to come to Allah's Messenger (saw) when he was with me;*

*Allah's Messenger (saw) used to continue praying while I lay in front of him;*

*Allah's Messenger (saw) passed away when he was in my chamber with me, while I was awake; and, He was buried in my room."*[253]

* * *

According to the Qur'an, the wives of the Holy Prophet (saw) are the mothers of the faithful. For them, this is an everlasting honour. They acquired this position because of their marriage to the Holy Prophet (saw), and because of their outstanding merits and qualities. Following the death of Allah's Messenger (saw), his wives perpetuated his lifestyle for approximately fifty years, with all its pleasantness, purity and freshness: they strived for their best so that Islam was taught and lived properly;

Therefore respecting them means respecting Allah the Almighty and His Messenger (saw).

Without doubt, Sayyidah Â'ishah (r.ah) holds a pre-eminent position among the mothers of the faithful, who are all exceptional people. She holds a lofty position, which cannot be blemished by the libelling of gossips: for Allah has absolved her and raised her dignity until the Day of Judgment. Indeed libelling Sayyidah Â'ishah (r.ah) because of the slander incident has been forbidden eternally in the verses of Surah an-Noor, which were revealed regarding her: *"Allah admonishes you that you should not return to the like of it ever again if you are*

---

253.   Havva Ergene Işık, Ibid., page: 295.

*believers.*"[254] Some of the scholars have concluded that if anyone continues to slander Sayyidah Â'ishah (r.ah), despite the explicit declaration of this verse, they would become infidels.[255]

The prominent historian and *mufassir*[256] Ibn Katheer says:

*"Generally, 'Ahlul Kitab wa Sunnah'[257] regard Â'ishah (r.ah) higher (among the wives of Allah's Messenger) from the point of virtues. First of all, she is the daughter of Abu Bakr (ra). She possesses an unprecedented mental faculty, knowledge and eloquence within the Ummah, and has more knowledge than Khadijah (r.ah)."*

*"Allah's Messenger (saw) didn't love any other of his wives as he loved her. Divine revelation was sent from seven heavens about her, declaring her innocence. Following the passing of the Holy Prophet (saw), she related a large amount of pure and blessed knowledge from him. Regarding her it was said: 'Take half of your religion from Humeira'.*

*Despite all these, instead of being wordy, it is more befitting to say 'Allah knows best' concerning this matter."*[258]

However, the evaluation of Ibn Qayyim al-Javziyya on this issue, who is the student of Ibn Katheer, appears to be more comprehensive and fitting:

*"If the intention in pre-eminence is pertaining to the rank in the next world, only Allah the Almighty knows this. On the other hand, if the intention is nobility, Fatimah az-Zahra is superior to all of them. If the intention is precedence in believing; believing in Islam, enduring the hardships suffered by Muslims in their earliest times and helping Allah's Messenger (saw); then Khadijah (r.ah) is superior to all of them. However, if the intention is perfection of knowledge, religious services and spreading the teachings and guidance of Allah's Messenger (saw), then no one can challenge Â'ishah (r.ah) in this matter."*[259]

---

254. Surah an-Noor 24:17
255. Ramazan Balcı, Ibid., page: 121-122.
256. A scholar of tafsir.
257. *Ahlul Kitab wa sunnah* literally means "the People of the Book (the Holy Qur'an) and the Sunnah (sayings and traditions of Holy Prophet, SAW)". This refers to the people who strive to follow the teachings of the Holy Qur'an and Prophet Muhammad (saw), without any deviations.
258. Ramazan Balcı, Ibid., page: 118-119.
259. Ramazan Balcı, Ibid., page: 119

## Lessons to be Learned From This Examplary Life

1- The house of Sayyidah Â'ishah (r.ah) consisted of a small room, arranged for a plain and modest life. The walls of this room were made of mud-bricks, and its roof was covered with date leaves, and it was not very high. The goods in the house were made up of a mattress and a pot. The person who lived in this house was Humeira, the mother of the faithful, who was crowned with verses from the Qur'an, and whose life presents an example for us. We should make our homes and lives humble and free from waste, like the house of Sayyidah Â'ishah (r.ah); at the same time striving to enrich our spiritual world like that blessed person. How can this be achieved? With affection towards Allah and His Messenger (saw) and following the *Sunnah* of His Messenger (saw)!

2- Sayyidah Â'ishah (r.ah) is also an example to be followed for women who do not have children, as a test by Allah the Almighty: she was not held back because of this test, and she did not consume her energy by complaining. To the contrary, she allotted her wit, understanding and capabilities; in short all her life, before all else, to her husband, and following his death, she served as one of the greatest women scholars, teaching for early fifty years. On the one hand she passed on the *ahadith* that she had learned, and on the other hand she became the soundest reference about legal issues concerning women. She took to her heart whoever was seeking knowledge, and imparted them with her wisdom.

3- The marriage of Allah's Messenger (saw) with Sayyidah Â'ishah (r.ah), who was much younger than him, has been a blessing for his ummah, because, Sayyidah Â'ishah (r.ah) observed the life of the Holy Prophet (saw) in the finest and most private details. She asked and learned about all matters that she did not understand, and related these to the companions, as if they were her own sons,- and their followers (sincerely and with all details).[260] Many companions and even Umar (ra) felt the need to consult with Sayyidah Â'ishah (r.ah), especially on issues regarding women.

4- Before he passed away, Umar (ra) asked Sayyidah Â'ishah's (r.ah) permission to be buried at the feet of Allah's Messenger (saw). Sayyidah Â'ishah (r.ah) relinquished this place voluntarily, (which she had thought for herself), by saying: "*I prefer Umar to myself*!"

---

260.　Surah al-Ahzâb, 33: 6.

In this way, in order to follow his sunnah, she forsook being close to Allah's Messenger (saw): the most beloved person to her in this world; because the Holy Prophet (saw) had said: *"Unless one desires for his brother what he desires for himself, he will not have sincerely believed."* Even this event on its own shows how far Sayyidah Â'ishah (r.ah) had absorbed the morals of Allah's Messenger (saw), putting others before her self.

Sayyidah Â'ishah (r.ah) was the most jealous, compared to the other wives of Allah's Messenger (saw). Jealousy is a trait which can be used for both goodness and evil. When it is done aimlessly, blindly and excessively, it turns into a wicked trait. However, some characteristics of Sayyidah Â'ishah (r.ah) justified her jealousy towards Allah's Messenger (saw). She was his youngest and the single virgin wife. She did not have a child from the Holy Prophet (saw), therefore her love towards him was never shared, and so, Allah's Messenger (saw) was the first and last man who had a place in Sayyidah Â'ishah's (r.ah) heart. Furthermore, the main reason that Allah's Messenger (saw) had an exceptional place in her heart was his lofty morals and unparalleled merits. If she had been married to a commoner instead of the Prophet, perhaps she would not have been so jealous of him. As a matter of fact, from time to time the Holy Prophet (saw) and Sayyidah Â'ishah (r.ah) used to have conversations as follows:

*"Do you feel jealous?"*

*"How can it be (that a woman like me) should not feel jealous in regard to a husband like you."*[261]

Sayyidah Â'ishah (r.ah) was speaking the truth. How could a wife like her not be jealous of a husband like Allah's Messenger (saw)?

As for the other wives of the Holy Prophet (saw), they had married others previously; some even had children from these marriages. This characteristic of Sayyidah Â'ishah (r.ah), which distinguishes her from the other wives of Allah's Messenger (saw), adds a distinct hue and beauty to her life and personality.

6- The life of Sayyidah Â'ishah (r.ah) is like a painting which depicts beautifully the surges taking place in the soul of a woman.

---

261.  Muslim, Book 039, Number 6759; (Muslim, Munâfikûn, 70).

Age was never an issue in the marriage of Sayyidah Â'ishah (r.ah) and the Holy Prophet (saw). Allah's Messenger (saw) knew how to connect with her at her level, and displayed an exemplary family life, showing men how to treat their wives. He did whatever was necessary; including playing (games) with her, allowing her to watch games, tolerating her, sometimes necessary, sometimes superfluous, jealousy.

7- Sayyidah Â'ishah (r.ah) displayed affection, respect and care towards the *Sunnah* and *ahadith* of Allah's Messenger (saw), as she had towards him during his lifetime. When she was relating hadith in her lessons, she displayed careful attention for having *wudu,* and when this was not possible, she made *tayammum*[262].

May Allah the Almighty be pleased with our upright mother for her love towards His Messenger (saw) and for conforming to his sunnah, and may he render each one of us a "Humayra", drawing lessons from her spiritual world.

---

262.  *Tayammum* literally means 'to intend to do a thing'. As an Islamic legal term, it refers to wiping one's hands and face with clean earth as a substitution for ablution when water cannot be obtained.

# SAYYIDAH HAFSA (r.ah),

## The Daughter of 'Umar (ra)

## The First Years of Her Life

Sayyidah Hafsa (r.ah) was the daughter of 'Umar (ra). She was from the Adiyy branch of the Quraysh Tribe and was married to the Prophet (saw) in 3 A.H. The lineage of 'Umar (ra) merges with the lineage of Allah's Messenger (saw) a few generations before. Her mother is Zainab bint Maz'un al-Jumahiyyah, the sister of 'Uthman bin Maz'un. According to 'Umar (ra), Sayyidah Hafsa was born in 605 A.D., in Mecca; five years before the advent of the Holy Prophet (saw).[263]

Sayyidah Hafsa became a Muslim during the Meccan period, and made *hijrah* (migrated) to Madinah with her first husband Hunais bin Huzaafa.[264] Hunais died in Medina, after he was wounded in the Battle of Badr.[265] His funeral was led by the Messenger of Allah (saw).

---

263. M. Yaşar Kandemir, the article of "Hafsa", DIA, XV, 119-120.
264. Muhammad Hamîdullah, II, p: 679; Celal Yeniceri, p: 82.
In the *"Diyanet Islamic Encyclopedia"* (DIA), a note has been written about this issue: *"It can be concluded that the marriage of Hafsa with Hunais bin Huzaafa took place after Hunais immigrated to Ethiopia and then came back to Makkah. (Then) Hafsa made hijrah to Madinah with her husband.*
With this information provided by the author of the article M. Yasar Kandemir, it occurs that Hafsa made *hijrah* only to Madinah, and not to Ethiopia.
265. Bukhari, Magazi, 12; DIA, article on "Hafsa", Afzalurrahman,vol: II, p: 175. In this connection some resources provide differing information. For example Muhammad Hamîdullah relates that Hafsa's husband died because of the serious wounds inflicted on him during the Battle of Uhud. (M. Hamîdullah,The Prophet of Islam, II, sh: 679). However, since there is an agreement that the marriage of Allah's Messenger and Sayyidah Hafsa took place 2 and half years after hijrah, this account seems historically incorrect as the Battle of Uhud had occurred in the third year of *hijrah*.

'Umar (ra) was very saddened to see his daughter widowed at such a young age. He felt this sadness intensify each time he would visit her and find her downcast in the remembrance of the husband she had lost, and thus, 'Umar (ra) resolved to get her remarried. Not only was he spurred into seeking another partner for her in the attempt to alleviate her distress, it was also the custom of the Arabs at the time to seek the marriage of one's daughters or sisters to someone virtuous as to do so was taken as an indicator that one cared for his relatives.[266]

## The Efforts of a Father

With this intention, 'Umar first turned to 'Uthman (ra) as a possible suitor for his daughter as 'Uthman too had suffered the loss of his wife Ruqayyah[267] (r.ah), the daughter of the Prophet (saw). However, 'Uthman (ra) asked for a few days to think it over, and then politely refused his offer by saying: "I am not considering marrying again for the time being".

Troubled by this answer, 'Umar (ra) went to see Abu Bakr (ra) and made the same proposal to him. Abu Bakr (ra) also declined. 'Umar was both hurt and confused and thus resorted to speak of the matter before the Prophet (saw). In response the Holy Prophet (saw) said, "Allah the Almighty has predestined a more righteous husband for your daughter than 'Uthman, and a more honourable wife for him than your daughter!", thereby declaring that he sought to marry Sayyidah Hafsa. Extremely pleased of this request, 'Umar immediately married his daughter to the Holy Prophet (saw).[268]

This matrimony took place in the month of Sha'bân, in the third year of *hijrah* (January 625, AD), with a *mahr*, wedding dowry of 400 *dirhams*.

Later on, when Abu Bakr (ra) met 'Umar (ra), in order to congratulate him, he said: "Perhaps you were angry with me when you offered Sayyidah Hafsa

---

266. DIA, the article of "Hafsa."
267. Ruqayyah, (ra) the wife of 'Uthman (ra) and the daughter of the Holy Prophet (saw) fell ill when she was returning from Ethiopia, just when Muslims were going to the Battle of Badr. Her husband 'Uthman had remained with her to take care of her. Because of this 'Uthman (ra) wasn't able to join the Battle of Badr. Ruqqayah (ra) passed away following the victory of Badr. (Ayse Abdurrahman, 76)
268. DIA, the article of "Hafsa".

to me in marriage and I declined?" 'Umar (ra) confirmed this: "Yes (honestly, I was hurt)!" Then Abu Bakr (ra) said: "Nothing prevented me from accepting your offer except that I learnt that Allah's Messenger (saw) had intended to propose to Sayyidah Hafsa and I did not want to disclose the secret of Allah's Messenger (saw), but had he (i.e. the Prophet) given her up I would surely have accepted her."

The Prophet (saw) got married to Sayyidah Hafsa bint 'Umar (ra) and Uthman (ra) got married to Ummu Kulthum bint Muhammad.[269]

## Being a Mother of the Believers

Thus Sayyidah Hafsa became one of the mothers of the faithful, and a beloved wife of Allah's Messenger (saw). With this happy event, Allah's Messenger (saw) became a relative to 'Umar (ra) and won his heart; the person whom he loved most after Abu Bakr (ra).[270]

## A New Home

Sayyidah Hafsa (r.ah) was one of very few people who were literate.[271] She was 22 years old when she married to the Holy Prophet (saw).

At that time, Sayyidah Sawda (r.ah) and Sayyidah Â'ishah (r.ah) were also married to Allah's Messenger (saw), sharing his house. Sayyidah Sawda welcomed Sayyidah Hafsa, just as she had received Sayyidah Â'ishah (r.ah) with a contented heart.

Although in the first years of her marriage she was a bit distant, in time she got on very well with Sayyidah Â'ishah (r.ah), and even in some occasions they acted together against the other wives of Allah's Messenger (saw).

Sayyidah Hafsa had an important position besides the Holy Prophet (saw).

---

269. Buhârî, Megâzî, 12; Nikâh, 33.
270. Muhammed Hamidullah, İslâm Peygamberi, II, 679.
271. Muhammed Hamidullah, İslâm Peygamberi, II, 679.

She was a knowledgeable, cultured, strong willed and devoted wife. Compared to the other wives of the Holy Prophet (saw), along with Sayyidah Â'ishah (r.ah), she had a more distinguished position to be envied for. Nevertheless, she had a strong temperament, perhaps inherited from her father.[272] Because of this, every so often 'Umar (ra) used to advise his daughter to never offend Allah's Messenger (saw).

There are several detailed accounts in the hadith books regarding this issue. One of these occurred when Umar (ra) felt uncomfortable about the way his wife had started to retort him, after they had made *hijrah* to Medina. Upon reprimanding his wife for her behaviour, she informed him that the wives of Allah's Messenger (saw) felt at liberty to speak back to him. Umar (ra) was enraged to hear this. He went to see his daughter, who was one of the wives of the Holy Prophet (saw), and asked her: "Do any of you stay irritated with Allah's Messenger (saw) throughout the whole night?" When her reply was "Yes", he cautioned her by saying: "She is a ruined loser (and will never have success)! Doesn't she fear that Allah may get angry for the anger of Allah's Messenger (saw) and thus she will be ruined? Don't ask Allah's Messenger (saw) too many things, and don't retort against him in any case, and don't desert him. Demand from me whatever you like!"

On another occasion he said: "O my daughter, if you offend Allah's Messenger (saw), Allah will grant him better (wives) than you! And you will be deprived!"[273]

These events demonstrate how Sayyidina 'Umar (ra) took care of his daughter and how worried he was that perchance she might offend the Holy Prophet (saw) and she might have to stay away from him.[274]

**The Honey Syrup**

According to the written sources, one of the important events which Sayyidah Hafsa (r.ah) was involved in, is the honey syrup incident. This was a conflict

---

272. Ziya Kazıcı, Ibid., page: 191.
273. Bukhârî, Mazâlim, 25.
274. See: Ziya Kazıcı, Ibid., page: 192-198; Elmalılı Muhammed Hamdi Yazır, Hak Dini Kur'ân Dili, Tafseer of Surah Tahrim, VII, s: 5084-5112.

between Allah's Messenger (saw) and his blessed wives, which started when he visited Sayyidah Hafsa, and she offered him honey syrup.[275]

This incident became quite complicated; and became the cause for the revelation of the first verses of *Surah al-Tahrîm*. Here we have an account of the event as narrated by Sayyidah Â'ishah (r.ah):

Allah's Messenger (saw) was fond of honey and sweet foods. It was his habit to visit his wives and stay the night with one of them after the asr prayer. One time he went to Sayyidah Hafsa, the daughter of Umar (ra) and stayed with her more than usual. I got jealous and asked the reason for that. I was told that a lady of her folk had given her a skin filled with honey as a present, and she made syrup from it and gave it to the Prophet (saw) to drink: and that was the reason for the delay. I said, "By Allah we will respond to him in such a way that it will prevent him from doing so." So I said to Sayyidah Sawda bint Zam'a "Allah's Messenger (saw) will approach you, and when he comes near you, say: 'Have you taken *maghafir* (a bad-smelling gum)?' He will say, 'No.' Then say to him: 'Then what is this bad smell which I smell from you?'

In one narration Sayyidah Â'ishah (r.ah) made this explanation: "The Messenger of Allah (saw) would be very unhappy if he perceived an unpleasant odor from himself. Because of this, certainly he will say, 'Hafsa made me drink honey syrup.' Then say: Perhaps the bees of that honey had sucked the juice of the tree of *Al-'Urfut*.' I shall also say the same. O you, Sayyidah Safiyyah, say the same." Later Sawda (r.ah) said, "By Allah, as soon as he (the Prophet -saw-) stood at the door, I was about to say to him what you had ordered me to say because I was afraid of you." So when the Holy Prophet (saw) came near Sayyidah Sawda, she said to him, "O Allah's Messenger (saw)! Have you taken *maghafir*?" He said, "No." She said. "Then what is this bad smell which I detect on you?" He said, "Hafsa made me drink honey syrup." She said, "Perhaps its bees had sucked the juice of *Al-'Urfut* tree." When he came to me, I also said the same, and when he went to Sayyidah Safiyyah, she also said the same. And when the Holy Prophet (saw) again went to Sayyidah Hafsa, she said, 'O Allah's

---

275. In some accounts, it is said that Sayyidah Hafsa (ra) offered the honey syrup, while some other accounts say that it was Zainab bint Jahsh. According to the latter, Sayyidah Hafsa and Sayyidah Â'ishah (ra) had led the event. (See. Elmalili Muhammed Hamdi Yazir, Hak Dini Kur'an Dili, VII, p: 5094-5097)

Messenger (saw)! Shall I give you more of that drink?" He said, "I am not in need of it." Sayyidah Sawda said, "By Allah, we deprived him (of it)." I said to her, "Keep quiet".[276]

There are several accounts regarding this incident. According to some of these, Allah's Messenger (saw) had forbid himself from eating honey, and Allah the Almighty warned him about this.[277]

### Keeping a Secret

Another account about Sayyidah Hafsa is a secret that Allah's Messenger (saw) had revealed to her. However, Sayyidah Hafsa couldn't conceal the secret and broke it to her confidant Sayyidah Â'ishah. Because of this incident, the third verse of *Surah at-Tahrîm* was revealed. While various theories have been put forward as to what this "secret" was, it is largely accepted that the Prophet of Allah (saw) had confided in Sayyidah Hafsa (r.ah) that he had sworn an oath never to have honey again as a result of the aforementioned event. Here are three different accounts in the written sources about what this secret was.

The first of these is about the "honey syrup incident": in which details are provided above. Allah's Messenger (saw) had made an oath not to drink honey syrup again.

The second account is about Allah's Messenger (saw) and his bondswoman Maria (r.ah) being together in Sayyidah Hafsa's house when she was not home. When Sayyidah Hafsa was hurt because of this, he told her that this would never happen again, and in fact he would never again be with Maria.

The third account is about Allah's Messenger (saw) informing her that Sayyidina Abu Bakr and Sayyidina 'Umar (ra) would be the head of state after him.[278]

---

276. Buhârî, Talâk 8, Nikâh 103, Et'ime 32, Eşribe 10, 15, Tıb 4, Hiyel 5; Müslim, Talâk 20; Ebû Dâvud, Eşribe, 11 (3715), Nesaî, Talak, 16. Ayrıca bkz: Elmalılı Muhammed Hamdi Yazır, Hak Dini Kur'ân Dili, Tahrim Sûresi Tefsîri, VII, page: 5084-5112.

277. Saliha Akgül, Ezvâc-ı Tâhirât, page:116-119.

278. DIA, the article of "Hafsa".

In response to this the verse of *Surah at-Tahrîm* regarding "forbidding what Allah made lawful to him, to please his wives" were revealed, as the Prophet of Allah (saw) had forbidden for himself that which Allah has made permissible.

Although the exact nature of the secret is not clear, it is related that Allah's Messenger (saw) had divorced Sayyidah Hafsa (with *talaq raji'i*) probably because of her weakness in keeping a secret. Umar (ra) was extremely upset because of this, since he considered that offending Allah's Messenger (saw) would mean offending Allah. Later, Allah the Almighty ordered the Holy Prophet (saw) to take Sayyidah Hafsa back.[279]

It is clear that this issue was so important that it caused verses of the *Qur'ân* to be revealed. In this way, it would serve as a lesson to the other members of *Ahl al-Bayt*.

Regarding the incident about keeping a secret, although the issue at hand was not very important, its implications were grave. The Holy Prophet (saw) was the head of the Islamic State and whatever he confided to his wife should be concealed at all costs. There was a great war taking place between the Muslims and non-Muslims, and Muslims were completely surrounded by their enemies. At the same time hypocrites were seeking opportunities to disturb the State in Madinah. Revealing any kind of confidential information before its due time could significantly harm the cause of the Holy Prophet (saw). For these reasons, the *Ahl al-Bayt* had to be warned regarding these delicate issues.[280]

Sometimes Umar (ra) would reprimand Sayyidah Hafsa, because of some incidents taking place between her and Sayyidah Â'ishah (r.ah) saying: "Neither yours, nor your father's position besides the Prophet (saw) is like Sayyidah Â'ishah's and her father's position."

For some time Allah's Messenger (saw) had considered divorcing Sayyidah Hafsa because of her strong temperament.[281] Umar (ra) became very upset when he heard this, and even according to some narrations, he threw dirt upon his own head.

---

279. Nesâî, Talak, 76; DIA, the article of "Hafsa".
280. Afzalurrahman, Ibid., II, sh: 176.
281. According to another report, the Prophet (saw) wanted to divorce her because she told a private secret to the other wives (the expaned information on this can be found in cause of the revelation of Surah Tahrim, verses 1-4 or in this book in the chapter entitled Hz. Mariya.)

## The Wife of Allah's Messenger (saw) in Paradise

Afterwards, Jibreel (as) came to the Holy Prophet (saw) and notified him to go back to Sayyidah Hafsa. Sayyidah Hafsa (r.ah) used to fast often in the day time and she constantly performed *tahajjud* at nights. Among all the things Jibreel (as) said, the most important was that Hafsa was to be the wife of Allah's Messenger (saw) in Paradise.[282] With this message, Sayyidah Hafsa received the good tidings of entering Paradise, while she was still alive. This alone is sufficient to indicate how virtuous she was.[283]

## The Great Choice

By the time Allah's Messenger (saw) ruled almost all of the Arabian Peninsula, the social conditions had changed significantly. Prosperity was widespread, instead of poverty. Under these conditions, the wives of the Holy Prophet (saw) had asked him for some jewellery and for better conditions of life, with the desire to share the common riches.

A divine inspiration which was revealed at this time commanded Allah's Messenger (saw) to practice asceticism, as before. The message of Islâm could not be conveyed to the people by a materialistic person who indulged in worldly pleasures, and strove to amass more and more power and wealth. If the Holy Prophet (saw) were to allocate a portion for his wives out of the common riches, no one would oppose him. However, he would never abandon his life style which was based on simplicity. No matter how much the common life standard changed, the temporary ornaments of this world would never find a place in his house. The household of the Prophet (saw) would remain distant from worldly ostentations, and thus would serve as a model for the rulers following him.

The following verses of *Surah al-Ahzâb* were revealed in response to the demands of the wives:

"O Prophet! Say unto thy wives: If ye desire the world's life and its adornment, come! I will content you and will release you with a fair release. But if ye

---

282. Ibni Sa'd, et-Tabakât, VIII, 84; Ibni Abdi'l-Berr, el-Istiâb, IV, 261.
283. Ziya Kazıcı, Ibid., page: 192.

desire Allah and His Messenger (saw) and the abode of the Hereafter, then lo! Allah hath prepared for the good among you an immense reward." (Ahzab 33: 28-29)

These verses, which were revealed about the inclinations of the wives of the Holy Prophet (saw) are called as "verses of *Tahyir* (liberation)".

Following the revelation of these verses, Allah's Messenger (saw) set his wives at liberty to choose either 'the life and ornament of this world' or 'Allah and His Messenger'. Thereupon they all chose Allah and His Messenger (saw), repented for their blunders and apologized to the Holy Prophet (saw).

## Her Last Moments

Sayyidah Hafsa (r.ah) stayed away from the political incidents which took place after the death of the Holy Prophet (saw), as much as possible. Because of this, she led a simple life even during the caliphate of her father. Hafsa (r.ah) used to receive her allotted portion from the revenues of Khaybar.[284] She modestly met her needs with this, and gave the rest as charity.

Towards the end of her life, she played an important role in Islamic history. The Qur'ân had been compiled into one book during the caliphate of Abu Bakr (ra). Following his death, this Qur'ân was handed over to Umar (ra). After 'Umar was martyred, it was kept by Sayyidah Hafsa (r.ah) for a long time.[285] Later, Uthman (ra) asked for this Qur'ân, made five or seven copies of it, and distributed it to the main regions of the Muslim world.

Sayyidah Hafsa (r.ah) narrated sixty hadiths from Allah's Messenger (saw); 10 of these are recorded in Muslim, 44 in the Musnad of Ahmad bin Hanbal, and 4 in both Bukhâri and Muslim.[286]

Sayyidah Hafsa (r.ah) passed away in the 41ˢᵗ year of hijrah, during the caliphate of Sayyidina Mu'âwiya (ra). Some accounts give the year of her death

---


284. Muslim, Musâkât, 1.
285. Bukhârî, Tefsîru'l-Kur'ân, 20; İsmail Cerrahoğlu, Tefsir Usûlü, Ankara, 1979, page: 71.
286. DIA, the article of "Hafsa".

as the 45th year of hijrah.[287] She was sixty years old when she died in Medina.[288] She was buried in the Cemetery of Baqi.

## Lessons to be Learned From the Life of Sayyidah Hafsa (r.ah)

1-There are a lot of lessons to be derived from the marriage of Allah's Messenger (saw) with Sayyidah Hafsa, especially for men who have wives with a strong temperament. The Holy Prophet (saw) was a human being and he experienced many incidents throughout his marriages which present an example for the believers.

On one occasion, Allah's Messenger (saw) wanted to divorce Sayyidah Hafsa. However, Allah the Almighty did not give permission for this, and informed him that Sayyidah Hafsa was to be one of his wives in Paradise. This is because she was devoted to prayer, she used to fast often, give charity and pray at nights (*tahajjud*). This shows clearly that worship is one of the ways we can gian value in the sight of Allah.

On the other hand, this divorce incident and the following events teach men how to react when they face irritable habits and temperament from their wives which they dislike. The principle to follow is to see the good in one's spouse and as long as they are conscious about worshipping Allah, to show patience against their bad attitudes for the sake of Allah.

2-Sayyidah Hafsa was a fortunate person who safeguarded the Qur'ân after her father died. This is a good example of displaying the level of confidence for her faithfulness and competency in the society. This event also demonstrates the value of women in Islam.

3-Sayyidah Hafsa was one of the rare women who received the good tidings of entering Paradise during her lifetime. She strove to refine her strong temperament with prayers and with her love for Allah's Messenger (saw).

4-Sayyidah Hafsa loved giving alms. Before she passed away, she requested

---

287. DIA, the article of "Hafsa".
288. Ziya Kazıcı, Ibid., 202.

that the good services she used to fulfil be carried out after her death.[289]

5-Sayyidah Hafsa preferred not to interfere in the political events which took place after the death of Allah's Messenger (saw). Even during the caliphate of her father, she provided an example to us, by leading a simple and unadorned life, even though during these times the Muslims were prosperous.

6-We should take a lesson from the way she looked upon life, by utilising our wealth for the sake of Allah and for charity. And we should opt for a modest life style, as much as possible.

7-Sayyidina Umar (ra) used to visit his daughter often, and he would advise her about her conduct towards her spouse. This is also a good example, showing that a father should take care of her daughter even after her marriage, and that he should support her in fulfilling her financial needs and in correcting her flaws.

---

289.   Ziya Kazıcı, Ibid., page: 199, 201.

# SAYYIDAH ZAINAB BINT HUZAYMA (r.ah)

## The Mother of the Poor and Needy

She was called *Ummu'l Masakeen,* the mother of the poor and needy. The reason for this was her inclination to share everything she owned with the poor, both during the days of Jahiliya, and after the advent of Islam.

This blessed mother of the believers lived with the Holy Prophet (saw) for a very short time, two or three months, and because of this the books of *Sirah* and historians rarely mention her name. Nevertheless, we can provide the following brief information about her past:

## Her Tribe

Her *kunya* from her father's side is as follows: Zainab bint Huzayma bin Harith bin Abdullah al-Amiriyya. Their lineage originates from the Nejd region. Her ancestors had migrated from there and settled in Mecca[290]. There is not much information about her mother, and scholars have expressed differing opinions regarding this lineage.

Amir ibn Sa'saa, or Amiriyya, the tribe of Zainab (r.ah), was one of the

---

290.   Celal Yeniçeri, Ibid., page: 83; Muhammad Hamidullah, İslâm Peygamberi, II, 679.

strongest tribes of the Arabian Peninsula in that period.[291] This tribe's contact with Islam was severed in the third year of *hijrah*, because a group of Muslims from various tribes, who had been sent to convey the message of Islam, were martyred. Two people from the tribe of Amiriyya had become Muslim, however they were killed inadvertently by the survivors of this incident.[292] This unwitting offence had angered the tribe.[293]

### Her Marriage with Allah's Messenger (saw)

The Holy Prophet (saw) wanted to do something to cease the enmity of this tribe[294] toward Islam, and his marriage with Sayyidah Zainab bint Huzayma happened for this reason. When the proposal was made to Sayyidah Zainab (r.ah), she displayed great submission and said: *"The decision on this matter belongs to the Messenger of Allah (saw)".*[295]

The Holy Prophet (saw) married her in the month of Ramadan, in the third year of *hijrah*. He gave her 400 dirhams as *mahr* (marital dowry).[296]

With this marriage, The Holy Prophet (saw) had established a kinship with the Amiriyya tribe, and had significantly alleviated their animosity and hatred.[297] However, within two or three months of this marriage, Sayyidah Zainab (r.ah) passed away. She was in her thirties when she died.[298]

According to one report, Sayyidah Zainab had several marriages before she married the Messenger of Allah (saw). Based on this account, she first married Tufayl bin Harith bin Muttalib, who was a relative of the Holy Prophet (saw), and after him she married his brother Ubaid bin Harith. After Ubaid was martyred in the battle of Badr, she married the Messenger of Allah (saw).[299]

---

291. Rıza Savaş, Ibid., Asr-ı Saâdette İslâm, I, page: 302.
292. Muhammed Hamidullah, İslâm Peygamberi, II, 679-680; Celal Yeniçeri, Ibid., page: 83.
293. Rıza Savaş, Ibid., Asr-ı Saâdette İslâm, I, page: 302.
294. Muhammed Hamidullah, İslâm Peygamberi, II, 679-680.
295. İbn-i Sa'd, Ibid., VIII, 115; Saliha Akgül, Ibid., 139.
296. Afzalurrahman, Ibid., II, 178.
297. Muhammed Hamidullah, İslâm Peygamberi, II, 680; Rıza Savaş, Ibid., Asr-ı Saâdette İslâm, I, 302.
298. There are those who say that this period of eight months. (See: Ziya Kazıcı, Ibid., page: 210-212)
299. Havva Ergene Işık, Ibid., page: 309.

However, according to another account, she was initially married to Abdullah bin Jahsh, the son of the Holy Prophet's aunt. After he was martyred in the battle of Uhud, she married the Holy Prophet (saw).


### Her Virtues

The Holy Prophet (saw) must have made the marriage proposal with the aim of both establishing a kinship with her strong tribe, and also to reward Sayyidah Zainab for her high morals, since she was known as *Ummu'l Masakeen,* the mother of the needy and the poor, because of her devotion in helping poor people. Maybe the Holy Prophet (saw) also considered the spiritual effect she would have on other people, because of her compassion, kindness and affection.[300]

Allah's Messenger (saw) had said *"The first one among you to reunite with me is the one with the longest hand."*[301] Upon hearing this, our blessed mothers had first started to measure the length of their hands. Whereas, by saying 'long hand' the Holy Prophet (saw) had meant 'one who gives a lot of alms'.

Scholars discussed about whether the person mentioned in this *hadith* could be Sayyidah Zainab bint Huzayma[302], but agreed that it could not have been her, because the *hadith* is about who would die first among the wives of the Holy Prophet (saw), following his death: and this was Sayyidah Zainab bint Jahsh. On the contrary, Sayyidah Zainab bint Huzayma died when the Holy Prophet (saw) was still alive, in the first years of the Medina period.

This is all the information we have about her life. However, what is important for us is that she was married to the Holy Prophet (saw) and she became one of the mothers of the faithful. The duration of this marriage, be it long or short, and the limited information we have about her cannot overshadow this distinction.

Sayyidah Zainab bint Huzayma was the first wife of the Holy Prophet (saw) to be buried at the Baqi Cemetery. Her funeral prayer was led by the Holy Prophet (saw).[303]

---

300.    Celal Yeniçeri, Ibid., page: 83.
301.    Muslim, Fedâilü's-Sahâbe, 101.
302.    See: İbn-i İshak, Sîret, page: 241; Ibn-i Hajar, el-ısâbe, IV, 309; Ziya Kazıcı, Ibid., 127 vd.
303.    Afzalurrahman, Ibid., II, 178.

## Lessons to be Learned from the Life of Zainab (r.ah)

1- When she received the marriage proposal, which would change her life, she displayed her affection and submission towards the Messenger of Allah (saw), and left the decision to him. This sets a beautiful example for the level of submission which Muslim men and women should display towards the instructions and even recommendations of the Holy Prophet (saw).

2- This blessed woman preferred to take care of the needy; and she took them to her heart and consoled them, instead of engaging with her peers. Just like Sayyidah Zainab bint Huzayma, we should also abandon the temporary struggles of the world and strive to alleviate the suffering of believers, thus preparing ourselves for the eternal life of the Hereafter.

3- Sayyidah Zainab bint Huzayma did not make requests which would burden the Holy Prophet (saw) and neither did she incline towards jealousy. Earning the recognition of the Holy Prophet (saw) and of the Muslims was sufficient for her[304]. Likewise, we should also refrain from requesting burdensome things from our spouses and should avoid causing distress with excessive jealousy.

4- Due to many reasons, one could experience many marriages in ones lifetime, and could face misfortune in any marriage. The important point is not to be overtaken by these events: but to preserve the sincerity of our hearts in worship and the purity of our intentions.

Sayyidah Zainab (r.ah) put her short life to best use, by first being "the mother of the needy" and then by becoming "the mother of the faithful" before she passed away. She lived in peace and was buried in peace in her eternal resting place. In reality, what matters is not the duration of the life, but how it is put to use. May Allah be pleased with her.

---

304.   Ziya Kazıcı, Ibid., page: 214.

## SAYYIDAH UMMU SALAMA (r.ah)

### Her Family

Sayyidah Ummu Salama (r.ah) was related both to the Holy Prophet (saw), and to the great commander Khalid bin Walid, who was nick-named "the sword of Allah". Her real name is Hind.[305] She is also known as Hind bint Abe Umayya.[306] She is from Mecca and belongs to the Mahzum tribe.[307] She is known as "Ummu Salama", because of her son Salama.

Abu Umayya, the father of Ummu Salama was known with the epithet of "Zadu'r-Rakeeb" The reason of this epithet was his habit of taking provisions sufficient for two people and sharing these with his companions, whenever he travelled.[308] He was a very generous person. The mother of Ummu Salama was Ateeka bint Amer.

### The Hijrah to Ethiopia

In the beginning, Ummu Salama had married to Abu Salama Abdullah bin Abd al-Asad. Abu Salama was the foster brother of the Holy Prophet (saw).

---

305. Ibn-i Abdi'l-Berr, IV, 436.
306. Afzalurrahman, Ibid., II, 178.
307. Celal Yeniçeri, Ibid., sh: 84; Muhammed Hamidullah, İslâm Peygamberi, II, 680.
308. Ziya Kazıcı, Ibid., 215.

He and his wife were among the first to believe in Islam and to make hijrah to Ethiopia.

They left everything behind and emigrated to Etpiopia, because of the suffocating torture of Mecca. There, they started to lead a peaceful life. They worshipped Allah to their heart's content. They also had a child

One day they received news from Mecca, which said all the pagans of had become Muslims. Believing into this, they set out for Mecca. Whereas the information they received was baseless; Mecca had not changed. To the contrary, the torture and oppression they applied was escalating with each passing day.

## The Hijrah to Medina

Thereupon, following the second meeting at *Aqabah*, they got permission from the Holy Prophet (saw) to make hijrah to Medina. They completed all their preparations, loaded their belongings onto their camel and set out for Medina. Ummu Salama was riding on the camel, with her son Salama.

Just when they reached the outskirts of the city, a group from the tribe and relatives of Ummu Salama intercepted them. They said that Abu Salama was free to go to Medina, but they would not let Ummu Salama and her son go. They even started to harass the child and pull him away from them.[309] Wrangling with them didn't bear a result. They forcibly separated Abu Salama from his wife and son. Abu Salama had to continue his travel to Medina on his own.

From this day on, Ummu Salama and her son were followed closely by her relatives -the Mughira family. As if this was not sufficient, they separated the child from his mother and gave him to the family of Abdulasad as security. This situation lasted for one year. Throughout the whole year, each morning Ummu Salama climbed to the place called Abtah (on the Safa Hill), turned towards Ka'bah and in tears, cursed her relatives who had broken the arm of her unweaned baby and broke up her family.[310]

---

309.   Afzalurrahman, Ibid., II, 178.
310.   Ziya Kazıcı, Ibid., page: 216-217; Muhammed Hamidullah, İslâm Peygamberi, II, 680.

One day, seeing her in this state, someone from the family of Mughira felt sorry asked about her situation. Then he went to the relatives of Ummu Salama and protested them and said: "You have separated this poor woman from her husband and son. Why do you still keep her and not release her?" Thereupon her relatives took pity on her and permitted Ummu Salama and said to her: "If you want, you can go to your husband!"

At last, Ummu Salama and her son were united and they were set free. But how would they go to Medina from Mecca on their own? How could they endure such a difficult, troublesome and dangerous journey under the circumstances of those days?

This resolute and bold lady decided to take all the risks and ventured to Medina on her (their?) own. She narrated her experience as follows:

"I prepared my camel and placed my son into the camel-litter. Then I set out to reach my husband in Medina. I had nobody accompanying me. When I reached the place called *Tan'im*, I met with Uthman bin Talha from the Abduddar family. He asked me: 'O Ummu Salama, where are you going?' I said: 'I want to go to Medina to my husband.' He inquired: 'Don't you have anyone with you?' I replied: 'No, I have no one other than Allah and this child of mine!' Then he said: 'I swear by Allah that you will not be left alone.' He held my camel from its bridle and set off with me. I swear to Allah that I haven't seen anyone in the Arabs as benevolent as him. Wherever we encamped he used kneel down my camel and then he would go far from me. Once, my camel went astry. He got hold of it and tied it to tree. Then he left it there, and rested under another tree. After a while he drove the camel towards me, told me to mount (on) it and stood away from me (went away). When I mounted and settled myself on the camel, he came back and held the bridle. And he didn't let go of the bridle until we reached our next encampment. When the village of the family of Amr bin Awf in Quba appeared, he said: 'Abu Salama is here. Go and enter there with the blessing of Allah.' After that he left us and went back to Mecca."[311]

In this way, Ummu Salama became the first of the companions to make hijrah to Medina in a camel litter.

---

311. See: Ibn-i Hacer, IV, 440; Ziya Kazıcı, Ibid., 217-218; Sâliha Akgül, Ibid., page: 146-148; Afzalurrahman, Ibid., II, 178-179.

## Umma Salama's Life in Medina

After Sayyidah Ummu Salama arrived in Medina and settled there, she lived a peaceful life with her husband. Here she was occupied with educating and raising her children. She was a woman who had an aptitude for poetry, who was clever, wise and cultured; at the same time she was very beautiful.

This blessed couple was so devoted to one another that they had promised that if the other should die they would not remarry: they sincerely believed that their true marriage would be in Heaven. It was for this reason that one day Abu Salama's wife made the following suggestion: "O, Abu Salama..! If a man deserving of Heaven dies he will be reunited with his wife, also worthy of Heaven, if she has not remarried. Likewise, if a woman deserving of Heaven dies, she will certainly be reunited with her husband, if he is deserving of Heaven and if he marries no other. Thus, let us make an agreement. If I die first, do not marry after my death, and if you die first, I shall not remarry."

Abu Salama, in response to his wife's suggestion, said: "Will you respect my wishes?" She promised to do so, and he said: "When I die, marry." Then he prayed for the wife he loved so much: "O Allah..! After my death grant Sayyidah Ummu Salama with a more blessed husband who will not sadden or hurt her!.."

Our mother, Sayyidah Ummu Salama loved her husband so much that she could not conceive of a husband that could be more blessed.[312]

* * *

Prophet Muhammad (saw) made Sayyidah Ummu Salama's husband, Abu Salama, a brother with Said bin Haysam of the Ansar. Abu Salama participated in the Battles of Badir and Uhud with Prophet Muhammad (saw). He was wounded in the arm by an arrow that had been shot by the polytheists during the Battle of Uhud. After a month of being treated the wound closed, and it was assumed that it had healed.

In the mean time news was received that the Sons of Huwaylid, from the Bani Asad tribe, were about to attack Medina. Prophet Muhammad (saw) called for Abu

---

312.   Saliha Akgül, Ibid., page: 149-150.

Salama and put him in command of a 150 strong force. This troop included leading Companions like Abu Ubayda bin Jerrah and Sa'd bin Abi Waqqas. When the force arrived at the Katan River in the Faid region there was an engagement and the Muslim force returned victorious with great spoils. However, Abu Salama's wound, which they thought had healed, reopened during this campaign and he lost a lot of blood. Abu Salama was dying, and Prophet Muhammad (saw) visited him and prayed for him, until he passed away. The death of this Companion in the 4th year of the Hijrah greatly saddened Prophet Muhammad (saw) and he prayed: "*O Allah!.. Forgive Abu Salama. Make him one of those who are close to You!.. Guard over those who remain behind. Forgive us and forgive him, O Lord of the Worlds!..*"[313]

Prophet Muhammad (saw) led the funeral prayer himself. During the prayer he uttered the *takbir* 9 times. After the prayer, when the Companions asked why he had done this, the Prophet of Allah (saw) replied: "*I swear that I neither forgot nor made an error. If I had uttered one thousand takbir for Abu Salama it would have been because that is what he deserves.*"[314]

Abu Salama was not just renowned for his heroism, but also for his superior morals and virtues.

The death of Abu Salama from the wound he had suffered at Uhud was a great sorrow and grief for his wife. It is said that she cried for days. In referring to those days Sayyidah Ummu Salama said: "One day (my husband) Abu Salama returned from being with the Prophet (saw) and said:

"I have heard something from the Prophet (saw) that has made me very happy. The Prophet (saw) said: '*When a Muslim experiences trouble or disaster, they should say: "Inna lillahi wa inna ilayhi rajiun."* (We belong to Allah and to Him we will return). *Then they should say: "O Allah, bless us with reward and recompense for this calamity. Grant that I am one who attains what is more blessed." If they say this then Allah will accept their prayer.*'"[315]

When Abu Salama died, I remembered this and immediately said "*Inna lillahi wa inna ilayhi rajiun,*" repeating the prayer that had been taught to us by

313. Saliha Akgül, Ibid., page: 151.
314. See: Taberî, Tarih, II, 414'den naklen Ziya Kazıcı, Ibid., page: 219-220; Ayşe Abdurrahman, Ibid., page: 92.
315. Ibn-i Hanbel, Musned, IV, 278.

Prophet Muhammad (saw). Then I said to myself: "Who could be more blessed than Abu Salama?"

Allah gave me what was more blessed and married me to Prophet Muhammad (saw).[316]

## Marriage to Prophet Muhammad (saw)

After our mother Sayyidah Ummu Salama's period of *iddet* (waiting period) was completed, leading members of the Companions like Abu Bakr (ra) and Umar (ra) offered her marriage, but she politely refused. In recognition[317] of the state of this great woman who devoted herself to her four children, Salama, Umar, Zainab and Durra, Allah's Prophet (saw) offered marriage to her.

Sayyidah Ummu Salama knew that this offer was an opportunity that she could not refuse. However, she was afraid that next to the other wives of the Prophet (saw), who were young and beautiful, she, who was old, a widow and a mother, would make the Prophet (saw) uncomfortable. For this reason, begging the forgiveness of Prophet Muhammad (saw), she sent the following message to him: "I am a jealous woman; I am old and I have children, moreover, the guardian to give permission for me to marry is not with me!.."

In response to these excuses, Prophet Muhammad (saw) sent the following reply: "You say you are old: I am older than you. You speak of jealousy: I pray to Allah and it is hoped that Allah will remove jealousy from you. As far as the children are concerned: they belong to Allah and His Prophet (saw). As far as the guardians who are here and not here: I do not think that they will oppose this union."[318]

Sayyidah Ummu Salama describes Prophet Muhammad (saw) coming to ask for her hand in marriage as follows:

---

316. Ibn-i Sa'd, VIII, 87-89.
317. Celal Yeniçeri, Ibid., page: 85.
318. Ibn-i Sa'd, VIII, 90; Ayşe Abdurrahman, Ibi.., page: 93; Saliha Akgül, Ibid., 154; Afzalurrahman, Ibid., II, page: 179.

*"I was tanning some leather for myself. I cleaned the material known as "karz", which is used in the process, from my hands. I asked permission from the Prophet and put down a leather cushion filled with plant fibers. He sat on the cushion and asked me to marry him."[319]*

From this account we can understand that Sayyidah Ummu Salama made contributions to the family budget and later dealt in tanning leather to provide for her children.[320]

Then Sayyidah Ummu Salama married Prophet Muhammad (saw) (saw) in the 4th year after the Hijrah[321] in the month of Shawwal (one year after Uhud) and saw the blessings of the prayer: being blessed with the honor of being a "mother of believers"

During the marriage ceremony the Prophet (saw) offered *walima* (a wedding feast) to the guests. After the wedding Prophet Muhammad (saw) settled Sayyidah Ummu Salama in the home of Umma'l Mesakin Sayyidah Zainab bintu Huzaima, who had died.[322] Prophet Muhammad (saw) spent three nights with Sayyidah Ummu Salama.[323]

This marriage was a means for the relatives of Sayyidah Ummu Salama, including the fiercest opponent of Islam at that time, Halid bin Walid, to soften their attitude to Islam.[324] Not long after this wedding Halid bin Walid became Muslim and gained the title of "The Sword of Allah".

## Sayyidah Ummu Salama's Morals

Umma Salama (r.ah) was a wise woman who spoke well and for this reason

---

319. Ibn-i Kesir, 111/174-175; Celal Yeniçeri, Ibid., page: 85.
320. Celal Yeniçeri, Ibid., page: 85.
321. Celal Yeniçeri, Ibid., page: 85.
322. Sayyidah Ummu Salama describes this room:
*"There was a clay pot and there was some barley, a hand mill, a pot made from stone and another earthenware pot. Inside the pot was a little melted butter. I ground the barley in the mill. Then I made a thick soup with this. I added some butter to this and made a meal. This was the food that the Prophet and his family ate on the night of the wedding."* (Afzalurrahman, Ibid., II, page: 182)
323. Ibn-i Sa'd, VIII, 92.
324. Muhammed Hamidullah, İslâm Peygamberi, II, 681.

she was listened to with respect. In fact, from time to time her words could even bring someone like Umar to a halt.

Indeed, at one time Umar (ra) heard that the wives of Prophet Muhammad (saw) had upset the Prophet (saw), the Sun of the Two Worlds, and he was infuriated. He started to speak in a hurtful manner, but Sayyidah Ummu Salama interrupted and said:

*"I am surprised at you, O son of Hattab!.. You interfere in everything… are you going to even interfere between the Prophet (saw) and his wives?"*

Umar (ra) was later to say: *"Her words affected me in such a way that my anger melted away."*[325]


### Advice to the Believers in Hudaybiyah

Sayyidah Ummu Salama was a knowledgeable and cultured woman. Prophet Muhammad (saw) would consult with her from time to time and sometimes act in accordance with her opinion. In fact, in the sixth year of the Hijrah, during the drawing up of the Hudaybiyah Treaty, that was made with the polytheists of Mecca, Prophet Muhammad (saw) asked for her opinion and acted accordingly.

To briefly recap this event, Prophet Muhammad (saw) had marched with the Companions towards Mecca to make the *umrah*, but he was prevented from doing this by the polytheists. After long arguments, a treaty was drawn up with the polytheists and it was decided to return to Medina without performing this *umrah*. The conditions of the treaty seemed to be against the Muslims. For this reason, everyone, including Umar (ra), did not know how to act. Thus it was that even though the Prophet of Allah (saw) ordered the Companions to sacrifice an animal, shave and take off their *ihram*, three times, the Companions remained motionless, quietly hoping that the Prophet (saw) would abandon the treaty.

Prophet Muhammad (saw) was saddened by their behavior and headed towards his tent. Sayyidah Ummu Salama said:

---

325.   Bukhârî, Tefsir, (66), 323.

*"O Prophet (saw), forgive them. They hoped that they would be able to circumambulate the Kaaba this year. Not only have they realized that this hope was in vain, but a treaty that fulfills the wishes of the polytheists has been made. You should go and slaughter a sacrificial animal and shave; when they see you do this, they will follow your lead."*

Prophet Muhammad (saw) left the tent and acted as Sayyidah Ummu Salama had suggested, and the Companions, understanding that the treaty was not to be broken, followed suit and made the sacrifice and shaved.[326]

Thus, at such a sensitive time, Sayyidah Ummu Salama was able to analyze the situation using her intelligence, perception and courage, and thus the matter ended happily in a way which upset no one.

## She was With the Prophet (saw) in War and Hard Times

Sayyidah Ummu Salama (r.ah) was with Prophet Muhammad (saw) during the Haybar Campaign, the Conquest of Mecca, the Seige of Taif, the Battles of Hawazin and Sakif, and the Farewell Pilgrimage.

In short, she was with Prophet Muhammad (saw) at all the battles, and was herself a soldier challenging disbelief and *shirk*. She was a battling lion who carried the same blood as the Sword of Allah, Halid bin Walid. She was a woman who managed to be a monument of modesty while at the same time being resolute, brave and wise.[327]

## The Wife Who Saw Jibreel

Our mother Sayyidah Ummu Salama saw Archangel Jibreel (AS) in the form of Dihya, one of the Companions. As reported by Usama bin Zaid:

"One day Jibreel (AS) came to Prophet Muhammad (saw). At that point

---

326. See: Bukhârî, Şurût, 15; Ziya Kazıcı, Ibid., 229-231; O. Nûri Topbaş; Nebiler Silsilesi, IV, 208-210; Afzalurrahman, Ibid., II, 179.
327. Celal Yeniçeri, Ibid., page: 86.

Sayyidah Ummu Salama was with the Prophet (saw). After talking to the Prophet (saw), Jibreel got up and left. Prophet Muhammad (saw) turned to Sayyidah Ummu Salama and asked: *"Who was that?"* She answered *"That was Dihya"*. Then Sayyidah Ummu Salama said *"I swear that until I listened to the speech Prophet Muhammad (saw) delivered in the mosque about the revelation that he had received from Gabriel (at that time) I thought Gabriel was Dihya."*[328]

### Her Respect for and Service to Prophet Muhammad (saw)

Sayyidah Ummu Salama tried to do all she could to ensure Prophet Muhammad's (saw) comfort and ease. She dedicated her slave, Safina, to the service of Prophet Muhammad (saw).

When Prophet Muhammad (saw) stayed in her house she prepared everything; the prayer mat, bed and everything else: whatever he would need would be ready.[329]

Sayyidah Ummu Salama kept a lock of Prophet Muhammad's (saw) hair and protected it as a memento throughout her life.[330]

### The House to Which the Revelation Came

Both Sayyidah Â'ishah and Sayyidah Hafsa, (r.ah) made great efforts to treat this new wife of Prophet Muhammad (saw) well.

The earlier revelations only came when Prophet Muhammad (saw) was in Sayyidah Â'ishah's house; this was a source of great pride for Sayyidah Â'ishah. This situation continued until Prophet Muhammad (saw) married Sayyidah Ummu Salama and verse 102 of *Surah Tauba*[331] was revealed.

---

328. Afzalurrahman, Ibid., II, page: 182.
329. Madni Abbâsî, *"Hz. Peygamber'in (sav) Âile Hayatı"*, Translated by: Ali Zengin, İstanbul, 2000, page: 206.
330. Madni Abbâsî, Ibid., page: 217.
331. This verse was concerned with Abu Lubaba, who had been sent by the Bani Qurayza, to betray Prophet Muhammad. During this envoy's visit, the Companions, thinking that he had behaved

After the revelation occurred in Sayyidah Ummu Salama's house, Sayyidah Â'ishah did not mention her special status again.

Prophet Muhammad (saw) greatly valued Sayyidah Ummu Salama. According to a report by Sayyidah Â'ishah, Prophet Muhammad (saw) would visit his wives after the afternoon prayer. He would start these visits first with Sayyidah Ummu Salama, as she was the eldest, and he would visit Sayyidah Â'ishah last.

## You and Your Daughter are of My *Ahl al-Bayt*

One day, Allah's Prophet (saw) was with Sayyidah Ummu Salama, and Sayyidah Ummu Salama's daughter Zainab was there too.

Fatimatu'z Zahra and her sons Hasan (ra) and Husayn (ra) came. The Prophet (saw) embraced them, saying: "My *Ahlil- Bayt*, may Allah's mercy and blessings be upon you. Allah deserves every type of praise. He is One of utmost honor!.."

According to what her daughter Zainab related, Sayyidah Ummu Salama started to cry when she heard this. The Prophet (saw) looked at her and said kindly: "What has made you cry?" She replied "O Allah's Prophet (saw), you have divided (Allah's mercy and blessings) between the *ahlil-bayt*, but you have forgotten me and my daughter."

The Prophet (saw) answered: "Both you and your daughter are of the *ahlil-bayt*."[332]

---

incorrectly, and without consulting the Prophet, tied Abu Lubaba to a pillar in the Masjid, to remain there until Allah and His Prophet had forgiven him. When Prophet Muhammad was informed about this event he waited for an edict from Allah Almighty but made no ruling himself. Abu Lubaba remained tied to the pillar, and it was after five days, whilst Prophet Muhammad was with Ummu Salama, that the 102nd verse of Surah Tauba was revealed. The verse reads as follows:

*"Others (there are who) have acknowledged their wrong-doings: They have mixed an act that was good with another that was evil. Perhaps God will turn unto them (in mercy): For Allah is Oft-Forgiving, Most Merciful"* (9,102).

There is a report that the same verse was revealed for those who did not participate in the Tabuk Campaign and tied themselves to the pillar of the Masjid.

332.  Ziya Kazıcı, Ibid., page: 224.

The daughter of our Mother Ummu Salama, Zainab, (r.ah) was a great canonist after Sayyidah Â'ishah. In fact, it was said that she was the person who knew *fiqh* (Islamic Law) the best among the women of her time.[333]

According to one report, while the Prophet of Allah (saw) was bathing, Umma Salama's daughter Zainab (r.ah) came near him, she was still a young child, and the Prophet (saw) sprinkled water on her face. The narrator tells us that Sayyidah Zainab still had the freshness of youth on her face even when she was old.[334] According to another report, Sayyidah Zainab, (r.ah), who had this water splashed on her face, had a beauty that was envied by those who saw her.

* * *

Prophet Muhammad (saw) loved the children of Sayyidah Ummu Salama as if they were his own and protected them thus. In fact, he married his stepson Salama to Umama, the daughter of his uncle Hamza who had died at Uhud. After marrying them the Prophet (saw) turned to the Companions and said: *"You see, I have rewarded him."*[335]

* * *

The calm and peaceful atmosphere of the Prophet's house continued until Prophet Muhammad (saw) became ill. Sayyidah Ummu Salama and the other wives of Prophet Muhammad (saw) willingly agreed that he should rest in the house of Sayyidah Â'ishah.[336]

## After the Death of Prophet Muhammad (saw)

After the death of Prophet Muhammad (saw), Sayyidah Ummu Salama retreated to her home and began to lead a secluded life. She refrained from involving herself in daily events in society and devoted herself to worship.

Sayyidah Ummu Salama (r.ah) was the last of the Prophet's wives to die.

---

333. Ziya Kazıcı, Ibid., page: 234.
334. Ziya Kazıcı, Ibid., page: 24-225.
335. Ziya Kazıcı, Ibid., page: 225.
336. Bkz: Ayşe Abdurrahman, Ibid., page: 331.

She died in the 61st year after the Hijrah and was 84 years old, though some reports state that she was even 90.[337] Yazid bin Muawiya was the Caliph at this time. She was buried in the Baki cemetery in Medina. Abu Huraira led the funeral prayer.

When Sayyidah Ummu Salama heard of the martyrdom of Husayn and his family at Karbala she fainted from sorrow, and it is stated that her death was due to the sadness caused by this event.[338]

### Level of Knowledge

Sayyidah Ummu Salama was a woman who knew how to write and she was also a poet.[339] Although Mahmud bin Labid explained that although the people had a great respect for all the wives of Prophet Muhammad (saw), Sayyidah Â'ishah and Sayyidah Ummu Salama held a special place due to their memorization and protection of hadiths.[340]

Sayyidah Ummu Salama (r.ah) was a Companion who was acquainted with *fiqh* and who narrated hadiths. In fact, of the Prophet's wives, after Sayyidah Â'ishah, she narrated the most hadiths and there are a total of 378 hadiths that were reported by Umma Salama,[341] moreover, 13 of these are in both Bukhari and Muslim. Dozens of people learned hadiths from her, including Abu Huraira and Ibn-i Abbas.[342]

### Lessons We Can Learn from the Life of this Blessed Mother

1- Sayyidah Ummu Salama's life was full of many examples of the difficulties and sacrifices she underwent for Islam. She was one of the first women believers, and she suffered persecution and torment at the hands of the disbe-

---

337. Saliha Akgül, Ibid., page: 155.
338. Ibn-i Sa'd, Tabakât, VIII, 96; Celal Yeniçeri, Ibid., page: 86.
339. Celal Yeniçeri, Ibid., page: 85.
340. Madni Abbâsî, Ibid., page: 206.
341. Afzalurrahman, Ibid., II, 181.
342. Bkz: Madni Abbâsî, Ibid., page: 214-215.

lievers of Mecca; and so she was forced to emigrate to Abyssinia and then to Medina. Thus, she abandoned the land in which she was born and raised, twice, in order to follow her religion.

2- While she considered emigrating to Medina she was separated from her husband and children and forced to remain apart from them for a long time; but this did not cause her to waver or to falter in her belief. On the contrary, her patience, reliance and submission to Allah increased.

3- In her deciding to emigrate from Mecca to Medina on her own, without husband and family, she personally demonstrated great bravery to other Muslim women. The life of our blessed mother was a great comfort for the women who were experiencing similar difficulties.

4- As we can understand from the sacrifices that Sayyidah Ummu Salama made in her life, Islam does not come us easily, it comes to us with great difficulty, but it never came with a concession. Sayyidah Ummu Salama is an exceptional example of a wife, mother and believer: one who endured the difficulties thrown up by this world of trials, bearing them without giving up her belief.

5- After the Hudaybiyah Treaty, when the Companions did not act despite the order of Prophet Muhammad (saw), Sayyidah Ummu Salama (r.ah) fulfilled the duty of the Mother of Believers, in that she did not react based upon her tumultuous feelings, but advised with reason and wisdom, and was an example of a faithful woman who *"did not incite, but soothed."*

6- Her reason, intelligence, modesty, morals and maturity made a great impression on both Prophet Muhammad's (saw) wives and on the Prophet (saw) himself; and because of this she was an example not only for the people of her era but also for those to come.

Sayyidah Ummu Salama, an intelligent, cultured woman who was also a poet, was accomplished enough to offer counsel to the Prophet (saw); and she followed the Prophet's life with great care, making great efforts to transfer his memory to his community. After Sayyidah Â'ishahh, she is one of the Prophet's wives to have reported the most hadiths.

7- The thousands of positive and negative zigzags that make up life most certainly affect husbands and wives, so that from time to time a variety of unforeseen events can occur in their home. Sometimes they experience joy, sometimes sorrow. However, with good intentions, the extended family and friends that are not part of the immediate family circle will try to help the husband and wife. Thus it is that the solutions for some simple problems, the details of which should have remained within the family and been resolved by husband and wife, can at times become untenable due to such "outside" interference. Thus, Umar's interference, which was completely well intentioned, could sometimes make things worse in the family life of Prophet Muhammad (saw). However, Sayyidah Ummu Salama resolutely reminded Umar (ra), despite him being a very strong minded person, that he was in danger of making such a mistake.

8- In fact, sometimes mothers, fathers, brothers and sisters or other close relatives interfere in the problems of married couples in order to help them find a solution to those problems or deficiencies, but generally this causes more problems than it solves. Not only are all people different from one another, but also all of the families have different characteristics, even if the general features are the same. Therefore, the older generation, rather than trying to dictate how a couple should solve their problems, should be content to present their knowledge as an "experience". The actual authority that will solve the problem belongs to the couple who have established the family. Such an approach will allow the young couple to be happier, more successful and confident in matters of marriage.

9- In the person of Sayyidah Ummu Salama we can see another value that Islam gives to women: she expressed her opinions as needed, when it was necessary and to whom it was necessary, with great courage, wisdom and self-confidence; and she did not receive any negative reaction to this behavior. Sometimes she offered advice to Prophet Muhammad (saw), and at other times she challenged Umar (ra). This shows that expressing the truth in the proper way at the proper time is something that will be accepted by all; even if the truth is spoken by a woman. Thus, people should be careful about the truth of what they utter, and also the timing and location: only in this way can words achieve the intended result.

10- May Allah bless us all with a share of the life of this blessed mother who was full of wisdom and who is a great example. May she be our intercessor.

# SAYYIDAH ZAINAB BINT JAHSH (r.ah)

## A Marriage Made in Heaven

Sayyidah Zainab bint Jahsh (r.ah), one of the two wives of Prophet Muhammad (saw) to be called Sayyidah Zainab, married the Prophet (saw) in the fifth year after the Hijrah, when she was thirty-six years old.

This marriage between Sayyidah Zainab bint Jahsh and Prophet Muhammad (saw) was a matter that aroused a great deal of discussion among the enemies of Islam; however, before talking about her marriage, let's take a look at her life.

## Family

Sayyidah Zainab bint Jahsh (r.ah) was related to Prophet Muhammad (saw) on her mother's side. Her mother, Umayma bint Abdulmuttalib, was the sister of Prophet Muhammad's (saw) father.[343] On her father's side, her father was Jahsh, the son of Riab, who was the son of Ya'mur. Her father came to settle in Mecca from another region.

Our mother Sayyidah Zainab (r.ah) was born in Mecca in 588.[344] And according to one report, her name was "Berre",[345] but Prophet Muhammad (saw) changed it to Zainab.

---

343. Ibn-i Abdi'l-Berr, IV, 306-307; Ziya Kazıcı, Ibid., sh: 247; Saliha Akgül, Ibid., page: 172.
344. Ziya Kazıcı, Ibid., page: 241.
345. Afzalurrahman, Ibid., II, page: 182.

Sayyidah Zainab bint Jahsh (r.ah) remained unmarried until she was 35 with the hope[346] that she would be able to marry Prophet Muhammad (saw). However, she first married the freed slave of the Prophet (saw), Zayd ibn Harithah (ra), on the Prophet's recommendation, but, as will be explained below in detail, this marriage did not last long and ended in divorce. After her divorce, Prophet Muhammad (saw) married Sayyidah Zainab (r.ah) after receiving a divine decree.[347]

Now, let us examine these events more closely:

## Zayd ibn Harithah's Past

Zayd ibn Harithah was a slave of Prophet Muhammad (saw) whom he had set free. In fact, he had been born the son of a free family, but was later taken prisoner and enslaved. This happened as follows:

One day while Zayd ibn Harithah was going with his mother to visit his relatives of the Ma'n ibn Tayy tribe, their caravan was raided and Zayd was taken prisoner and sold in the Arab market as a slave. Zayd, who was only eight years old, was sold for 400 *dirhem* to Hakim ibn Hathim who had bought the slave for his aunt Sayyidah Khadîjah (r.ah), in Mecca. Our mother Sayyidah Khadîjah (r.ah) loved this slave very much and so made a gift of him to the person she loved best, the Prophet Muhammad (saw).

Prophet Muhammad (saw) wanted to free Zayd when he was ten years old, but Zayd did not agree to it. At this point in time Zayd's family had traced their child's whereabouts and his father Harithah and his uncle Ka'b came to Mecca to ask Prophet Muhammad (saw) to allow them to take their child back to their homeland. Prophet Muhammad (saw) suggested that they ask Zayd about this matter: *"If Zayd so desires, he can return with you and you need not pay anything!.."* he said.

---

346. Celal Yeniçeri, Ibid., page: 186; Muhammed Hamidullah, İslâm Peygamberi, II, page: 681.
347. *"Truly, there were such special conditions and disputes in the matter of marriage with Zainab that these could only be solved by a divine revelation. And no other wedding preoccupied Mecca as much as that of Zainab."* (Ayşe Abdurrahman, Ibid., 101)

His uncle and father were very happy, as they thought that Zayd would be very keen to come with them, but this is not how things worked out. Zayd preferred to stay with Muhammad (saw), who had not yet received the revelations, rather than return with his father. His father was very surprised: *"You would rather be a slave then return with your father?"*

Zayd replied *"I have seen such things with Muhammad (saw) that I cannot leave him before the end of time."* There was nothing else to be done. His father and uncle returned to their homeland, empty-handed and sad.

When Zayd chose Prophet Muhammad (saw), in keeping with the traditions of that time, the Prophet (saw), being the owner of loyalty, climbed on a rock in the middle of a crowd of Qurayshi and said *"From this time on Zayd is not my slave, he is my son!.."* thus adopting him; those who were there were witnesses to this act.[348]

Zayd never left the Prophet's (saw) side from that day on and he had the good fortune to be one of the first to follow Prophet Muhammad (saw). After Hamza (ra) became Muslim, Prophet Muhammad (saw) made him Zayd's brother. Zayd shielded Prophet Muhammad (saw) with his own body from the stones that were thrown in Taif and showed his affection for Prophet Muhammad (saw) at every opportunity. Allah's Prophet (saw) took Zayd to his breast like a father and protected him throughout his life.[349]

Prophet Muhammad (saw) one day said: *"Whoever wants to wed a woman of heaven should marry Ummu Ayman, who was my mother after my mother!.."* Zayd then requested Ummu Ayman's hand and they were wed. Their son was the famous commander Usama bin Zayd.

---

348.  See: Tirmîzî, Tefsîru Sûreti Ahzâb, 9,12; Ziya Kazıcı, Ibid., page: 244-245; Ayşe Abdurrahman, Ibid., 101-103.

349.  Prophet Muhammad said the following about Zayd ibn Harithah: *"He is truly worthy of commandership. And he is truly of my most beloved."*
Ibn-i Umar said: "When my father Umar (ra) gave Usama (son of Zayd) a larger salary than mine and I asked him about this he said: 'He was more beloved by the Prophet and the Prophet loved his father more than he loved your father.' " (Tirmidhi, 1633)
As can be understood from these hadiths, there was a strong bond of affection between Zayd and Allah's Prophet. It was such a bond of love that it was preferred to the love of parents, relatives and country. (Saliha Akgul, page: 163)

### The Wedding of Zayd and Zainab

Later young Zayd wanted permission from his elderly wife Ummu Ayman to marry again. She told him to ask Prophet Muhammad (saw), saying *"He will know best what is most blessed for you!.."*

Then Zayd told Prophet Muhammad (saw) about his intentions. Prophet Muhammad (saw) arranged for Zayd to marry the daughter of his aunt, Sayyidah Zainab bint Jahsh.

### Equality Between People in Islam

However, Sayyidah Zainab and her family responded that it would not be possible, according to the traditions and customs of the time, for Zayd, who had been a slave, to marry Sayyidah Zainab, who was from a free and noble family. However, the aim of Prophet Muhammad (saw) was to actively demonstrate that in Islam all people were "equal, like the teeth of the same comb."[350] Indeed, the measure of this sublime religion is determined in the following verse: **"Verily the most honored of you in the sight of Allah is (he who is) the most righteous of you."**[351]

Prophet Muhammad (saw) said: *"O people! You Lord is one, your father is one. There is no superiority of Arab to non-Arab, of non-Arap to Arab, of red to black or black to red. Superiority is only with taqwa* (God consciousness)."[352]

*"Allah does not examine your appearance or your property. He only examines your hearts and your deeds."*[353]

Islam is a religion that removes the differences between rich and poor, between noble and slaves, and which establishes absolute equality between people.[354] For this reason, Prophet Muhammad (saw) wanted very much for

---

350. Muhammed Hamidullah, İslâm Peygamberi, II, 681; Celal Yeniçeri, Ibid., sh: 87.
351. Surah al-Hujurât, 49: 13.
352. Ahmad bin Hanbal, 5/411.
353. Muslim, Birr, 33; Ibn-i Mâjah, Zuhd, 9; Ahmad bin Hanbal, 2/285.
354. In this matter Muhammed Hamidullah says: *"In no other religion but Islam have I found freed slaves who have established kingdoms and their descendants have made history. In Egypt the Mamluks,*

Sayyidah Zainab, the daughter of his aunt, to marry the freed slave whom he had adopted, Zayd. There were other divine wishes in this marriage which would become apparent with time.

Let me indicate another matter here: one of Prophet Muhammad's (saw) methods of teaching Islam was to apply Allah's orders and rules to himself or his close relatives first.[355]

## When Allah and His Prophet (saw) Performed Something

Even though Prophet Muhammad (was) spoke insistently of Zayd's value in Islam and in his own family to Sayyidah Zainab and her family, stating that he was in fact a member of his own noble family, Sayyidah Zainab and her family, despite their affection for the Prophet (saw), could not accept Zayd.

Then the following verse was revealed: **"It is not fitting for a Believer, man or woman, when a matter has been decided by Allah and His Messenger to have any option about their decision: if any one disobeys Allah and His Messenger, he is indeed on a clearly wrong Path."[356]**

When this verse was revealed Sayyidah Zainab bint Jahsh changed her mind, and obeying the order of Allah and His Prophet (saw), agreed to marry Zayd. Our Lord, who places love and friendship in our hearts, who is **Al Wadud**, could have placed a beautiful love and friendship between Zayd and Zainab but in keeping with the Divine desire, this was not the case. This marriage, which lasted about a year, did not bring either party contentment or happiness. The differences between the two came to the fore quite often and caused them unhappiness. Both sides treated each other with irritation and they constantly spoke in hurtful ways to one another.[357]

---

*in Northern India the Gulamans, in Southern India Adil Shah and Kutb Shah were all freed slaves. These all achieved high posts that enabled them to establish ruling families that controlled empires. These former slaves, who rose to the position of ruler, were accepted at the head of the country by free Muslims without the least hesitation and were recognized by all. There is no need to list the viziers, military commanders, and other similar statesmen who were freed slaves here"* (İslam Peygamberi, II, 683)

355. Afzalurrahman, Ibid., II, 183.
356. Surah Ahzâb, 33: 36.
357. Muhammed Hamidullah, İslâm Peygamberi, II, page: 681.

One day Prophet Muhammad (saw), wanted to go and visit their house with the intention of changing Zayd's attitude toward his wife; however, he did not find Zayd at home. Although Sayyidah Zainab bintu Jahsh invited him inside, he turned at the door and left. Seeing the sad state of Sayyidah Zainab in this house he said: *"How mighty is Allah, Who transforms the hearts from one state to another!..."*

Muhammed Hamidullah makes the following interpretation of Prophet Muhammad's (saw) words: *"This is an expression of surprise that Zayd, who had earlier married someone who was older than himself, Ummu Ayman, and had had a happy marriage, was now married to someone who he could not get along with, despite her being beautiful and attractive and from a good family, someone who had good manners and character: he admits to himself that the failure of people to feel emotions towards one is a condition from Allah."*[358]

### Keep Your Spouse

At every opportunity Zayd informed Prophet Muhammad (saw) that he wanted to divorce his wife, and each time Prophet Muhammad (saw) told him: *"Fear Allah and hold on to your spouse! Do not divorce her!.."*[359]

Unable to tolerate the situation any longer, Zayd divorced Zainab without informing Prophet Muhammad (saw). Prophet Muhammad (saw) in fact learned through a revelation that Zayd had divorced Zainab and that Zainab was being presented to him as a spouse. Prophet Muhammad (saw) hesitated to make this known.

The first part of that divine revelation had been manifested, and was proof that there was no difference in class or distinction between people other than according to their *taqwa*.

### The Abolition of Adoption

The divine edict after this stage was to set out to abolish another practice from the Age of Ignorance: this was *tebenni*, or adoption. Before the advent of

---

358.   Muhammed Hamidullah, İslâm Peygamberi, II, page: 682.
359.   Surah al-Ahzâb, 33: 37.

Islam, Arabs would adopt a child who was not of their family, for any reason, and announce this to all. After adoption, the child would possess the same rights and authority as the other children of the family, despite being the offspring of another family. Even though there was no blood tie, this child would be called by the father's name and have the same rights as regards inheritance and marriage.

However, this was not correct according to Islam, and Prophet Muhammad (saw) set an example of how everyone is the child only of their mothers and fathers, and how adoption does not create a biological relationship.

### The Marriage of Zainab bint Jahsh and Prophet Muhammad (saw)

Despite the repeated warnings from Prophet Muhammad (saw), Zayd bin Harithah divorced his wife without informing the Prophet (saw). Prophet Muhammad (saw) learned about this situation via a revelation, in which he was also ordered to marry Sayyidah Zainab bint Jahsh when her period of *iddet* was finished. Thus, this marriage was to be performed without witness, guardian[360] or dowry[361], as clearly proclaimed in the Qur'ân.

Prophet Muhammad (saw) thought to keep this revelation, that had been sent to him, secret for a while worried about the slander of the unbelievers. However, a second revelation not only made his marriage mandatory, but also completely abolished the practice of adoption in a cautionary verse: *"Behold! Thou didst say to one who had received the grace of Allah and thy favour: "Retain thou (in wedlock) thy wife, and fear Allah." But thou didst hide in thy heart that which Allah was about to make manifest: thou didst fear the people, but it is more fitting that thou shouldst fear Allah. Then when Zayd had dissolved (his marriage) with her, with the necessary (formality), We joined her in marriage to thee: in order that (in future) there may be no difficulty to the Believers in (the matter of) marriage with the wives of their adopted sons, when the latter have dissolved with the necessary (formality) (their marriage) with them. And Allah's command must be fulfilled."*[362]

---

360. Sâliha Akgül, Ibid., page: 161.
361. Afzalurrahman, Ibid, II, page: 183.
362. Surah Ahzâb, 33: 37.

As can be seen, this verse clearly states three matters:

1-Prophet Muhammad's (saw) insistence that Zayd continue his marriage with Zainab.

2-Prophet Muhammad (saw), even though Allah Almighty had informed him that he was to marry Sayyidah Zainab bint Jahsh, was worried about how people would react to this due to the matter of "adoption customs" and for this reason was "warned" not to delay any further.

3-After Zayd had separated from his wife of his own free will, the intention of Prophet Muhammad (saw) to marry Sayyidah Zainab was not forbidden; that is the wives of adopted sons are not *mahram*, while the wives of biological sons are.

An important detail of this verse is that Zayd bin Harithah (ra) is the only one of the Companions named in the Qur'ân.

Due to this divine order Prophet Muhammad (saw) offered marriage to Sayyidah Zainab bintu Jahsh. The fact that this marriage took place upon Allah's order and was commanded in a revelation that would be recited until the Day of Judgment caused Sayyidah Zainab to say: *"My marriage was performed by Allah Almighty"* and she thanked Allah for this blessing.

## The First Reactions to this Marriage

When Prophet Muhammad (saw) married Sayyidah Zainab (r.ah) the gossip and slander began immediately. Things went so far that people were saying: *"Muhammad, even though he knows that the wife of the son is forbidden for the father to marry, has married the wife of his own son."*

The answer to this is given in the Qur'ân: *"Muhammad is not the father of any of your men, but (he is) the Messenger of Allah (saw), and the Seal of the Prophets: and Allah has full knowledge of all things."*[363]

---

363.   Surah al-Ahzâb, 33: 40.

The strength of these first reactions indicates that Prophet Muhammad (saw) was correct in wanting to keep secret the revelation of this event. However, Allah Almighty provided Islam as a whole, and as He desired it to be without fault and complete in itself, He was not pleased when our beloved Prophet kept this matter secret; even though it was only for a short time. This is one of the most important pieces of evidence that the Qur'ân we hold in our hands today is still as it was revealed by Allah: if Prophet Muhammad (saw), a human being, had been able to change or interfere with the Qur'ân, then without a doubt he would have changed this particular verse and other cautionary ones that were revealed concerning him. Certainly Allah Almighty has protected the Qur'ân from human hands. In fact, the Qur'ân says about this:

**"This is a Message sent down from the Lord of the Worlds. And if the messenger were to invent any sayings in Our name, We should certainly seize him by his right hand, and We should certainly then cut off the artery of his heart: Nor could any of you withhold him** (from Our wranth). **But verily this is a Message for the Allah fearing."**[364]

On the other hand, the matter that Prophet Muhammad (saw) kept secret was not a revelation that was to be declared to the people: it was only an inspiration about what would happen in the future, however, the dimension of the event caused Prophet Muhammad (saw) to hesitate about whether to immediately make an explanation about this matter or not. If this had been an inspiration that he had been ordered to declare to the people Prophet Muhammad (saw) would not have hesitated, he would have had no doubts, and he would not have felt the need to keep it secret, whether the matter was in his favor or not.

In fact, Sayyidah Â'ishah (r.ah) speaks of the difficulties that Prophet Muhammad (saw) found himself in because of these events as follows: "*If Allah's Prophet (saw) had hidden something from the revelation that came to him, it would have been the verse concerned with this marriage.*"[365]

In conclusion, all of these events were desired by Allah Almighty and thus the matter of adoption was abrogated by the hand of Prophet Muhammad (saw).

The orientalists and other enemies of Islam claimed that Prophet Muham-

---

364. Surah al-Hâkka, 69: 43-48.
365. Bukhârî, Tevhid, 22; Müslim, Iman, 288; Ahmad bin Hanbal, 2/5.

mad (saw) had once seen Sayyidah Zainab bint Jahsh in the corner of a window or door and had fallen in love with her, thus wanting to marry her.[366]

However, this claim was totally groundless and untrue: as we mentioned at the start, Sayyidah Zainab was Prophet Muhammad's (saw) cousin. They had had many opportunities over the years to see one another and become acquainted. On the other hand, the verses about *hijab* were not revealed until after both Sayyidah Zainab's wedding to Zayd and her marriage to the Prophet (saw). Thus, Prophet Muhammad (saw) would have seen her many times without *hijab*.

In addition, if Prophet Muhammad (saw) had proposed marriage to Sayyidah Zainab before her marriage to Zayd, she would hardly have refused him. In fact, it is because both Sayyidah Zainab and her family were expecting such a proposal that Zayd dragged their feet.[367]

Another matter is that if Allah's Prophet (saw) had wanted to marry Sayyidah Zainab rather than marrying her to someone else he could have married her while she was still a virgin. Prophet Muhammad (saw) was insistent that Zayd and Zainab's marriage continue; and he encouraged Zayd (ra), who had come to his house to complain about his wife, to work at the marriage. If his intention had been to marry Sayyidah Zainab (r.ah) then why did he marry her to someone else and why did he encourage them to stay married?

For this and many similar reasons it is indicated that the marriage between Prophet Muhammad (saw) and Sayyidah Zainab was not the result of human effort, but rather that of a divine order and direction.

Allah Almighty gradually revealed the truths that were necessary for us to realize what is right and necessary for humanity. Although the realization of these rights and truths sometimes caused Prophet Muhammad (saw) to have difficulties with them, Allah Almighty created many blessings and wisdoms in this. Allah Almighty never refrains from announcing these truths and educating people about them using a number of means.[368]

---

366. See: Ziya Kazıcı, Ibid., page: 249-254.
367. Celal Yeniçeri, Ibid., page: 89.
368. In the 53rd verse of Surah Ahzab, which was revealed for another reason, the following is stated: "*O ye who believe! Enter not the Prophet's houses,- until leave is given you,- for a meal, (and then) not*

## Why was Adoption Abolished?

The following question might occur to you: 'Why was the adoption of children abolished in Islam?'

Many instances of wisdom can be discovered in this. However, so as not to stray too far from our subject, we will only focus on one or two matters. Without a doubt, one of the most disastrous results of adoption was that over time lineage would become confused, and it would be difficult to determine which family a person belonged to. A child, outside of the environment of the family he or she had joined, would not recognize their own mother or father or close relatives, and this could lead to people who are forbidden from marrying one another unwittingly marrying. There have been many examples of such sorrowful situations in history. For this reason, if a child must be adopted, they should not be remembered as an actual member of the family, but as the child of their biological mother and father. In this matter the fifth verse of Surah Ahzab tells us:

*"Call them by (the names of) their fathers: that is more just in the sight of Allah. But if ye know not their father's (names, call them) your Brothers in faith, or your maulas. But there is no blame on you if ye make a mistake therein: (what matters is) the intention of your hearts: and Allah is Oft-Returning, Most Merciful."*

Also, the adoption of children leads to serious problems of *mahramiyat* and *haremlik* and *selamlik*. If the person adopted is a girl, in the future it would be possible for her to marry her adoptive father. The opposite is also true: if the child is a boy he could eventually marry his adoptive mother. If we are to think of the same situation for the adopted person and other members of the family; it is abundantly clear that they would not be able to stay in the same house and move about with ease.

---

*(so early as) to wait for its preparation: but when ye are invited, enter; and when ye have taken your meal, disperse, without seeking familiar talk. Such (behaviour) annoys the Prophet: he is ashamed to dismiss you, but Allah is not ashamed (to tell you) the truth. And when ye ask (his ladies) for anything ye want, ask them from before a screen: that makes for greater purity for your hearts and for theirs. Nor is it right for you that ye should annoy Allah's Messenger, or that ye should marry his widows after him at any time. Truly such a thing is in Allah's sight an enormity."*

Another matter that needs to be considered is the child wrongly being given rights to inheritance, thus coming between those who actually possess the rights due to blood ties. Over time this could lead to serious, or even deadly, conflicts within the family.

In Islam, adoption does not mean making another person a member of the family, but rather taking them under protection. Children who have no parents should be looked after and brought up by those who are closest to them: however, they will not be recorded as part of the family and they have no right to inheritance or other rights. This method is what is known today as a "foster family". To adopt in this way, and to raise a child and take care of them, is a reason for great rewards from Allah.

## The Wedding Feast

After receiving the revelation Prophet Muhammad (saw) sent news to Sayyidah Zainab, according to some by the servant Salma[369], and according to others with Zainab's former husband Zayd bin Harithah[370], that he wanted to marry her.[371] Zainab, hearing this news, was very pleased, and made a gift of all the jewelry she was wearing to the person who had brought her the glad tidings[372], prayed in thanks and swore to fast for two months.[373]

According to what was reported by Anas bin Malik (ra), a miracle occurred in connection with the *valima* (wedding feast) that Prophet Muhammad (saw) gave during his marriage to Sayyidah Zainab.[374] It occurred thus: Anas bin Malik's mother, Ummu Sulaym, brought a dish called *hays*[375], saying that there was only a little of this. Prophet Muhammad (saw) said to Anas bin Malik: "*Go to such and such a people and invite any of the Muslims you meet*" and gave him the names of some of the people he should invite. Anas invited many of the

---


369. Celal Yeniçeri, Ibid., page: 88; Afzalurrahman, Ibid., II, page: 183.
370. Havva Ergene Işık, Ibid., page: 307.
371. See: Muslim, Nikâh, 15.
372. Muhammed Hamidullah, İslâm Peygamberi, II, 681.
373. Ibn-i Sa'd, VIII, 102; Celal Yeniçeri, Ibid., page: 88; Havva Ergene Işık, Ibid., page: 307.
374. Afzalurrahman, Ibid., II, page: 183.
375. *Hays*: A traditional dish of Medina dates mixed with butter.

people named and that people he met, and although approximately 300 people came, they were able to eat their fill. Thus, a meal that was only enough for 3 to 4 people was able to feed 300 hundred people.[376]

## The *Hijab* Verse

This feast took place in the fifth year after the Hijrah, and following it, the 53rd verse of Surah Ahzab was revealed: *"O ye who believe! Enter not the Prophet's houses,- until leave is given you -for a meal- (and then) not (so early as) to wait for its preparation: but when ye are invited, enter; and when ye have taken your meal, disperse, without seeking familiar talk. Such (behaviour) annoys the Prophet: he is ashamed to dismiss you, but Allah is not ashamed (to tell you) the truth. And when ye ask (his ladies) for anything ye want, ask them from before a screen: that makes for greater purity for your hearts and for theirs. Nor is it right for you that ye should annoy Allah's Messenger (saw), or that ye should marry his widows after him at any time. Truly such a thing is in Allah's sight an enormity."[377]*

As can be seen, it was ordered that no one enter Prophet Muhammad's (saw) house without permission, and that after having eaten they should not sit for a long time without being invited; and that the wives of the Prophet (saw), the mothers of the *ummah,* were only to be asked something from behind a curtain. The Qur'an also forbade the wives of Prophet Muhammad (saw) from marrying another person after the death of the Prophet of Islam.

Formerly the Arabs would go into one another's houses without paying any attention to the time: if a person wanted to see someone they did not think that it was necessary to knock on the door or to attain permission, on the contrary they would immediately enter the house and ask the women and children in the house if the head of the house was at home. This ignorant practice was often the cause of some evil or negative consequences. For this reason, to start with, a rule was made that no one, not even if they were a close friend or relative, would

---

376.   Muslim, Nikâh, 94-96; See: Buhârî, Tefsîru'l-Kur'ân, 8.
377.   Surah Ahzâb, 33: 53.

be able to enter the Prophet's house without permission. Later the 27th and 28th verses of Surah Nur stated:

*"O ye who believe! enter not houses other than your own, until ye have asked permission and saluted those in them: that is best for you, in order that ye may heed (what is seemly). If ye find no one in the house, enter not until permission is given to you: if ye are asked to go back, go back: that makes for greater purity for yourselves: and Allah knows well all that ye do."* (Surah An-Nur, 24: 27-28) Thus the rule was expanded to include the houses of all Muslims.[378]

This verse was called the "Hijab verse". Bukhari reports from Anas (ra) that on numerous occasions Umar (ra) said to Prophet Muhammad (saw): *"O, Messenger of Allah (saw), many people, good and bad, visit you. Order your wives to cover themselves!"*

According to another hadith, Umar (ra) once said to the wives of the Prophet (saw): *"If what I say about you is accepted, my eyes will never see you again."*

Prophet Muhammad (saw) waited for a Divine order as he was not free in making rules. After the Divine decree, revealed in a verse of the Qur'an, that no one other than the men who were *mahram* could enter the house of Prophet Muhammad (saw), and that anyone who spoke to the mothers of Islam was to do so from behind a curtain.[379] After this order had been given the mothers of the believers hung curtains at their doors.[380]

## After the Wedding

The marriage of Prophet Muhammad (saw) to Sayyidah Zainab bint Jahsh (r.ah), because Sayyidah Zainab was a relative of the Prophet (saw) and her wedding had been carried out in keeping with a Divine order, led to a gentle

---

378. Saliha Akgül, Ibid., page: 178-179.
379. The close relatives asked: *"Are we too to talk to you through a curtain?"* The following verse was then revealed: *"There is no blame (on these ladies if they appear) before their fathers or their sons, their brothers, or their brother's sons, or their sisters' sons, or their women, or the (slaves) whom their right hands possess. And, (ladies), fear Allah. for Allah is Witness to all things."* (Ahzab, 33: 55).
380. Saliha Akgül, Ibid., page: 179.

rivalry with the other wives. As a result Sayyidah Zainab (r.ah) said to Prophet Muhammad (saw): *"There are three privileges that I have that your other wives do not possess:*

*1-Your grandfather was my grandfather (Abdulmuttalib;)*

*2-Allah ordered your marriage to me; and,*

*3-The go-between was Gabriel (as)."*[381]

Sayyidah Â'ishah expressed her jealousy of Sayyidah Zainab because of these privileges at every opportunity, and competition and argument among the wives would sometimes take place in front of Prophet Muhammad (saw). He would sometimes witness these with a smile, but at other times he would get up and leave so that they could let out their feelings with ease.[382]

However, according to a report by Bukhari which we have given above concerning the issue of slander against Sayyidah Â'ishah, while many people were talking about Sayyidah Â'ishah, Prophet Muhammad (saw) asked Sayyidah Zainab bintu Jahsh what she thought about the matter. She replied: *"O Prophet! I protect my ears and my eyes against that which I have not seen or heard myself. I swear to Allah that I know nothing but good about Â'ishah."*[383]

Sayyidah Â'ishah, hearing these words, said: *"Zainab was a woman who was my rival. But due to her taqwa Allah protected her (from participating in the slander)."*[384] Thus, the rivalry between the wives of the Prophet (saw) was not so great that it caused Sayyidah Zainab bint Jahsh to speak against Sayyidah Â'ishah during the period when she was being slandered.[385]

One of the greatest reasons for misunderstandings and arguments among individuals, families and even states, is the making of decisions based on

---

381. Bukhârî, Tevhid, 21.
382. Â'isha Abdurrahman, page 103.
383. These words of Zainab remind us of verse 36 of Surah Isra: *"And pursue not that of which thou hast no knowledge; for every act of hearing, or of seeing or of (feeling in) the heart will be enquired into (on the Day of Reckoning)."* This reminds us to witness only what is good.
384. Bukhârî, Shahâdah, 15; Ziya Kazıcı, Ibid., page: 259.
385. Ziya Kazıcı, Ibid., sh: 258-259.

assumptions and suppositions which lack thorough investigation.[386] Allah Almighty orders us to investigate any news, action or event thoroughly before making a decision, and not to arrive at conclusions based on suppositions or possibilities: *"O ye who believe! If a wicked person comes to you with any news, ascertain the truth, lest ye harm people unwittingly, and afterwards become full of repentance for what ye have done."*[387]

Due to Sayyidah Zainab's piety Allah protected her; Sayyidah Zainab was a woman with *taqwa*, piety and religiousness. She was sincere in her belief, and her standing up for Sayyidah Â'ishah (r.ah) is evidence of this. In fact, Sayyidah Â'ishah (r.ah) stated that she had not seen anyone who was more blessed than Sayyidah Zainab bin Jahsh in their religious life: *"She had a great deal of taqwa towards Allah. She told the truth. She maintained her connections with her relatives. She gave a great deal in charity and did every thing possible to come closer to Allah."*

In fact, a hadith shows us how fond she was of worshipping and how much *taqwa* she had: Anas bin Malik reported: The Prophet (saw) went into the *masjid* and saw that a rope was tied between two pillars. When he asked *"What is this rope for?"* the Companions answered: *"That rope belongs to Zainab. When Zainab becomes tired (from standing up during prayer) she holds on to this rope."* Then Prophet Muhammad (saw) said: *"No. (Worship should not be difficult). Undo this rope. When you are fit and strong pray standing up. When you are tired, sit down."*[388]

### After the Prophet's Death

Sayyidah Zainab bint Jahsh (r.ah) had an allowance of 12,000 Dirhem, which had been allocated wholly to her. However, as soon as she received her money she would immediately distribute it to the poor. In fact, it is reported that one time she received the money she said: *"Allah! Do not send me this money next year…It is a provocation!.."*[389] Here, I would like to examine an important event in a little more detail:

---

386. Saliha Akgül, Ibid., page: 183.
387. Surah al-Hujurat, 49: 6.
388. Bukhârî, Tahajjud, 18; Muslim, Salâtu'l-Musâfirîn, 31.
389. Ziya Kazıcı, Ibid., page: 260.

When the income in the treasury increased Umar gave some of the Companions, the family of the Prophet (saw) and those who were in need among the community an allowance. The first allowance was sent to Sayyidah Zainab. Seeing this much money Sayyidah Zainab was shocked and asked: "Allah, *forgive Umar. Are the shares of my other sisters and brothers included in this?*"

The person who had brought the money told her that the money was just for her and she said *"Subhanallah!"* and covered the money with a cloth and said to her servant: *"Put your hand in, take a handful of money and take it to the son of such and such a person. Take another handful and take it to such and such a person,"* and thus distributed the money to her relatives and to people who were without family. After taking out handfuls of the money, eventually little was left. The servant said: *"O mother of believers, may Allah forgive you, this is our share."* Then Sayyidah Zainab said *"What is left under the cover is yours."*[390] Thus, she distributed all the money that had been sent to her. When the servant lifted the cover and counted what was left, there was 85 *Dirhem* and none of the monet was left for Sayyidah Zainab.[391]

When the second caliph Umar (ra) learnt of this situation he stopped in front of her door, sending his greetings inside and said *"I have heard that you distributed all the money I sent to you. I am sending one thousand more Dirhem to you; these are for you."*

Umar (ra) sent one thousand more dirhem, but Sayyidah Zainab's were the same as before and she distributed everything she had.[392]

The prayer that Sayyidah Zainab (r.ah) had made was accepted and she died before Umar (ra) was able to send another allowance to the "mother of the believers".[393]

Sayyidah Zainab (r.ah) gave much to the poor, to those who were in need and to widows. She had prepared her own shroud before she died; though Umar (ra) sent her a shroud, and when she died the shroud she had prepared was given away in charity by her sister Hamna.

---

390. Ibn-i Sa'd, VIII, 108-109; Sâliha Akgül, 180.
391. Afzalurrahman, Ibid., II, page: 184-185.
392. Ibn-i Sa'd, Tabakat, VIII, 110.
393. Afzalurrahman, Ibid., II, page: 185.

When Sayyidah Zainab (r.ah) died it is reported that Sayyidah Â'ishah (r.ah) said: *"One who is worthy of praise, who worshipped much has gone to the shelter of orphans and widows!.."*[394]

Her virtues created such a spiritual condition that Sayyidah Zainab (r.ah) and charity became one.

Sayyidah Zainab was a woman who worked with her hands: she would tan leather, and sew leather goods out of them. The money she earned from these would be spent in the way of Allah.[395] It soon became clear that these efforts were not in vain, as according to a report, close to his death Prophet Muhammad (saw) said: *"Those who will reach me quickest and first are those with the longest hands."*

What was understood by the expression "the longest hands", at the time of Sayyidah Zainab's death, was one who gives the most in charity; as she was not tall, her hands were not long in comparison to those of the other wives of Prophet Muhammad (saw), but she did receive great pleasure in distributing both the money she earned with her own efforts as well as the allowance from the Caliphs to others.

This report reminds us of another matter: it was said that Sayyidah Zainab would be with Prophet Muhammad (saw) in Heaven. In other words, she was told that she would have a place in Heaven while she was alive.


**Her Death**

Sayyidah Zainab (r.ah) died in the 20th year after the Hijrah (641) when she was 53 years old, during the caliphate of Umar (ra). He led the funeral prayer himself and she was buried in the Baqi Cemetery. There are eleven hadiths that were reported by Sayyidah Zainab. Two of these are found in both Bukhari and Muslim.

---

394.    Ibn-i Hajar, el-Isâbe, IV, 308; Ayşe Abdurrahman, Ibid., page: 105.
395.    Muhammed Hamidullah, İslâm Peygamberi, II, page: 683.

## Lessons to be Learned From Her Life:

1- Sayyidah Zainab bint Jahsh (r.ah) is an example to us all with her meticulous worship, her mercy to the poor, her generosity, her efforts to earn her own living and in giving from what she possessed.

2- At first, our mother Sayyidah Zainab (r.ah) did not want to marry Zayd bin Harithah (ra), but the persuasion of Prophet Muhammad (saw), and because she did not want to disregard the 13th verse of Surah Hujurat, she agreed to the marriage. What we can understand from this is that the most important consideration when making choices about whom to marry is that the person should have the qualities recommended in the Qur'ân and Sunnah, and should be someone who will direct us towards *taqwa*.

3- It is very difficult to eliminate traditions and practices that are well embedded in society and which almost have taken on the nature of a religion. Going against such traditions that are generally accepted in society will often cause extreme reactions in the society. For this reason Allah Almighty removed traditions carried on since the Age of Ignorance, by the actions of His Prophet (saw). The marriage of the Prophet's own cousin to a former slave shows that one tradition of the Age of Ignorance, which prevented a rich person marrying a poor person and a noble person a slave, were invalid.

However, it would be a good idea to stress an important point here: that a couple who are about to marry should occupy positions in society that are as close to one another as possible, even though there is no difference or superiority between people. In Islamic law this is called *kufuw* (balance). This balance, even though it is not one of the preconditions of a marriage, has become accepted as one of the principles that make it easier for the marriage to continue in peace and to last for many years.

That Sayyidah Zainab bint Jahsh (r.ah) was chosen for the ordering and implementation of such a serious legal matter, and that she was not condemned for it, is a matter that has instilled great breadth in the rights of women.

4- Sayyidah Zainab bint Jahsh (r.ah) sold the leather she herself tanned and decorated., and is thus an example of a working woman, and therefore, we can understand that women are able to work in tasks that are not against their nature and in legitimate surroundings. In addition, Sayyidah Zainab (r.ah) did not use what she earned for her own purposes, but used it to help others: preferring to be a mother to the poor. This is a good example of how working women should use their income. The rewards for such services and sacrifices will be, in the words of Prophet Muhammad (saw), the blessings of Heaven.

5- When Sayyidah Â'ishah (r.ah) was in a most difficult position, Sayyidah Zainab bint Jahsh (r.ah) defended her, despite the fact that there was rivalry between them, and Sayyidah Zainab (r.ah) did not remain under the influence of the jealousy she had felt against Sayyidah Â'ishah (r.ah) from time to time. She taught us that we must restrain our feelings, particularly where justice is due, and that in situations where people are being harmed by slander or instigation, we must not abandon what is right and true.

6- At a time when her ego became oppressive to Sayyidah Zainab (r.ah), Allah Almighty arranged her marriage in heaven and appointed her as the wife of Prophet Muhammad (saw), as she had remained faithful to the orders of Allah and His Prophet (saw). This shows us that in order to be blessed, we must strive to obey the orders of Allah and His Prophet (saw), even if it is difficult for us.

## SAYYIDAH JUWAYRIYA BINT HARITH (r.ah)

### The Beauty from the Bani Mustalik

### The Bani Mustalik Battle

It was the fifth year of the hijrah. After fighting fiercely for 27 days in the Battle of the Trenches the Muslims received a signal from Archangel Jibreel (as)[396] to immediately set out for campaign against the Bani Qurayza Jews, who had committed treason during the battle. Prophet Muhammad (saw) told the muezzin Bilal to announce: *"Let those who obey the orders of Allah pray the afternoon prayer in the land of the Bani Qurayza!..."*[397]

Barely even a month had passed after all those exhausting events, the Bani Mustalik, whose leader was Harith bin Abi Dirar, and which was a branch of the Huzaa Tribe, made preparations to attack the Muslims and came as far Medina. Prophet Muhammad (saw) had an envoy investigate the reports, and when the reports were confirmed, Allah's Prophet (saw) decided to march upon the enemy. During this battle he was accompanied by his blessed wives Sayyidah Â'ishah and Umm Salama. There were many men who participated

---

396.  Prophet Muhammad had returned from the Battle of the Trench around noon. After praying the noon prayer he went to Zainab's room, removed his weapons and started to wash his face. At once Jibreel (AS) came and said: "O Prophet… the angels have not yet put down their weapons. Allah desires that you march against the Bani Qurayza." (Ibn Hisham, es-Siyreh, III, 138; Ziya Kazıcı, Ibid., page: 267)
397.  The Bani Qurayza castle fell after a 25-day long battle.

in this battle with the sole intention of obtaining wealth from their share of the victory spoils.[398]

The Muslim army consisted of 700 people, and the two armies met at the edge of a body of water that was known as the *Muraysi*. The Mustalik tribe, not expecting to see the Muslims facing them this quickly, were surprised and unprepared. If Prophet Muhammad (saw) had so desired, he could have easily killed all the Mustalik in their moment of panic. However, he was a merciful prophet. For him, guiding people to the Truth was more important, and in any case, the aim of Islam was to conquer hearts rather than lands. For this reason, the merciful Prophet requested that Umar (ra) invite the enemy to Islam. Umar (ra) stood up, and called upon the Mustaliks to accept Islam. However, they responded to this invitation with arrows and thus a fight was inevitable. After a fierce battle, the Bani Mustalik were defeated, and they abandoned the battle-field, leaving behind hundreds of prisoners, and great spoils, consisting of five thousand sheep and two thousand camels.[399]

The chief and commander of the tribe, Harith bin Abi Dirar fled, but his daughter Berre was one of the prisoners. According to their rules of engagement, the spoils of war and prisoners were to be divided up between the soldiers who had participated in the battle. In this division, Berre fell to Sabit bin Qays, one of the Companions of the Prophet (saw).[400]

## The Captive Daughter of the Tribal Chief

Berre, the daughter of Harith bin Abi Dirar, the chief of the Bani Mustalik which was a branch of the Huzaa tribe, was born in AD 607.[401]

---

398. These men were the hypocrites, and because of their large numbers in the battle, serious disputes arose, but Prophet Muhammad was able to solve these peacefully before the problems escalated out of control. However, once again proving contentious during this battle, the hypocrites began slandering Prophet Muhammad's (saw) family, namely Â'ishah, and this had a serious effect on the Muslims for a long time. (See: Osman Nûri Topbaş, Hazret-i Muhammed -Medine Devri-, page: 276-294)
399. Rıza Savaş, DIA, "Juwayriya bint Hâris", VIII, page: 146.
400. Ibn-i Hişam, Sîre, III, 154.
401. DIA, "Juwayriya bint Hâris".

She had married her cousin[402], Musavi bin Safwan, who was of the same tribe.[403] They had no children but they had a happy marriage. However, the Muraysi battle occurred and her life was changed for ever: she was a prisoner and her husband was dead, killed during the battle.

Berre, who before the battle had been the daughter of the chief, was now a prisoner as a consequence of the battle and was being taken to Medina. However, before she had even arrived in Medina, she had made a deal with her master, asking him to set a price on her: she would work to earn the money to purchase her freedom. Now she was held as a captive in Medina, far from her homeland, and her master was Sabit bin Qays.[404]

She could purchase her freedom was all well and good; but where was the money to come from? She had to find a solution. She was influenced by a dream she had had three days before the battle, and she thought of presenting this matter to Prophet Muhammad (saw). In her dream she had embraced a moon that appeared in Medina. She had not told anyone in her tribe about her dream because she sensed that in it were indications of the defeat of her tribe and her being taken to Medina.[405]

She went to Prophet Muhammad (saw) and told him that she wanted to attain her freedom, and she mentioned the agreement she had made with her master and the ransom that was to be paid. Prophet Muhammad (saw) listened to her carefully. Then he said: "Shall I suggest a more blessed way for you?"

Berre was surprised; what could be more blessed than her freedom? After hesitating for a moment, she said: "O Prophet of Allah!... What can be more blessed than being emancipated?"

Prophet Muhammad (saw) said: *"I will pay your ransom and take you as my wife."*[406]

---

402. DIA, "Juwayriya bint Hâris".
403. Afzalurrahman, Ibid., II, page: 187.
404. However, according to one report Berre actually fell to the share of two Companions, and they decided rather than sharing the prisoner that she, as "the daughter of a chief" should be set free for *fidy-i najat* (a form of ransom). (See: Muhammed Hamidullah, Ibid., II, page: 684)
405. Ziya Kazıcı, Ibid., page: 277 from Ibn-i Kethir, "el-Bidâye ve'n-Nihâye".
406. Ayşe Abdurrahman, Ibid., page: 108-109.

Berre was shocked by this reply. Never had she met such a great example of morals and kindness: if Prophet Muhammad (saw) had so desired he could have bought her as a concubine,[407] yet, this lofty person was offering her not only her freedom, but the honor of marrying him. With great excitement she replied: "O Prophet! If you present me with such an honor, there can be no doubt that this will be more blessed for me!.."

## Berre Becomes Juwayriya

At the time that Allah's Prophet (saw) was asking Berre to marry him in Medina, Berre's father Harith bin Abi Dirar had set out for Medina, taking camels with him to exchange for his daughter. When he arrived in Akik, he decided not to present the two best camels and hid them in an obscure place in this valley. He continued on his way. As soon as he arrived in Medina he went to Prophet Muhammad (saw): "O Muhammad!… You have captured my daughter. Look, I have brought you camels. Let them be her ransom. Set her free!.."

Prophet Muhammad (saw) knew just what to say: "Why did you not bring the two camels that you hid in the valley in Akik?"

Harith was shocked. He was sure that no one but himself knew where those camels had been hidden. How could this be? The only way this man could have such knowledge was if he were receiving information from a Lord who knew both what was hidden and what was apparent. In such a state of confusion, the light of belief shone in his heart and the words of the shahada (*kalima shahadah*) tripped off his tongue. When Harith became Muslim, his two sons and the leading members of the tribe were also honored with Islam.

Prophet Muhammad (saw) paid the ransom for Berre himself. He set her free and delivered her over to her father. Then he asked for her hand in marriage. He gave her 400 *dirhem* for her dowry (*mahr*).[408] Harith, surprised at all that had happened in such a short time, gladly gave his daughter in marriage.[409] He greatly admired the lofty morals of Allah's Prophet (saw). This is how the

---

407. Ziya Kazıcı, Ibid., page: 272.
408. Afzalurrahman, Ibid., II, 187-188.
409. Ibn-i Hişâm, Sîre, III, 157.

marriage between Prophet Muhammad (saw) and Berre (Juwayriya) took place.

Our Mother Berre was given the name Juwayriya by Prophet Muhammad (saw) himself. Berre means "blessed woman without fault". To take such a name was not approved of by the Prophet (saw) as it was considered inappropriate to praise one's self. Thus, Prophet Muhammad (saw) gave her the name Juwayriya, meaning "little woman, girl".[410]

## The Most Blessed Woman of the Tribe

Prophet Muhammad's (saw) marriage to Sayyidah Juwayriya (r.ah) was an occasion for great blessings: as the Companions said: "O Prophet, it is not appropriate that the relatives of your wife are our slaves!…" and thus they set free all the members of the Mustalik Tribe.[411]

Many of the members of the Mustalik tribe, now freed and hearing about the marriage of Prophet Muhammad (saw) and Sayyidah Juwayriya, became Muslim, influenced by their admiration for these generous and high-minded acts.[412] In fact, even men who had fled from the Muslims on the battle field came to Medina and accepted Islam.[413]

Thus, once again Prophet Muhammad (saw) occasioned many blessings with a marriage. For this reason Sayyidah Â'ishah said: "I know of no woman who was more blessed for herself and her tribe than Sayyidah Juwayriya."[414]

In truth, Sayyidah Juwayriya was a blessed woman. In one day she went from captivity to freedom, from freedom to the Truth, and then became the wife of Prophet Muhammad (saw). Again, through her, hundreds of people from her tribe -according to one report 100, according to another 700 people- were immediately set free and became Muslim.

As we have seen, this marriage was a matter based on political and social

---

410.   DIA, "Juwayriya bint Hâris".
411.   Ibn-i İshak, Sîre, page: 245; Ebû Dâvud, Itk, 2; Ayşe Abdurrahman, Ibid., page: 109-110.
412.   DIA, "Juwayriya bint Hâris"; Muhammed Hamidullah, Ibid., II, page: 684-685.
413.   Celal Yeniçeri, Ibid., page: 92.
414.   Ibn-i Abdi'l-Berr, el-Istiâb, IV, 253.

needs. The Qur'an also confirms that Prophet Muhammad (saw) was not acting for his personal pleasure, but in accordance with the revelation:

*"By the Star when it goes down,- Your Companion is neither astray nor being misled. Nor does he say (aught) of (his own) Desire. It is no less than inspiration sent down to him."* (Surah an-Najm, 53: 1-4)

The most important wisdom and purpose behind this marriage was to warm hearts to Prophet Muhammad (saw) and thus to Islam. Tribes grow through marriages and blood relations, and in this way the Bani Mustalik were a help to Islam. It is a well-known fact that when a person marries into a tribe or clan, a distinct closeness and friendship arises between these people. This naturally leads to mutual cooperation. In fact, after Sayyidah Juwayriya's marriage the Bani Mustalik captives were set free, and more importantly they became Muslims.[415]

### Sayyidah Juwayriya's Virtues

Our Mother Juwayriya (r.ah) was a woman who had incredible *taqwa*. She was very sincere in her devotions, she would pray and fast often. So much so, that Prophet Muhammad (saw) would try to discourage her from some of her supererogatory prayers, and ask her to break her fast.

Sahih-i Muslim gives us a hadith from Sayyidah Juwayriya:

*"One day I was in my area for praying and Allah's Prophet (saw) had prayed his morning prayer and left. He returned in the midmorning and said: 'Are you still sitting there and counting your tasbih (prayer beads)?' I replied that I was and he said 'Shall I teach you a prayer that is equivalent to all the prayers you have said from the morning until now?' He said, 'Say three times: Subhanallahi wa bihamdihi adada halkihi. (I give thanks and praise to the number of beings Allah has created). Then three times: wa ridhae nefsihi (I praise You for Your approval), three times: wa zinata arshihi (I praise You to the weight of the Ninth Heaven) and three times: was midada kalimatihi (I praise You to the extent of the ink of Allah's words).'"*[416]

---

415.   Celal Yeniçeri, Ibid., page: 92.
416.   Muslim, Zikr ve Duâ, 19; Ibn-i Mâjah, Adab, 56; Afzalurrahman, Ibid., II, 188.

Our Mother Juwayriya (r.ah) was married to Prophet Muhammad (saw) for six years and reported seven hadiths.[417]

Sayyidah Juwayriya (r.ah) was very tender and merciful towards the poor and needy. She would feed others and go without food herself, and give others water foregoing her own drink. One day Prophet Muhammad (saw) entered her room and said: "Do you have anything to eat?" Sayyidah Juwayriya (r.ah) said: "No, Prophet! I have nothing to eat but a mutton bone that the concubine we set free gave me to give in charity!.." Prophet Muhammad (saw) said "Bring it here… It has found its place." (Muslim Zakat, 52).[418]

*　*　*

Sayyidah Juwayriya died when she was in her 70 in the 56th year of the *hijrah*.[419] In some sources it states that she died in the 50th year (670) when she was 65.[420] She is buried in the Baki Cemetery.

May Allah bless us all with her most beautiful morals and allow us to be her neighbor and friend in heaven. Amen.

**The Messages We Can Take from the Life of This Blessed Mother Today**

1- In the ups and downs of life we can suddenly find ourselves elevated high, only to be hurled into obscurity the next day. In such situations we need to keep our inner balance alive and not let our istiqamah (direction) be confused. We must act with trust in Allah, and in accordance with developing conditions, because life in a palace and life in a prison are both tests, and in both conditions the good behavior and actions that we display are reflections of our inner world. Sayyidah Juwayriya (r.ah) was the daughter of the chief of the tribe one day, and then the next she tasted the life of a prisoner, on the following day she was set

---

417. DIA, "Juwayriya bint Hâris".
418. It is worth nothing that Prophet Muhammad (saw) would accept presents that were sent to him, but he would distribute those things that were brought as *sadaqa* or *zakat* to the Companions or the poor, and would not eat or drink of them himself. The mutton bone that he is asking about in the hadith was most likely for someone in need.
419. DIA, "Juwayriya bint Hâris".
420. Afzalurrahman, Ibid., II, 188.

free and then not only was she blessed with guidance, but she became the wife of Prophet Muhammad (saw). All of these changes in fortune did not destroy her personality or character: she did not allow them to disturb her inner balance.

2- Life is like a large field in which we gather together the results of all the choices we have made. We reap what we have sown. Therefore, we should show great care to choose the most blessed of the choices that are ranged in front of us: because blessed things will bring more blessings. Sayyidah Juwayriya (r.ah), tried in many ways to escape captivity: first by bargaining with her master, and then resolutely presenting her desire for freedom, her greatest desire, to Prophet Muhammad (saw). As soon as she saw his grace and perfect character, even though she was the daughter of the chief and without contemplating that her father would sooner or later come to rescue her, she accepted the Prophet's suggestions. This certainly demonstrates her courage and resolution. On the other hand, it also is a good examlple to understand Islam's trust and submission, because after doing all that she could to change the negative conditions in which she found herself. Sayyidah Juwayriya (r.ah) then chose the best of the options before her, and when it was necessary to completely submit, she submitted to the best person. This clearly shows us that idleness in looking for the easy way out in the difficult situations that life presents to us, saying: "This is my fate, I will submit…", is incorrect and is not the way to be followed. That is an "incorrect belief in fate".

3- Moreover, when choosing our future spouses we should turn towards those among us and in our surroundings who are blessed people, and who are people with positive qualities. Thus our marriage, like that of Sayyidah Juwayriya (r.ah), will be a means of guidance.

4- Our mother Sayyidah Juwayriya (r.ah), are her marraige, strove to adorn her faith with worship and piety, and preferred the asthetic life. Even though she was married to a prophet and was a *Mother of Believers* she constantly strove for the life in the next world. We should fill our lives and our homes with the decorations of *taqwa* and be of those who always prefer the Hereafter.

5- Like Sayyidah Juwayriya (r.ah) and the other wives of the Prophet (saw), we should give generously in charity to cleanse our souls, so that they become tender, and to distance our nafs from selfishness and stinginess.

# SAYYIDAH SAFIYYAH BINT HUYAY (r.ah)

## The Lineage of our Mother Safiyyah

Safiyyah's father, Huyay bin Ahtab, was the chief of the Jewish tribe the Bani Nadir. Her mother was Bera bint Samuel, who was the daughter of the chief of another Jewish tribe, the Bani Quraytha. Thus, because of her mother and father, Safiyyah was the inheritor of the leadership.

As we can see, Safiyyah's ancestors stretch back to the Children of Israel, Prophet Moses and Prophet Aaron, and thus as far back as Prophet Jacob.

Before marrying Prophet Muhammad (saw), Sayyidah Safiyyah (r.ah) had been married twice. Her first husband was the poet Sallam bin Mishkam, one of the prominant members of the tribe. After some time they were divorced; and her second marriage was to the commander of the Kamus castle, Kinana bin Rabi.[421]

We take that view that Sayyidah Safiyyah (r.ah) was the only person of Jewish descent among the Prophet's wives.[422]

Sayyidah Safiyyah converted to Islam before her marriage, and her real name was Sayyidah Zainab. At that time, the share of the loot that fell to the

---

421. Ziya Kazıcı, Ibid., page: 279.
422. Even though Reyhane was also one of the Prophet's wives who was of Jewish descent, there is some controversy about whether she was only a *jariya*, or first a *jariya* and then a wife. As this is a matter of debate, we prefer to state that the only Jewish wife was Safiyya, thus focusing only on those wives with whom a marriage ceremony had categorically taken place.

chief in Arabia was referred to as *"Safiyy"*, and as this lady fell to the share of Prophet Muhammad (saw) she was called Safiyyah.[423]

Now let us become acquainted with this blessed wife of Prophet Muhammad (saw) and study their marriage in a little detail.

## The Jews in Medina

As is known, when Prophet Muhammad (saw) emigrated from Mecca to Medina there were three Jewish tribes living in Medina: the Bani Kaynuka, the Bani Nadir and the Bani Kureytha. When these three Jewish tribes originally came to Medina, where only Arabs had lived before, they talked with the descendants of two brothers, the Aws and the Hazraj tribes, and asked for a corner of Medina to be given over to them. They Arabs agreed to this and the Jews were shown a region where they could reside. However, as time passed the Jews started to make problems, and were not living at peace in the area that had been allocated to them, and they frequently instigated trouble between the Aws and Hazraj.

When Prophet Muhammad (saw) came to Medina these two Arab tribes were involved in a very bloody war. First Prophet Muhammad (saw) sorted out the problems between the two tribes and then he made an agreement with the Jews. According to this agreement, if an attack was to be made on the city, the two sides would act together and fight to defend against the mutual enemy. Everyone would settle their own internal disputes with their own religious representatives and when there was a problem between the Muslims and the Jews, the litigants would apply to Prophet Muhammad (saw). This and similar rulings were accepted in a constitution of the Medina City State, in which an equal number of representatives from the Muslims, polytheists and Jews who resided there participated.

However, at certain intervals this agreement was violated by the three Jewish tribes that were living in Medina. The first of these infractions was carried out by the Bani Kaynuka Jews. They could not accept that the Muslims had

---

423.　Saliha Akgül, Ibid., page: 198; Afzalurrahman, Ibid., II, 191; Celal Yeniçeri, Ibid., 98.

won the Badir Battle (2<sup>nd</sup> year Hijra) and attacked a Muslim woman who was shopping in a jewelers, thus starting a war.

After this, the Meccans carried out the Battle of Uhud (third year of the Hijra), and the Muslim defeat served to increase the Jewish hostility. The Bani Nadir attempted to assassinate Prophet Muhammad (saw), and as a result of this they were exiled from Medina, like the Bani Kaynuka tribe.

The last Jewish tribe left in Medina was the Bani Quraytha; and during the Battle of the Trench (5<sup>th</sup> year of the Hijra) they made a pact with the enemy, taking advantage of the siege of the city, and attacked the Muslims from the rear. With the aid of Allah, after repelling the 10,000 strong enemy force that was attacking Medina, the Muslims marched against the Bani Quraytha to settle this score. After a long, seige the Jews were forced to surrender the castle in which they had sought refuge.

This last tribe had violated the existing agreement and it was decided to exile them from Medina. Thus only Arabs, most of whom were Muslim, remained in Medina. However, the Jews who had been expelled from Medina failed to learn from their errors, rather becoming more incensed: they gathered around Haybar and did not refrain from acting out of enmity towards the Muslims at every opportunity. Thus Haybar became a hive of intrigue.

**In Front of Haybar**

During the Battle of the Trench, the Jews in Haybar had turned to many tribes and tried in vain to form a front to attack Medina. They were incensed that they had been unable to attain this aim.

However, the Hudaybiya Treaty which the Muslims drew up with the Meccans (6<sup>th</sup> year of the *hijra*) gave new hope to the Jews, because they mistakenly thought that the Muslims had drawn up this treaty because they were in no position to withstand even the Meccans. In return for the crops of Haybar, the Jewish tribes began to make preparations to destroy the Muslims. They sent news to all the surrounding tribes. In particular, envoys went between the Gatafan Tribe and Mecca.

In reaction to this behavior, Prophet Muhammad (saw) sent Abdullah bin Rewaha of the Companions to Haybar to negotiate a peace settlement. However, when this was refused the Prophet (saw) announced to the Companions that the Battle of Hayber would commence, saying: *"Let only those who want jihad come with us."*[424] Battle was now inevitable. However, Medina lay between Haybar and Mecca; therefore, if a battle was to be waged against with the hypocrites, Haybar presented a great danger behind the Muslims.

Prophet Muhammad (saw) set out to conquer Haybar Castle with 1,400 infantry and 200 cavalry (7th year of the Hijrah). In addition, almost twenty women came with them to look after the wounded. The army arrived in Haybar at night, then they waited because the Master of the Light of Creation would never attack an enemy at night, but rather would wait until morning.[425] When morning came, the Jews were shocked: Prophet Muhammad (saw), whom they had thought was far away, had arrived at their very door with his army.

Prophet Muhammad (saw) had set up camp in a region known as Raji, between Haybar and the Gatafan Tribe, to prevent the latter sending help. Thus, the Jews were firmly trapped. As a result of the siege, which lasted for days, the Muslim provisions began to run out and their strength and energy began to wane. At this point, Prophet Muhammad (saw) said: *"Tomorrow I will place our standard in the hand of one whom Allah will bless with the conquest of Haybar. That person loves Allah and His Prophet (saw) and Allah and His Prophet (saw) love that person!"*

The Companions, hearing these glad tidings, were all very eager to carry out this task. Each one of them wanted to carry Allah and His Prophet (saw) and each one of them wanted to carry that standard and be the one whom Allah and Prophet (saw) loved. On the following morning, Prophet Muhammad (saw) gave the standard to Ali (ra) and the conquest was accomplished. There were eight castles in Haybar. Two of these were taken without a struggle. Thus, the miracle of the Prophet (saw) was realized. In this battle 93 Jews died, while only15 Muslims were killed.

---

424. Ibn-i Sa'd, II, 92, 106.
425. Ziya Kazıcı, Ibid., page: 281.

## In the Presence of Prophet Muhammad (saw)

After the victory of Haybar, the Jews requested to continue to work the land as shaecroppers.[426] As a result, Prophet Muhammad (was) did not exile all the Jews. With the precondition that he could exile them when he wanted, this fertile land was to be worked and half the earnings were to be given to the Jews, who were accepted as shareholders. With this condition the Jews remained in their homes until the caliphate of Umar (ra). This agreement made by Prophet Muhammad (saw) and his subsequent marriage to Sayyidah Safiyyah (r.ah) were the result of a policy of *"striking accord and understanding with the defeated"*.[427]

Among the prisoners captured was Sayyidah Safiyyah (r.ah), the daughter of Huyay, the chief of the tribe. She had been captured together with her cousin by Bilal and brought in front of Prophet Muhammad (saw). Bilal (ra), as he was bringing them from the battle field, led the two women through the wounded and dead soldiers. The women, seeing their friends and family lying on the ground threw themselves on the corpses and, covered in dust, wept; so this was the condition in which they were brought before Prophet Muhammad (saw). He did not approve of Bilal bringing the women to him in this manner and said to him: *"O, Bilal, has the mercy been torn from your heart?"*[428]

Then Prophet Muhammad (saw) turned to Sayyidah Safiyyah bint Huyay (r.ah) and said: *"If you like, become Muslim and we will get married. If you like, remain a Jewess, and I will set you free and you may return to your tribe!.."*

Sayyidah Safiyyah (r.ah) was shocked by this offer, because at that time the rules of engagement meant that Prophet Muhammad (saw) could keep her with him as his *jariya*. He did not need to free her, marry her, nor give her *mahr*.

Sayyidah Safiyyah bint Huyay (r.ah) said: *"O Prophet of Allah! Before you even called me to Islam I was thinking of converting to this religion."* What Sayyidah Safiyyah (r.ah) was referring to here is that a few days before Prophet Muhammad (saw) arrived in Haybar, Sayyidah Safiyyah (r.ah) was married to one of the leading Jews. On her wedding night she had a dream in which the

---

426. Ziya Kazıcı, Ibid., page: 182.
427. Muhammed Hamidullah, İslâm Peygamberi, II, 686.
428. İbn-i İshak, Sîre, p. 246.

moon came from Medina and entered her lap. When she told her husband about this he was enraged and said: "*You only want to be with the ruler of the Hijaz, Muhammad!*" and slapped her across her face, giving her a black eye. Her husband was killed during the battle. When Sayyidah Safiyyah (r.ah) married Prophet Muhammad (saw), the bruise from her husband's slap was still visible on her face.

She went on to say: "*I agree with you. Now I have no father, no brother nor any other relative among the Jews. Therefore, as you have left me free to chose, Allah and His Prophet are more pleasing to me than being released and returning to my tribe.*"[429] Prophet Muhammad (saw) then released her and they were married.

According to what can be understood from the information given in the sources, the Prophet of Allah (saw) did not marry any woman or take on any *jariya* who had not become Muslim nor did he spend the night with them before they had converted.[430]

## A Couple of Notes on Slavery in Islam

The "prisoners of war", which at this time meant the same as "slave" or "*jariya*", was part of the rules of engagement. There would be fierce fighting during the war and the victor would either kill the prisoners they took, or return them to their tribe for ransom, or keep them as their personal slaves or *jariya*s.

Prophet Muhammad (saw) would not have been able to eliminate this well-established practice over night, because no matter how much he might say: "*you cannot take prisoners in war*", the enemy would continue to take people prisoner, although this would be in contravention of the treaties. Moreover, the prisoners captured harbored antagonistic feelings and thoughts towards the Muslims. The only way to correct the error in their thoughts was for them to see Muslim daily life and how the Muslims interacted with other people. Thus, the slaves and *jariya*s who remained among the Muslims had an opportunity to

---

429.  Afzalurrahman, Ibid., II, 191.
430.  Celal Yeniçeri, Ibid., page: 99.

become closely acquainted with Islam. Significantly, this aspect is demonstrated in the fact that many of the greatest individuals raised in Islamic history were the liberated slaves or the children of *jariya*s.

As reported by Muhammed Hamidullah[431], in the history of no other state can one find the children of liberated slaves establishing a state. In the following hadith, Prophet Muhammad (saw) indicates what kind of education and training the slaves and *jariya*s should undergo:

*"When any man has a jariya (a female slave or prisoner is called a jariya) they should teach them science and educate them well, they should train them and teach them well; later they should liberate them and if the (man) marries her, then there are two rewards for this person."*[432]

Islam puts a great responsibility on Muslims who own slaves or *jariya*,in that the slaves should be perceived almost as a member of the family: they should eat the same as the family, drink the same as the family, wear the same clothing as the family and not be given any work that is beyond their strength, nor be burdened with heavy loads to carry. Cruelty to slaves is absolutely forbidden. They are accepted as "human beings" who have been deprived of their freedom. In the Age of Ignorance, a time deprived of Islam, and throughout long centuries in Europe which did not enjoy the mercy of Islam, slaves and *jariya* were not accepted as "human beings" and they had to survive under very bad conditions.

In this way Islam not only raised the living standards of slaves and *jariya*, it also supported their being liberated by any means, and in the shortest time possible. In a similar way, the repentance for some sins was "setting a slave free", and great bounties were promised for those who liberated slaves. Slaves also had the right to sit and barter with their master to purchase their freedom.

In short, Islam did not completely abolish slavery, due to the necessities of the time; however, it established the necessary foundation and conditions for slavery to disappear over time.[433]

---

431. See: Muhammed Hamidullah, İslâm Peygamberi, II, 683.
Moreover, one can refer to the section: "Equality among People in Islam", mentioned in the discussion of Zainab bint Jahsh (ra).
432. Bukhârî, Nikâh, 13.
433. For more information on this matter, see the related section at the end of the book.

## The Marriage Between Prophet Muhammad (saw) and Sayyidah Safiyyah (r.ah)

After the above conversation between Prophet Muhammad (saw) and Sayyidah Safiyyah (r.ah), Allah's Prophet (saw) set her free. Even if he wanted to give her a *mahr*, Sayyidah Safiyyah considered her liberation to be her *mahr*. In this way, their wedding was contracted. Prophet Muhammad (saw) wanted to spend the night with Sayyidah Safiyyah (r.ah) on the return from Haybar, but she refused. Although Prophet Muhammad (saw) was a bit upset by this situation, he refrained from saying anything. They continued on their way. When they reached the place called Sahba, Prophet Muhammad (saw) told Anas bin Malik's mother Ummu Sulaym to make preparations for a wedding.[434] Then Ummu Sulaym (saw) and the other wives prepared Sayyidah Safiyyah (r.ah) for the wedding and Prophet Muhammad (saw) spent the night with her.

According to a report by Ummu Sulaym the next morning she went to Sayyidah Safiyyah to talk to her. Sayyidah Safiyyah said that the Prophet (saw) had been happy, that he had not slept that night, but had continuously wanted to talk with her.[435] A few days before she had lost some of her close relatives, including her father and husband, and thus she was in great need of this sort of close attention, and Prophet Muhammad (saw) had not begrudged her this.[436]

During this conversation Prophet Muhammad (saw) reassured his new wife about the damage and loss her tribe had incurred, and while explaining the reasons and events that made battle with the residents of Haybar compulsory, he explained that the responsibility for the battle was completely with the people of Haybar.[437]

After this explanation, Prophet Muhammad (saw) asked her why she had not wanted to spend the night with him at the first stage they had reached after the battle. Sayyidah Safiyyah answered him that the place that they had reached was very close to the Jews and that she was afraid that they might try to harm Prophet Muhammad (saw) . The Prophet (saw) was very pleased by this answer.[438]

---

434. Bukhârî, Cihad ve Siyer, 73.
435. Celal Yeniçeri, Ibid., page: 100.
436. Afzalurrahman, Ibid., II, page: 192.
437. Muhammed Hamidullah, İslâm Peygamberi, II, 686.
438. Ibn-i Sa'd, et-Tabakât, VIII, 121-122; Ibn-i Hacer, el-Isâbe, IV, 338; Ayşe Abdurrahman, Ibid., 115-

The magnificent and perfect character of Prophet Muhammad (saw), his righteousness, kindness, and his ability to guide to the truth left many positive impressions on Sayyidah Safiyyah (r.ah). She accepted Islam with all sincerity. She started to practice the Sunnah of Prophet Muhammad (saw) with great sincerity and devotion.[439]

## I Feared That They Would Cause You Harm!

Sayyidah Safiyyah's fear that the Jews might cause harm to Prophet Muhammad (saw) was not misplaced, because even when she was a child her family would speak of the qualities of the Prophet (saw) who was to come and for whom they were waiting with great anticipation. However, when they heard that the Prophet (saw) had appeared in Mecca and, subsequently, had emigrated to Medina, their pleasure waned and their joy turned to disappointment. Sayyidah Safiyyah (r.ah) described those days with her family, and particularly her father, as follows:

*"I was the favorite child of my father and my uncle Abu Yasir. Whenever I met them they would pay attention to me before all the other children. One day, on their return home, they brought with them a tense atmosphere: it was as if the sun had set and darkness had surrounded us."*

*"As they were coming home they were staggering, and it was as if they would fall down. I wanted to cheer them up, as always. I swear to Allah, the greatness of the sorrow prevented them from even looking me in the face. However, I heard Abu Yasir ask my father: 'Is that he?' 'Yes, I swear to God it is he.' My father answered."*

*"Then my uncle said: 'Can you recognize and acknowledge his attributes?' My father answered in the affirmative, and my uncle asked again: 'What do you feel in your nafs towards him?' My father answered: 'I swear to God as long as I live I will be his enemy.'"[440]*

---

116.

439.   Afzalurrahman, Ibid., II, page: 192.

440.   See: Ayşe Abdurrahman, Terâcim Seyyidât Beyti'n-Nubuwwah, p. 368-369.

This event, which occurred in Sayyidah Safiyyah's childhood, was so terrible as to make her fear her father and uncle: she knew what kind of understanding the Jews had. In addition, the wife of Sallam bin Mishkem fed the Muslims, including Prophet Muhammad (saw), poisoned mutton to try to kill them.[441] Sayyidah Safiyyah (r.ah) was well aware of this treachery.

Without a doubt, this fear did not just worry her, but others as well. An example of this was Abu Ayyub Halid bin Zaid of the Ansar. He stood guard outside the Prophet's tent with his sword in his hand, not sleeping, the entire wedding night of Prophet Muhammad (saw) and Sayyidah Safiyyah. When Prophet Muhammad (saw), who was not aware of the situation, saw Abu Ayyub Halid bin Zayd (ra) in the morning he asked him what he had been doing. The answer came: *"Oh, Prophet of Allah, I was afraid for you because of this woman. You have killed her father, brother, husband and many of her tribe. She is still very close to her time of being an infidel. She is only a new Muslim. I was afraid that she might harm you."* Prophet Muhammad (saw), hearing these words of concern from Abu Ayyub Halid bin Zaid (ra) smiled and prayed for him.[442]

## First Reactions in Medina

The marriage of Sayyidah Safiyyah (r.ah) and Prophet Muhammad (saw) caused the Companions to worry. Some, like Halid bin Zaid above, were worried that Sayyidah Safiyyah (r.ah) would cause some harm to Prophet Muhammad (saw), while others thought that he had taken her not as a wife, but as *jariya*. In fact, during their return to Medina they tried to understand whether he saw her as a "spouse" or as a "*jariya*" from the way he treated her.

This situation did not change for some time after they had arrived in Medina: difficult times lay ahead for Sayyidah Safiyyah (r.ah). The people around her sometimes denigrated her because she had been a Jewess, and Prophet Muhammad (saw) would interfere, reminding them that she was now a Muslim and that they should not talk about her tribe for any reason. In fact, some of the Prophet's wives were unkind to Sayyidah Safiyyah (r.ah) in this first period.

---

441.   Ziya Kazıcı, Ibid., page: 283-283; Ayşe Abdurrahman, Ibid., 116-117; İbn-i Hişâm, Sîre, III, 177-184
442.   Ibn-i Hişam, Sire, III, 185; Ibn-i Sa'd, et-Tabakat, VIII, 126; Afzalurrahman, Ibid., II, page: 190.

Prophet Muhammad (saw) sent Sayyidah Safiyyah to the house of Harith bin Numan when they arrived in Medina. After staying there for a while he took her to his dwelling that was connected to the Masjid.[443] While Sayyidah Safiyyah was residing in Harith bin Numan's house the women of Medina came to see her in groups. Sayyidah Â'ishah (r.ah) was among them.

Prophet Muhammad (saw) saw Sayyidah Â'ishah leaving the house, looking from side to side. He followed her. She went into Harith bin Numan's house. Prophet Muhammad (saw) waited until she came out and when she did, he took hold of her dress and asked her what she thought of his new bride. She answered sharply: "*I found a Jewess. Send her back to the Jews.*"

Prophet Muhammad (saw) told her she should not speak like this, as Sayyidah Safiyyah was now a Muslim.[444] Sayyidah Â'ishah (r.ah) did not say another word but went straight to the house of Sayyidah Hafsa, who was wondering what her thoughts were about the new bride.

A similar event happened between Sayyidah Zainab bint Jahsh (r.ah) and Sayyidah Safiyyah (r.ah). During a campaign Prophet Muhammad's (saw) wives Sayyidah Safiyyah bint Huyay (r.ah) and Sayyidah Zainab bint Jahsh (r.ah) were with him. Sayyidah Safiyyah's camel was lame and Prophet Muhammad (saw) turned to Sayyidah Zainab (r.ah), who had more camels with her, and said: "Sayyidah Safiyyah's camel is lame. *Can you give her a camel?*" (According to another report, "*Can you give your sister a camel!*") Sayyidah Zainab (r.ah) answered: "*What? You want me to give a Jewess one of my camels?*"

In response to these words Prophet Muhammad (saw) turned his face away enraged. He did not go near Sayyidah Zainab (r.ah) for two or three months. According to one report, Prophet Muhammad (saw) left Sayyidah Zainab (r.ah) alone in her bed during the months of Dhul Hijjah, Muharram and part of Safar. Later he started to visit her again.[445]

Here, it would be useful to mention the following matter: the fact that Prophet Muhammad (saw) took a girl from among the Jews should be examined

---

443.   Ziya Kazıcı, Ibid., page: 295; Ayşe Abdurrahman, Ibid, page: 117.
444.   Ibni Sa'd, et Tabakât, VIII, 126; Ibn-i Mâjah, Nikâh, 50; Ibn-i Hacer, el-Isâbe, IV, 338.
445.   Ibn-i Sa'd et-Tabakât, VIII, 127; Ziya Kazıcı, Ibid., page: 295-296.

more carefully today. The Qur'an is not opposed to the Jews as a race, but to their opposition to the divine injunctions, their instigation and mischief making. Allah Almighty would not reject any people, race or nation that He has created. It is not suitable for Him to create a thing which he does not like. However, Allah opposes those who oppose His mighty will.[446]

**My Father is Aaron, My Uncle is Moses (as)**

After some time Sayyidah Safiyyah (r.ah) moved into one of Prophet Muhammad's (saw) houses. Here she fell into the friendly competition and light jealousy that existed between his wives.

"On the one side were Sayyidah Â'ishah (r.ah) and Sayyidah Hafsa (r.ah), on the other side were the other wives of Prophet Muhammad (saw), who were supported by his daughter Fatima (r.ah)… She tried to hold her place between the two sides."[447] However, no matter how much she tried to be close to them, they, starting with Sayyidah Â'ishah (r.ah) and Sayyidah Hafsa (r.ah), then the other wives of Prophet Muhammad (saw) pressured Sayyidah Safiyyah (r.ah) and they talked about her past. This saddened Sayyidah Safiyyah (r.ah), who kept it all bottled up within her.

One day, she could stand no more and she complained to Prophet Muhammad (saw) about Sayyidah Â'ishah (r.ah) and Sayyidah Hafsa (r.ah), who had said to her that *"As they were from the Quraysh, they were closer to Prophet Muhammad (saw)."*

Prophet Muhammad (saw) then said: *"Why did you not tell them: 'How can you be more blessed than me? My husband is Prophet Muhammad (saw), my father is Prophet Aaron (as) and my uncle is Prophet Moses (as)?"* thus teaching her how to respond to them and comforting her.[448] This comfort reduced the pain in the heart of Sayyidah Safiyyah (r.ah) and like a cool breeze caused her to realize that Prophet Muhammad (saw) was a safe harbor for her to shelter in.

---

446.  Celal Yeniçeri, Ibid, page: 102.
447.  Ayşe Abdurrahman, Ibid., page: 118.
448.  Ibn-i Abdi'l-Berr, el-Istîab, IV, 339.

## Last Memories of Prophet Muhammad (saw)

Prophet Muhammad (saw) continued to stretch his protective wings over Sayyidah Safiyyah (r.ah) until the day he died. Sayyidah Safiyyah (r.ah) also loved Prophet Muhammad (saw) very much. In fact, according to the reports, the mothers of believers gathered at his bed during his final illness. Sayyidah Safiyyah (r.ah), greatly saddened by his illness, said: *"O, Prophet of Allah, I swear to Allah I wish that the trouble you are undergoing now would come to me."* The other wives of Prophet Muhammad (saw), hearing these words, began to gesture to one another with their eyes and eyebrows, and whisper to one another. Prophet Muhammad (saw) then said to them: *"Wash out your mouths."* The wives, surprised at this response said: *"Why, O Prophet?"* Prophet Muhammad (saw) then answered *"You are gossiping about your friend. I swear to Allah that she is sincere."*[449]

## The Morals and Virtues of Sayyidah Safiyyah

The marriage of the Pride of Humanity to Sayyidah Safiyyah (r.ah), the daughter of Huyay, one of the leading Jews, was a means for the Haybar Jews to become closer and for the enmity between the Muslims and the Jews to be reduced, marking the start of friendly relations.

Sayyidah Safiyyah (r.ah) demonstrated closeness to the Jews to a degree that was noticeable and about which people complained: in fact, she was their representative in the households of happiness. One day, during the caliphate of Umar (ra), the *jariya* of Sayyidah Safiyyah (r.ah) came to the caliph and complained: *"O chief of the believers! Safiyyah loves Saturdays and continues the practices of the Jews."*

Umar (ra) sent a man to investigate the truth of the situation. Our respected mother said: *"You ask me about Saturdays. Ever since Allah has blessed me with Fridays I have not loved that day. When it comes to your questions about the Jews, we are related and I am maintaining my ties with my relations."*

---

449.   Ibn-i Sa'd, Tabakât, VIII, 128; Ibn-i Hacer, el-İsâbe, IV, 339; Ayşe Abdurrahman, Ibid, page: 120.

Sayyidah Safiyyah (r.ah) later turned to her *jariya* and asked here why she had slandered her owner. The girl replied *"The devil made me do it"*, confessing to her crime. The reaction of Sayyidah Safiyyah (r.ah) to this answer is magnificent in showing us to what a great degree she had adopted the morals of Islam. She said to the slave who had slandered her: *"Go, I give you your liberty!"*[450]

As we have seen, Sayyidah Safiyyah (r.ah) had lofty morals and the maturity to respond to those who treated her badly with kindness. She was a person who was intelligent, gentle and virtuous. However, she had no patience for injustice. In fact, during the political upheaval that began during the caliphate of Uthman she was on the side of the caliphate of the believers and did not join in opposition to him; and at the same time she helped him to what extent she could. In this matter her slave, or according to another report, her nephew whom she had adopted, Kinana, tells us:

*"Safiyyah (r.ah) mounted a mule and came to the rebels to defend Uthman. While going there she met Ashtar an-Nahai. Ashtar, not knowing who was sitting on the mule, struck the mule on the face. Then Safiyyah (r.ah) turned to me and said: 'Protect me, do not allow me to be humiliated!..' Later she made a secret path between her house and Uthman's. She stretched a plank between the two houses. In this way she took food and water to his house."*[451] This action shows how courageous she was.

### After the Death of Our Prophet (saw)

When they had returned from Haybar, Prophet Muhammad (saw) allocated 80 *wasq* (one camel-load) of dates and 20 *wasq* of barely (and wheat) to Sayyidah Safiyyah (r.ah), as he had done with his other wives.[452]

The income that was allocated to Sayyidah Safiyyah (r.ah) by the State Council during the caliphate of Umar (ra) was 10,000 *dirhem* a year. This amount was the same for all the wives of Prophet Muhammad (saw), except for Sayyidah Â'ishah (r.ah).[453]

---

450. Ibn-i Abdi'l-Berr, el-İstiâb, IV, 339; Ayşe Abdurrahman, Ibid., page: 120-121.
451. Ibn-i Sa'd, et-Tabakat, VIII, 128; Ayşe Abdurrahman, Ibid., page: 121-122.
452. Ibn-i Sa'd, et-Tabakât, VIII, 127.
453. See: Ziya Kazıcı, İslâm Müesseseleri Tarihi, page: 93-94.

When Sayyidah Safiyyah (r.ah) died in the 50th or 52nd year of the *Hijrah*, she left behind a field worth 100,000 *dirhem*.[454] One-third of this was left to her sister's son. When people protested about giving anything to this nephew, who was still Jewish, Sayyidah Â'ishah (r.ah) intervened and stated that it must certainly be given.[455] Then thirty thousand *dirhem* were given to this man.[456]

While Sayyidah Safiyyah was alive she loved to give in charity and to do good for others: in fact, she gave her entire house in charity.

Amina bint Abi Qays al Gifariyya, according to what was reported by Sayyidah Safiyyah (r.ah) herself, says that she was seventeen when she married Prophet Muhammad (saw).[457] According to another report Sayyidah Safiyyah (r.ah) was 27 when she married the Prophet (saw).[458]

This mother of believers, who died during the caliphate of Muawiya (ra) bin Abi Sufyan, was buried in the Baki cemetery.[459] She reported ten hadiths.[460] One of these can be found in both Bukhari and Muslim. May Allah be pleased with her.

## Lessons to be Learned from Her Life

1-Sayyidah Safiyyah (r.ah) first heard about Islam while still young and a Jewess. Her tribe and family looked on Prophet Muhammad (saw) with hatred as he had not come from the Jewish people, and Sayyidah Safiyyah (r.ah) grew up in such an environment. Despite this environment of blind bigotry, intransigency and hatred, her heart was not blackened, her perception and discernment were not blinded, and her heart was not hardened. At the first opportunity, when she

---

454. Celal Yeniçeri, Ibid., page: 102.
455. In this matter, the important point is the impartiality of the law. (Celal Yeniçeri, Ibid., page: 102-103) One must remember that the relationship between Â'isha and Safiyya when the latter first married the Prophet was not good, but after his death Â'isha did whatever she could to ensure that Safiyya's will was carried out and in fact took her side. This shows that nothing ever preceded justice and equity in the inner world of the wives of Prophet Muhammad (saw).
456. Ibn-i Sa'd, et-Tabakât, VIII, 128.
457. Ibn-i Sa'd, et-Tabakât, VIII, 129; Saliha Akgül, Ibid., page: 208; Ziya Kazıcı, Ibid., page: 300.
458. Ayşe Abdurrahman, Ibid., page: 113.
459. Ibn-i Sa'd, et-Tabakât, VIII, 129; Ibn-i Hacer, el-Isabe, IV, 339.
460. Afzalurrahman, Ibid., II, page: 193.

felt free to do so, she chose Islam. In fact, when in a position to choose freely for herself, rather than choosing freedom and her own tribe, she preferred belief in Allah and His Prophet and became one of Prophet Muhammad's (saw) pure wives. Our own preferences should always be with Allah and His Prophet (saw).

2-In a short time the affection she felt for Prophet Muhammad (saw) became so great that immediately after their marriage Sayyidah Safiyyah (r.ah) was afraid that her tribe, which was misled, would cause him harm and she undertook the protection of the Prophet (saw) against every kind of danger.

3-Prophet Muhammad (saw) did not hold back from responding to this affection and respect, and was with her constantly during the incertitude and pressure that occurred upon her return from Haybar. This situation of Prophet Muhammad (saw) is a good example of how a man should protect his wife against pressure and problems that come from those around them and how he should reassure and comfort his wife in times of trouble.

4-After becoming Muslim, Sayyidah Safiyyah (r.ah) gave importance to the ties of kinship, and did not break off relations with relatives and friends; and thought of them even when she was dying. Sayyidah Â'ishah (r.ah) defended Sayyidah Safiyyah (r.ah) against those who complained to her, when Sayyidah Safiyyah (r.ah) left an inheritance to her non-Muslim relatives, that it was necessary to respect the love and affection that Sayyidah Safiyyah (r.ah) had for her relatives.

5-The forgiveness shown by our Mother Sayyidah Safiyyah (r.ah) to the *jariya* who slandered her is a good example of how Muslim women should not harbour resentment, but rather forgive and thus be granted the forgiveness of Allah.

6-Like the other wives of Prophet Muhammad (saw) this holy Mother had impeccable morals, was generous, and her actions of charity and assistance encourage us to good actions.

7-There are two different reports about how old Sayyidah Safiyyah was when she married Prophet Muhammad (saw), either 17 or 27. If we accept that she was 17 then, if we remember that she had been married twice before marrying Prophet Muhammad (saw), then she had been married at a very young age for the Arab traditions. This event shows that the customs of marriage changes according to the climate, geography, culture, traditions and customs, and that it also changes throughout history.

8-It is very significant that Sayyidah Â'ishah (r.ah) acted not according to her emotions in the matter of Sayyidah Safiyyah's (r.ah) will, but rather according to justice and equity. This shows us which side we should uphold when caught up in a conflict.

9- The fact that Prophet Muhammad (saw) spent the first night after being married to Sayyidah Safiyyah (r.ah) just talking and not sleeping shows us to what degree he was concerned with the problems of his wives. Sayyidah Safiyyah (r.ah) was in need of a great deal of comforting and reassuring, having just lost her father and husband in battle; to the same extent women today are in need of the same interest and love when they become oppressed by the troubles of life. The matter that Prophet Muhammad (saw), as the "head of the family", gave the most importance to was "conversation with the members of the family." He made great efforts to not neglect this and it can even be said that he took precautions to ensure that he had "quality time" with his wives.

Prophet Muhammad (saw) was a wonderful example in this way, because women, as part of their nature, are inclined to conversation and in particular are in need of someone to listen to them. For this reason, to ensure and bolster the peace of the family, a husband should devote a special time for listening to his wife's troubles; and he should take her seriously, thus showing her that he values his partner.

10- Finally, the following point should be made clear: the religion of Islam has never been a religion that belongs to any one race, tribe or class. According to Islam, there are two nations, the Nation of Believers and the Nation of Unbelievers. After a person believes in Islam, no matter what tribe, race or social status they come from, they are considered to be a "sibling" of other believers, with equal rights.

This marriage of Prophet Muhammad (saw) was also directed against lessening the resentment, grudge and hatred felt by the Jews; as with this marriage Prophet Muhammad (saw) became a relative of the Jewish tribe. Some of the Companions, including the wives of Prophet Muhammad (saw), had doubts about Sayyidah Safiyyah (as), remembering the former hostility, and remained distant from her. However, Prophet Muhammad (saw) was not pleased by this behavior and from time to time he was forced to seriously reprimand them for these actions.

In truth, both in the eras of the earlier Prophets and in that of Prophet Muhammad (saw), true believers emerged from the Jews, a people recognized for their life-long betrayal and enmity to Islam: true believers can still emerge from them today. Guidance to Islam is determined by Allah and no one can know when, or to whom, or for what reason guidance will be granted.

For this reason, it is our responsibility to be aware of the tricks and traps set by people with bad intentions and to take precautions against them. However, this defensive attitude must not used against one who says that they have chosen Islam, rather we are to embrace the believer who has received guidance, even if they come from among our enemies. We cannot judge what is in their hearts: only Allah can know that. This is one of the most magnificent characteristics of our religion.

Muslims can never be the enemy of a tribe as a whole, even if they are the most ferocious enemies! In such an "enemy" society, the good and the bad, the leaders and those who are just merely living their lives, can never be held as one, even during battle, as this situation is contrary to the essence of Islam: humanity, justice, equity and fairness.

# SAYYIDAH UMMU HABIBAH BINT ABI SUFYAN (r.ah)

## Her Lineage

Ummu Habibah (r.ah) was born 17 years before the start of the Prophet-hood. She was of the Umayya tribe and her father was the chief of the Quraysh, Abu Sufyan Sahr bin Harb.[461] Her mother was Safiyye bint Abi'l-As bin Umayya.

Ummu Habibah's (r.ah) lineage was joined to that of Prophet Muhammad (saw) with their mutual ancestor Abdumenâf.

Ummu Habibah's (r.ah) real name was Ramla. She was called Ummu Habibah (r.ah) after her first daughter, Habibah, was born, in keeping with Arab tradition. Her first marriage was to Prophet Muhammad's (saw) cousin, Ubaydullah bin Jahsh.

## During the Age of Ignorance

Our mother Ummu Habibah was a member of the *hanif* religion before the advent of Islam. Her husband, Ubaydullah bin Jahsh, was one of the four *hanif*s

---

461.    After the Battle of Badr the head of the Meccan city state became Abu Sufyan.

who lived during the lifetime of Prophet Muhammad (saw).[462] However, before the advent of Islam Ubaydullah converted to Christianity.

Ubaydullah bin Jahsh and his wife Ramla (Ummu Habibah), who were among the first people to believe in Islam when Prophet Muhammad (saw) started to call people to the religion, were subjected to torture and oppression in Mecca. It was for this reason that they joined the second group that emigrated from Mecca to Abyssinia so that they could practice their religion freely, and abandoned the land in which they had been born and raised.

**The Ever Increasing Torment of Homesickness in Abyssinia**

Najashi, the king of Abyssinia, welcomed the members of this new religion from Mecca. The convoy decked out with expensive presents from the city, which had been sent out from Mecca to force the return of those Muslim emigrees back to Mecca, returned without them. The Muslims had now found their own peaceful country. They could carry out their worship in safety and comfortably fulfill the orders of the religion. Only one thing saddened them: that Prophet Muhammad (saw) and the other Muslims in Mecca, were still suffering torment.

Abyssinia was a Christian country, and the Muslims that settled there generally lived together, helping and supporting one another. During this time Sayyidah Ummu Habibah's (r.ah) husband, Ubaydullah, who was said to be fond of alcohol[463], apostatised and became Christian again. Ubaydullah asked his wife Ramla (Ummu Habibah) to become Christian: and in fact he exerted pressure on her to convert.[464] However, Ummu Habibah (r.ah) strongly opposed this and resisted her husband. Before much time had passed he divorced her.[465]

---

462. These four *hanifs* were called the *Hunefa-i Erbaa*. The other *hanifs* were Waraqa bin Nawfal, Osman bin Huwayris and Zayd bin Amr. One day, these four people, after watching a grand ceremony held for the idols, said: *"It is clear that our people are (lost) in heresy. They have perverted the true and real religion of their ancestor Abraham. Let us examine our own religion..!"* They then left the country and started to look for the laws of the Hanif religion and Abraham. (Aynur Uraler, Peygamberimizin Hanımı Hz. Ümmü Habibe ve Rivâyetleri, page: 32)
463. Celal Yeniçeri, Ibid., page: 93; Muhammed Hamidullah, Ibid., II, page: 685.
464. Muhammed Hamîdullâh, Ibid., II, page: 685.
465. Ibn-i Hişam, "es-Sîre", I, 238.

Ubaydullah was not content with only attempting to force his wife to convert: he called for all the Companions in Abyssinia to follow him, and he carried out "apostasy propaganda". He was to die in Abyssinia as a Christian.

Ummu Habibah (r.ah), ashamed of the actions of Ubaydullah, her husband and the father of her daughter, tried to distance herself from other people; but this merely increased her feelings of homesickness. She could not reside in peace in Abyssinia and she could not return to Mecca, because her father Abu Sufyan had started a merciless war against Prophet Muhammad (saw), the blessed prophet of the religion in which she believed. Here in Abyssinia her husband had betrayed her and their religion. She no longer knew who she could rely or who she could trust. Moreover, she was a member of one of the leading families of Mecca and for this reason the men felt uncomfortable in offering her marriage. She was in a hopeless situation.

**A Blessed Dream**

One day while Sayyidah Ummu Habibah (r.ah) was withdrawing more and more into mournful seclusion, she found comfort in a dream. In the dream someone called to her: "*Ya, Ummu'l mu'minin!.. (O, Mother of Believers!..)*" She interpreted this dream to mean that she would marry Prophet Muhammad (saw).[466] This dream comforted her somewhat, lightening her sorrow.

Sayyidah Ummu Habibah (r.ah) then tells us: "*While in Abyssinia nothing thrilled me as much as the news that a concubine called Abraha had been brought by Najashi's envoy. Abraha took care of Najashi's clothing and perfumes. She informed me that she wanted to talk to me and I agreed to meet with her.*

*She said: "The Prophet of Allah (saw) has written a letter[467] to the King of Abyssinia saying he wants to marry you." I responded: "May Allah give you*

---

466. Afzalurrahman, Ibid., II, page: 189.
467. At this time there was correspondence between the Prophet (saw) and Najashi. Prophet Muhammad's (saw) letters were sent with an envoy called Amr bin Umayya ad Damri. In one of those letters Prophet Muhammad (saw) called Najashi to Islam, in another he stated that he wanted to marry Ummu Habibah, and in another he asked for a ship to bring the Abbysinian Muslim refugeesback to Mecca. It is understood that Najashi did not refuse any of the suggestions or requests of Prophet Muhammad (saw), including conversion to Islam. (See: Celal Yeniçeri, Ibid, page: 93-94)

*even more blessed tidings!" But in order to be sure that what I had heard was correct I made Abraha repeat what she had said a few times. Finally Abraha said: "The king has asked you to appoint a representative for the marriage." Then I called my cousin Halid bin Said bin As'i and made him my representative. I was so happy that I gave all the jewelry I had on my hands and feet to Abraha".*

## Wedding Presents from the King of Abyssinia

The day after Prophet Muhammad (saw) and Sayyidah Ummu Habibah (r.ah) had been betrothed Najashi ordered Jafer bin Abi Talib to call together all the Muslims in the area. After a short speech, in keeping with the request of the Prophet (saw), Najashi gave Sayyidah Ummu Habibah (r.ah) 400 dinar (4,000 dirhem) as a *mahir* and a necklace.[468]

Prophet Muhammad (saw) gave his wives either four hundred[469] or five hundred dirhem as *mahir*.[470] That Sayyidah Ummu Habibah was given relatively more is due to the fact that Najashi, as a king, wanted to make a gift. Of course, there could be other reasons why Najashi gave such a large *mahir*. For example, Prophet Muhammad (saw) might not have stipulated an amount for the *mahir*, or it could have been because Sayyidah Ummu Habibah's father was one of the administrator's of Mecca, or it could have been because Sayyidah Ummu Habibah (r.ah) was in great need, as she was so far from her home....

After this verbal contract of marriage, Najashi, turned to the Companions, who were about to leave and said: *"It is the sunnah of the Prophet (saw) to give a meal after a marriage"* and offered them a wedding feast.[471]

The next morning Najashi's concubine Abraha knocked on Sayyidah Ummu Habibah's (r.ah) door. She had with her the gifts sent by Najashi's harem. These included aloe, incense and perfumes. After Sayyidah Ummu Habibah (r.ah) had received the gifts she took fifty dinar out of her *mahir* and called the concubine, saying: *"Yesterday I had no money, and I was only able to give you*

---

468. Ibn-i Sa'd, Tabakat, VIII, 99; Abû Dâvud, Nikah, 28/4.
469. Ibn-i Abdilber, Istiâb, IV, 305.
470. Hâkim, Müstedrek, VI, 22.
471. Ibn-i Abdi'l-ber, el-Istiâb, IV, 423.

*two bracelets. Today Allah Almighty has sent these.*" Abraha did not accept the money and handing back the bracelets, she said: "*Our ruler has given me many generous gifts and he warned me not to take anything from you.*"[472]

Each time that Abraha, who had become Muslim, came to see Sayyidah Ummu Habibah she asked her to give her salam to Prophet Muhammad (saw) when she returned to Medina and to inform him that Abraha had now become Muslim.

When Sayyidah Ummu Habibah (r.ah) returned to Medina she told Prophet Muhammad (saw) about the wedding ceremony and showed him the perfumes she had been presented with, Prophet Muhammad (saw) did not forbid her from using these. In addition, she told him of the services performed for her by Najashi's concubine Abraha and relayed her salam to the Prophet (saw): he received this with a smile.[473]

### Not a Man to Be Refused

This marriage, which took place in the 7th year of the hijrah, was a great reward for Sayyidah Ummu Habibah's (r.ah) devotion to Islam.[474] At the same time, this marriage also acted as a means for a weakening in the hostility and enmity towards Prophet Muhammad (saw) by the fierce enemy of Islam, Abu Sufyan. Although Sayyidah Ummu Habibah (r.ah) expected Abu Sufyan to be incensed that she had married Prophet Muhammad (saw) without asking his permission, this is not how things turned out.

When Abu Sufyan learned about this marriage he said: "*He (Prophet Muhammad) is a man who is not to be refused!*" and approved of the marriage.[475]

In addition, this marriage was a means for a warming in the attitude of the Quraysh, and Abu Sufyan himself, to Islam.[476] Thanks to this marriage, the

---

472. Ayşe Abdurrahman, Ibid, s.126-127.
473. İbn-i Sa'd, Tabakât, VIII, 97-98; Hakîm, Müstedrek IV, 20
474. Muhammed Hamidullah, İslâm Peygamberi, II, page: 685.
475. İbn-i Sa'd, Tabakat, VIII, 99; İbn-i Abdi'l-Berr, el-İstiâb, IV, 298.
476. Celal Yeniçeri, Ibid, page: 96; Rıza Savaş, Ibid., I, page: 305; Muhammed Hamidullah, İslâm Peygamberi, II, page: 685.

Quraysh understood that Prophet Muhammad (saw) was not their enemy, that in fact, he only desired what was good for them, and therefore that fighting with a relative was not the correct course to be followed.[477]

Ibn Abbas (ra) tells us that the verse: ***"It may be that Allah will grant love (and friendship) between you and those whom ye (now) hold as enemies…"***[478] was revealed upon the marriage of Prophet Muhammad (saw) and Sayyidah Ummu Habibah and that this marriage was interpreted as being for the purpose of the "friendship" mentioned in the verse.[479]

## The Reasons for and Wisdom of This Marriage

The other reasons for, and the wisdoms that lay behind this marriage are as follows: As indicated above, Sayyidah Ummu Habibah (r.ah) did not hesitate to go to a foreign land due to her devotion and efforts for her religion, leaving behind the land in which she had grown up and everything she had known. However, while far from home, her husband Ubaydullah changed his religion and put pressure on her, even treating her cruelly, so that she would change her religion. She withstood all these difficulties and did not allow herself or her child to be dragged into her husband's depravity. Because of this, she even was divorced by her husband and left on her own. Her noble and brave behavior increased her value and worth among the Muslims. In order to reward this religious constancy and fidelity Prophet Muhammad (saw) married her and took her under his patronage. Thus, Sayyidah Ummu Habibah (r.ah) was an example to Muslims of how a religious life requires one to be resilient and constant in the face of severe trials.

On the other hand, Prophet Muhammad's (saw) marriage with Sayyidah Ummu Habibah (r.ah) not only was a reward for her patience and efforts in the name of the religion, but also contains a separate significance from the perspective of *fiqh*: the marriage between the Prophet (saw) and Sayyidah Ummu Habibah (r.ah) was a "marriage by proxy" and the legitimacy of such

---

477.  Afzalurrahman, Ibid., II, page: 189.
478.  Surah al-Mumtahine, 60: 7.
479.  Ibn-i Sa'd, Tabakat, VIII, 99; Aynur Uraler, Ibid, page: 54; Rıza Savaş, Ibid., I, 305.

a practice is demonstrated here. The sunnah, a source of Islamic law, was thus creating a precedent.

## Return to Medina

While all this was happening in Abyssinia, Prophet Muhammad (saw) had left with the Companions for Medina, and achieved great comfort in completing the building of a mosque there. At this point in time Prophet Muhammad (saw) wrote a letter to Najashi to inform him of the condition of the Muslims and told him to send the Companions who were living in Abyssinia to him.

Najashi sent the Muslims in two ships. During this journey Sayyidah Ummu Habibah (r.ah) was accompanied by Shurahbil bin Hasana. On the day that Sayyidah Ummu Habibah (r.ah) and the Muslims reached Medina Prophet Muhammad (saw) was returning from the conquest of Haybar. For this reason Prophet Muhammad (saw) was doubly pleased on that day: by both the arrival of the Muslim and the conquest of Haybar.[480]

Prophet Muhammad (saw) had a room prepared for Sayyidah Ummu Habibah (r.ah); this was the room furthest from the mosque.

On the order of Prophet Muhammad (saw), Bilal Habashi took Sayyidah Ummu Habibah (r.ah) to her room. Sayyidah Ummu Habibah (r.ah) found a broom in her new home and dividing up the work with her slave, she swept out the room, then laid down a cloth made from camelhair. In the evening, when Prophet Muhammad (saw) came to the room he was aware of a lovely scent and after seeing the floor covering said: *"Qurayshi women are ones who decorate everything and make a home, they are not like the Bedouins or Arabs."* These words were in appreciation of Sayyidah Ummu Habibah's (r.ah) cleanliness and skill at setting up the home.[481]

## My Beloved!..

Sayyidah Ummu Habibah's (r.ah) affection for Prophet Muhammad (saw)

---

480.   Celal Yeniçeri, Ibid., page: 97.
481.   Aynur Uraler, Ibid., page: 53.

was very great; in fact, there is an hadith that suggests that she used the term "beloved" when talking about him.[482]

This situation should be considered to be normal as she was a lady who had undergone great trials for Islam. Her love and affection for the Prophet of Islam (saw) was not just for his person, but for any object that belonged to him. An event that occurred in Islamic history presents a good example of this.

The Hudaibiya Treaty was a ten-year treaty that the polytheists of Mecca had contracted with the Muslims. However, this treaty did not put an end to the hatred and resentment of the polytheists towards the Muslims. They were merely looking for an opportunity to cause harm to them. Finally, in contravention of the articles of the treaty, the polytheists incited the Bani Bakir tribe, who were affiliated with them against the Huzaa tribe, and they attacked them. In fact, some of them went so far as to commit (foul) murder.

The Huzaa tribe, with which the Prophet of Allah (saw) was affiliated, were Muslims. They were praying when they were attacked. In a great massacre they were martyred, some whilst in *sajda*, some in *ruku* and others while in *qiyam*… Amr bin Salim, who managed to escape with his life from this massacre, told the Prophet (saw) about this event, and as he was talking Prophet Muhammad's (saw) eyes filled with tears. The tear drops, like pearls, wet his rose-like cheeks. The Prophet (saw) was very saddened by this event and the Prophet (saw) said to Amr in consolation *"O Amr, You are helped."*

The Holy Prophet (saw) immediately consulted with the leading Companions and the decision made was to attack and conquer Mecca. However, this was not to be made public, so that secret preparations were carried out in Medina and the neighboring tribes. At the same time, news was sent to Mecca that the murderers should pay blood money to the Huzaas or forego the patronage of the Bani Bakir tribe, and if neither of these offers were accepted the Hudaybiya Treaty would be considered null and void. The cruel polytheists, whose eyes were full of vengeance and thirst for blood, accepted the third of these proposals made by Prophet Muhammad (saw): That is they decided to nullify the agreement. This was nothing less than an invitation to the Muslims to attack Mecca.

---

482.   Nesâî, Kıyâmu'l-Leyl, 67/10, ayrıca bkz. Aynur Uraler, Ibid., page: 65.

Even if the polytheists had come to their senses, it was too late: the treaty had been nullified by both sides. In order to rectify the problem, the chief of the Quraysh, Abu Sufyan, set out for Medina, desperate and without hope. He tried to meet with a number of people, including Prophet Muhammad (saw), Abu Bakr (ra) and Umar (ra). However, none of them agreed to meet with him. He was to return empty-handed to Mecca. As a last attempt, he decided to visit his daughter, Sayyidah Ummu Habibah (r.ah), who was married to Prophet Muhammad (saw).

As her father was about to sit down, Sayyidah Ummu Habibah (r.ah) withdrew a floor cushion from under him, even though he had come so far to visit her in her house. Abu Sufyan was surprised and asked: *"My dear, is the cushion not worthy of me, or am I not worthy of the cushion?"*

Sayyidah Ummu Habibah (r.ah), one who was devoted to Prophet Muhammad (saw), answered: *"This cushion belongs to Prophet Muhammad (saw). A filthy infidel like you could never be worthy of sitting on it!.."*

Abu Sufyan was shocked when he heard this reply: *"My dear, you have become strange since you have left us!.."* he said.[483]

However, Sayyidah Ummu Habibah said: *"No, Allah has honored me with Islam…"* thus reminding her father that belief is more sublime than any other value.[484]

This is a beautiful example of what a Muslim must do when they are fully aware of their religion. No matter what the relationship is, Muslims should not be with relatives who are opposed to Islam just because they are connected by blood.

Faced by such an attitude on the part of all the Companions, led by Prophet Muhammad (saw), Abu Sufyan had no choice but to return to Mecca. He was unable to hide his shock when telling the residents of Mecca, who had gathered around him, that a peace was not possible: *"I have never met a tribe this devoted, even to their ruler."*

---

483.   Muhammed Hamidullah, İslâm Peygamberi, II, page: 685-686.
484.   Afzalurrahman, Ibid., II, page: 189.

## The Character of Sayyidah Ummu Habibah (r.ah)

After becoming Muslim, Sayyidah Ummu Habibah (r.ah), one of the first people in polytheist Mecca to accept Islam[485] (in other words, a *sabikun*), was subjected to the oppression inflicted by her father Abu Sufyan and the other unbelievers in the name of the religion.[486] At that time, despite being pregnant, she displayed great bravery and resolution by emigrating to Abyssinia.

She was an active member of the community in Abyssinia. Even when her husband apostatised and became Christian, Sayyidah Ummu Habibah (r.ah), who had a strong belief, was not affected: she remained a devout Muslim. She took on the challenge of remaining in Abyssinia as a single mother and did not think of returning to Mecca, where her father Abu Sufyan was chief.

In general, the **Ummuhatu'l Muminin** (Mothers of Believers), that is the Prophet's wives, were all women who were devout and who possessed *taqwa*: and Sayyidah Ummu Habibah (r.ah) was no exception.[487] An intelligent, clever and articulate woman, Sayyidah Ummu Habibah (r.ah) takes her place among the Companions as one who gave *fatwa* on one or two matters.[488]

Sayyidah Ummu Habibah (r.ah) is known as someone who wished for the good and was charitable toward others. In this aspect, she wished fervently, from her heart, that other women would also be honored by becoming the wife of Prophet Muhammad (saw), even though this would mean that she would have to share her husband.

A hadith reported by Umma Habibah (r.ah), the daughter of Abu Sufyan, reads as follows: "*Once I said: 'O Prophet! Marry my sister, the daughter of Abu Sufyan!..' The Prophet (saw) said: 'How strange, you (are not jealous and) wish for this?' I replied: 'Yes, I desire this, because I am afraid of sharing you. I would like that my sister to be my partner in this!' In response to this Prophet Muhammad (saw) said: 'You must understand that your sister is not halal for me!' I then said: 'Fine, but I have heard that you want to marry the daughter of Abu Salama.' Prophet Muhammad (saw) said: 'The daughter of Ummu Salama*

---

485. Ibn-i Hacer, Tezhib, XII, 419.
486. Aynur Uraler, Ibid., page: 63.
487. Aynur Uraler, Ibid., page: 65.
488. Aynur Uraler, Ibid., page: 66.

*(r.ah)?' I said yes. Then the Prophet (saw) said: 'The daughter of Ummu Salama (Zainab) is my step-daughter, who grew up as my ward and under my hand. Marrying her is haram for me. Even if this were not the case, she would not be halal for me because she is the daughter of my suckling brother. Suwayba nursed both me and Abu Salama.' He then added: 'Do not offer me any of your daughters or sisters again!'"*[489]

When studying the above example, we must remember that Sayyidah Ummu Habibah (r.ah) was a person renowned for her fidelity in religion and for remaining in Abyssinia for a long time. It was not known at the time of the above hadith that two sisters could not marry the same man, and it is perhaps for this reason that she made such an offer.

Sayyidah Ummu Habibah (r.ah) reported 65 hadiths from Prophet Muhammad (saw), though it is possible that this number is higher.[490] When she reported hadiths she would make ablution and would request the person who was listening to also have ablution.

Sayyidah Ummu Habibah (r.ah) was the midwife at the birth of Dawood bin Asim bin Urwe[491], who was later to marry her daughter. From this we can deduce the possibility that she acted as midwife for other people as well. Also, according to a hadith reported by Ibn Asakir, Prophet Muhammad (saw) reported that Sayyidah Ummu Habibah (r.ah) was blessed with Paradise.[492]

Sayyidah Ummu Habibah (r.ah) remained married to Prophet Muhammad (saw) for four years, and she continued to live with asceticism and *taqwa* for thirty-four years after his death. Sayyidah Ummu Habibah (r.ah), like the other wives of the Prophet (saw), was shown great respect and was greatly valued by the other Muslims, and it was for this reason that during the time when her brother Muawiya (ra) was caliph he was referred to as the *'uncle of believers'*.[493]

Sayyidah Ummu Habibah (r.ah) did not participate in the instigation that arose among Muslims after the death of Prophet Muhammad (saw). However,

---

489.    Bukhârî, Nikâh, 20; Muslim, Reda', 4.
490.    Aynur Uraler, Ibid., 75-76.
491.    Abû Dâvûd, Janâiz, 32; Aynur Uraler, Ibid., page: 66.
492.    Aynur Uraler, Ibid., page: 67.
493.    Zehebî, Siyer, II, 222; Aynur Uraler, Ibid., page: 57.

when her cousin Uthman's house was attacked, she went there; and a man in the house pulled back her headscarf and not recognising her, started to list her physical attributes. In response to this disgusting behavior Sayyidah Ummu Habibah (r.ah) said: *"What is going on here! May Allah smite your hand – leave the area of mahram."* Another person there cut off the right hand of the person who had pulled off her scarf. The man whose either way, had been cut off started to flee, holding on to his gown with his left hand (or his mouth); however, his genital area was exposed.[494]

Sayyidah Ummu Habibah (r.ah) died when she was seventy years old, in the 44th year of the *hijrah*,[495] during the reign of her brother Muawiya (ra). May Allah be pleased with her.

**Lessons to be Learned From the Life of Sayyidah Ummu Habibah (r.ah)**

1- Sayyidah Ummu Habibah (r.ah) was a member of one of the leading families of Mecca. She could have lived a life of nobility, wealth, luxury and comfort. However, she listened to her heart and the instant she found out about Islam she became a follower. She was a living example of the hadith uttered by Prophet Muhammad (saw): *"The real life is the life of the Hereafter."*

2- She underwent much torment and oppression because of her enthusiasm for her faith, but the troubles she experienced did not force her back to her former life from the Age of Ignorance. She was able to protect her beliefs and even to abandon the country in which she was born and grew up to go to Abyssinia, where she could practice her faith in safety. The fact that during this emigration she was pregnant and that she was going to a country which was unfamiliar to her shows us how sincere and devoted Sayyidah Ummu Habibah (r.ah) was to the religion. She underwent great difficulties and trouble to protect her faith and to practice her religion. She is a great example for those who, when faced by the smallest trial, cry out: "There is no way out," "I can't practice my religion", "my husband/wife, my job prevents me from practicing my religion…"

---

494. Ibn-i Asâkir, Tarih, VI, 91; narrated by Aynur Uraler, Ibid., page: 58.
495. Afzalurrahman, Ibid., II, page: 190; Celal Yeniçeri, Ibid., page: 97.
Muhammed Hamidullah, stated date of death as 59 AH. (İslâm Peygamberi, II, sh: 686)

3- Her husband changed his religion and became Christian, but this did not turn her from Islam. Even though she was alone, she did not deviate from the correct path. She took her child under her wing and set up ramparts against her husband's propaganda. All of this behavior demonstrates her courage, intelligence, bravery, obedience, submission and resolution. She withstood the troubles of her life without giving way; in short, she is an example of one who chose the Hereafter rather than this world.

4- The torment that she underwent for the religion left echoes in the hearts of the other Muslims and Prophet Muhammad (saw), and she was honored by becoming a member of the Prophet's family and one of the "Mothers of Believers". This shows that torments endured for the sake of Allah do not go unnoticed, and that sooner or later they are the means for blessings.

5- After marrying Prophet Muhammad (saw) and because she preferred the brotherhood of Islam over her own family ties, she did not allow her own father, Abu Sufyan, who was not yet Muslim, to sit on the cushion of Prophet Muhammad (saw). This action alone is a perfect example of how deeply rooted belief was in her heart, and demonstrates how one should love for the sake of Allah, and how one should dislike for His sake as well.

6- Sayyidah Ummu Habibah (r.ah) married Prophet Muhammad (saw) and came to Medina, and he allocated her a room there. Sayyidah Ummu Habibah (r.ah) cleaned this room, decorated it and enhanced it with lovely fragrances. Prophet Muhammad (saw) praised her for these actions. This event tells us that a Muslim woman should always try to fulfill the order "ahsinû" to make every thing as beautiful or good as possible. This means that, our houses, without falling into luxury or waste, should be as beautiful as possible, and we should strive to be as clean as possible, to care for our children as well as possible and to carry out our duties as well as possible.

7- This blessed mother was very intelligent, very articulate and was one of the Companions who had enough knowledge to give fatwas, showing the way for all women believers in knowledge, *taqwa* and state.

May Allah bless us with being her neighbour in Paradise. Amen.

# SAYYIDAH MAYMUNAH BINT HARITH (r.ah)

## The Last Wife of Prophet Muhammad (saw)

*"Maymunah has left this world... She had more taqwa than anyone. She feared Allah, obeyed his orders and watched over relatives and close one."*[496]

Sayyidah Â'ishah (r.ah)

### *Qadha* Umrah

According to the Hudaybiyah, the believers were not to enter Mecca that year, but they would be able to one year later. Now it was time for that Umrah, and when the month of Dhul Qiddah of the seventh year of the Hijrah arrived Prophet Muhammad (saw) told all of those who had joined in the Hudaybiyah Campaign to prepare for Umrah.

Prophet Muhammad (saw) set out with 2000 Companions from Medina. During the journey they stopped at Abwa. Prophet Muhammad (saw) requested permission from Allah to visit his mother's grave. During the visit he straightened out the grave with his hands and sadly wept. The Muslims who saw him cry were unable to refrain from crying too. Later, they asked him why he had wept like that, and he replied: *"I wept because I remembered the mercy and*

---

496.   Ibn-i Sa'd, et-Tabakat, VIII, 138; Ibn-i Hacer, el-Isâbe, IV, 399.

*tenderness my mother showed to me."*[497]

In keeping with the Hudaybiyah treaty the polytheists left Mecca for three days, leaving it entirely to the believers. They went up to the mountains to watch with curiosity what the Muslims would do. The hearts of the believers, seeing the Ka'bah after a long time, started to utter the *talbiya (Laybbayk Allahumma...)* in unison with great enthusiasm.

Ibn Abbas (ra) tells us that when Prophet Muhammad (saw) was met by the small children of the Muttalib tribe he took one of them in front of him and one behind on his mount.[498]

In order to show the hypocrites that rumors that the Muslims had fallen victim to the Medina fever were not true, Prophet Muhammad (saw) ordered the Muslims to walk quickly and proudly.[499]

*"May Allah have mercy on the person who shows themselves to the Quraysh as strong and powerful!"*[500]

The Muslims, despite their exhaustion from having walked about four hundred kilometers from Mecca to Medina in the conditions of that time to visit the Ka'bah, carried out their Umrah with solemnity and grandeur in keeping with Prophet Muhammad's (saw) instructions. In fact, in the first three *shawt* of the tawaf, and in the *sa'y* between where there are two green poles today, they ran in an impressive manner.

On the other side, the polytheists were observing the Muslims from the hills. If they had seen any indication of exhaustion or laxity, they would have thought different things, but they could not help but be amazed by the liveliness and energy that they saw: *"Who said that these had been weakened by fever? They are healthier and more alive than we are!"* they said.[501]

The magnificent sight of the Muslims started to have an effect upon the

---

497.   Ibn-i Sa'd, I, 116-117.
498.   Bukhârî, Umre, 13; Libâs, 99.
499.   Bukhârî, Hac, 55; Muslim, Hajj, 240; Ahmad, I, 305-306.
500.   Ibn-i Hişâm, III, 424-425.
501.   Muslim, Hajj, 240.

Meccans, and in fact, the heart of one of the noble women of Mecca began to beat with affection for Prophet Muhammad (saw).

## The Believing Sisters

This woman was Berra, the daughter of Harith, and she was one of four sisters who were known as *"the believing sisters"*.

The second of these four sisters was the wife of the Prophet's uncle Abbas (ra), and she was Ummu'l Fadl Lubaba, the first woman to believe in Islam after Sayyidah Khadîjah (r.ah). Ummu'l Fadl, Berra's older sister, was one of the most zealous defenders and supporters of Islam. She was the only woman to beat Abu Lahab, the enemy of Islam. This event happened as follows:

One day as Abu Lahab was going to the house of his brother Abbas he picked up Abu Rafi, a slave who had accepted Islam at that time, and threw him to the ground. Swooping down on him he started to beat the slave for being a Muslim. Ummu'l Fadl, seeing this, picked up a thick stick and attacked Abu Lahab with it, saying: *"So you beat him because his master isn't around?"* hitting Abu Lahab on the head. A defeated Abu Lahab left, and a week later he became seriously ill and died.

Berra also had two half-sisters from her mother, the first was the wife of Jafar bin Abi Talib, Asma bint Umays, and the other was Salma bint Umays who was the wife of Hamza bin Abdulmuttalib, who fell at Uhud.

## Berra's Family

Her full name was name was Berra bint Harith bin Hathn al Hilaliyya, and she was born in Mecca around 590.[502] Her mother was Hind (Hawla) bint Hawf. Berra married Mas'ud bin Amr as-Sakafi some time before the advent of Islam, and after separating from him married Abu Ruhm bin Abduluzza.[503] After her husband had died she told her sister Ummu'l Fadl that she wanted to marry Prophet Muhammad (saw). Her sister told her husband, Abbas about this situation giving him the authority to marry Berra to the Prophet (saw).

---

502.   M. Yaşar Kandemir, "Maymûna", DIA, XXIX, 506.
503.   DIA, the article of "Maymûna".

### From Berra to Maymunah

Abbas did not hesitate but immediately went to the Prophet (saw), who was his nephew. He spoke of Berra, who was 36 years old at that time[504], and suggested that they marry[505]. Prophet Muhammad (saw) accepted this offer and appointed Jafar, his cousin and Berra's brother-in-law, to go ask for her hand.

When our Mother Berra learned that Prophet Muhammad (saw) wanted to marry her she dedicated herself to him. Upon this, the 50th verse of Surah Ahzab was revealed.[506] The translation of this verse is as follows:

*O Prophet (saw)! We have made lawful to thee thy wives to whom thou hast paid their dowers; and those whom thy right hand possesses out of the prisoners of war whom Allah has assigned to thee; and daughters of thy paternal uncles and aunts, and daughters of thy maternal uncles and aunts, who migrated (from Mecca) with thee; and any believing woman who dedicates her soul to the Prophet (saw) if the Prophet (saw) wishes to wed her;- this only for thee, and not for the Believers (at large); We know what We have appointed for them as to their wives and the captives whom their right hands possess;- in order that there should be no difficulty for thee. And Allah is Oft- Forgiving, Most Merciful.*

The phrase in the verse: *"who dedicates her soul to the Prophet (saw)"* is reported to have been used to refer to Berra.[507] There is the following report about this "dedication":

When the marriage proposal from Prophet Muhammad (saw), who had not been to Mecca for 7 years, reached Berra via an envoy she was riding a camel. When the envoy came to her she said with great joy and excitement: "Let this camel and she who is on it be the Prophet's!"[508]

The time-period determined for the Hudaybiyah Treaty was drawing to a close. Prophet Muhammad (saw) requested, from the Meccans, that he be allowed to remain in Mecca until his marriage with Berra was completed. He thought that with this he could gain time to soften the hearts of the polytheists.

---

504. Celal Yeniçeri, Ibid., page: 103; Muhammed Hamidullah, İslâm Peygamberi, II, page: 687.
505. Afzalurrahman, Ibid., II, page: 193.
506. DIA, the article of "Maymûna".
507. Celal Yeniçeri, Ibid., page: 105.
508. Afzalurrahman, Ibid., II, page: 193.

However the Quraysh sent two people to the Prophet (saw) to inform him that the time period was up and that they wanted him to leave the city as soon as possible. To keep his promise the Prophet (saw) complied with the request of the Meccans and gave the order to the Muslims to set out. His servant Abu Rafi was appointed to be Berra's companion, and they remained in Mecca, but were later due to catch up with the rest. The Muslims left the city.

Berra and her companion Abu Rafi caught up with the Muslim caravan in Sarif, near Tan. Here Prophet Muhammad (saw) and Berra were married. He gave her 500 *dirhem* as *mahr* (dowry).[509] Prophet Muhammad (saw) had been married to Berra while still wearing *ihram*, but they had their wedding night after he had removed the *ihram* in Sarif.[510] Thus the Prophet (saw) carried out his last marriage in the seventh year of the Hijrah in the month of Shawwal.

As he was able to enter Mecca without fear and in safety for the first time in seven years with Berra, he gave her the name *Maymunah*, meaning "good fortune."[511] Prophet Muhammad (saw) gave her the name Maymunah instead of the name Berra, meaning "perfect, blessed woman" as he did not approve of people giving names that were boastful of their good character.[512]

Sayyidah Maymunah (r.ah) entered the house of Prophet Muhammad (saw) in peace. She had the joy of being blessed by Allah with becoming Muslim and the honor of being the wife of Prophet Muhammad (saw), and she desired nothing else in the world.

## The Wisdom of This Marriage

One of the greatest reasons for this marriage was to seal the friendship with the tribe of Amir bin Sa'saa, because this tribe, as we stated when discussing Sayyidah Zainab bint Huzayma, was a strong and influential tribe, and an unintentional but unpleasant event had damaged the relationship between them. Sayyidah Maymunah's step-sister Sayyidah Zainab bint Huzayma had died a

---

509.   DIA, the aricle of "Maymûna".
510.   Afzalurrahman, Ibid., II, page: 194.
511.   See: Ibn-i Hisham, Sîre III, 202-203; Ibn-i Kesîr, el-Bidâye, IV, 229-230.
512.   DIA, the article of "Meymûne"

few months after being married to Prophet Muhammad (saw), thus preventing him from attaining the outcome he had hoped to by that marriage. However, by marrying another from the same tribe as Sayyidah Zainab, it did not take long for him to attain the news that he had hoped to, because the members of the tribe of Amir bin Sa'saa began to visit the Prophet (saw) to talk to him, and later all the people of the tribe accepted Islam.

Muhammed Hamidullah reports the following two reasons as being among those that caused Prophet Muhammad (saw) to marry Sayyidah Maymunah:

1-Sayyidah Maymunah had eight sisters, all of whom were married to the leaders of a number of different tribes.

2-The Prophet (saw) wanted to achieve conciliation and understanding between Mecca and Medina.[513] The atmosphere of peace and tranquility that was provided by the Hudaybiyah Treaty provided the perfect opportunity for this.

 In fact, the original plan was to hold the wedding in Mecca and to invite all the residents of the city, but the Meccans wanted the city emptied of the Medinans as the period set out in the treaty had run out, and they refused the hand held out in peace by the Prophet (saw).[514]

It is very clear that all the marriages that we have studied up to now were carried out in pursuance of an important agenda in the name of Islam by Prophet Muhammad (saw). He was trying to make the tribes, families and clans, which had been divided, one united tribe with Islam, to form a nucleus ummah. When the development of historical events is examined it can be seen that this was realised finally, although it was not easy.[515]

## Sayyidah Maymunah's House

Abdullah bin Abbas would sleep at Sayyidah Maymunah's house to see how the Prophet (saw) worshipped during the night, asking his aunt to wake

---


513.    Muhammed Hamidullah, İslâm Peygamberi, II page: 687.
514.    Celal Yeniçeri, Ibid., page: 102; Afzalurrahman, Ibid., II, page: 194.
515.    Celal Yeniçeri, Ibid., page: 103-104.

him when the Prophet woke, and he reported on this matter.[516]

According to the *sahih* hadith sources, the illness that led to Prophet Muhammad's (saw) death first started in Sayyidah Maymunah's house. The hadith that are found in Muslim's Sahih on this matter, as reported by Sayyidah Â'ishah, is as follows:

Sayyidah Â'ishah (r.ah) reported: *"The Prophet (saw) first became ill in the house of Maymunah. Then he asked his wives for permission to be cared for in my house. They gave permission. He placed one hand on Fadl bin Abbas, the other on another man (Ali). They left, the Prophet's feet dragging."*[517]

## The Final Days

After Prophet Muhammad (saw) died, Sayyidah Maymunah always remembered the blessed day she had met him and the blessings in Serif where she had had the honour of being married to him. She wanted to be buried in the place where this had occurred, and that did happen. When Sayyidah Maymunah died she was buried there, and her funeral prayer was led by her nephew Abdullah bin Abbas.[518] There are different reports about the date of her death, but it was probably before[519] the 58th year of the Hijrah, in the 51st year of the Hijrah[520] that she met her Lord.

Ibn Jurayj reports from Ata that *"I was with Ibn Abbas at the funeral of Prophet Muhammad's (saw) wife Sayyidah Maymunah in Sarif. Ibn Abbas said: 'This woman was the wife of Allah's Prophet (saw). Do not shake or rattle the coffin. Hold her well'."*

Sayyidah Maymunah reported 76 hadith of the Prophet (saw). Of these seven are both in Buhârî and Muslim, one appears only in Buhârî, five are only in Muslim, 60 in Ahmed bin Hanbel's *"Musnad"*[521], and the number in *Kutub-i Sitte* is forty-six.

---

516. See: Müslim, Musâfirûn, 181, 182, 185-195 DIA, the article of "Meymûne".
517. Muslim, Salât, 21.
518. DIA, the article of "Meymûne".
519. DIA, the article of "Meymûne".
520. Muhammed Hamidullah, İslâm Peygamberi, II, 688.
521. DIA, the article of "Meymûne".

Let us end with one of the hadith reported by her:

Sayyidah Maymunah would take loans from some people. One time the amount was quite large and people asked her: *"O mother of believers! What is the assurance you have when you take a loan. How will you repay it?"* Sayyidah Maymunah answered Prophet Muhammad (saw) with the following hadith: *"There is no servant who has the intention to repay a debt who is not assisted by Allah."*[522]

May Allah be pleased with her.

---

522.    Bukhârî ve Muslim'den naklen Afzalurrahman, Ibid., II, 194.

# ṢAYYIDAH MARIYA FROM EGYPT (r.ah)

## The Mother of Ibrahim, the Son of Prophet Muhammad (saw)

### A Life Begun in Egypt

Mariya (r.ah) was born in Upper Egypt, in the village of Hifn, on the eastern bank of the Nile River. The first part of her life was spent in this village with her sister Sirin. Her father was an Egyptian and her mother was an Orthodox Christian.[523]

When she was quite young she and her sister were brought to the palace of Juraij bin Mina al-Kipti, the *Muqawqis* of Egypt.[524] From that time on her life was spent in the palace.

At this point in time, the news that a prophet had emerged on the Arabian Peninsula came to the Egyptian palace. Before long this same Prophet sent a letter to Juraij bin Mina, and to the Byzantine governor of Alexandria via an envoy.[525]

---

523. Muhammad Hamidullah, having collected different reports about the lineage of Mariya, says the following: "It is likely that her father was an Iranian who married a Christian Greek woman when Egypt was invaded by the Iranians."
524. *Muqawqis* was a title like "sultan" or "king" that the rulers of Egypt called themselves.
525. Aynur Uraler, DIA, the article of "Mariye", XXVIII, 63.

## The Letter of the Prophet of Allah (saw)

Hatib bin Abi Beltaa, who was received into the presence of the *muqawqis*, presented the letter of Prophet Muhammad (saw) to the ruler. The letter was opened with great curiosity. The text of Prophet Muhammad's (saw) letter read as follows:

*"From the servant and Prophet of Allah, Muhammad, to the great Muqawqis of the Coptic nation..!*

*May greetings be upon those who find guidance and the correct way!*

*I invite you to Islam. Come to Islam and find peace and may Allah reward you twofold!*

*If you do not accept my invitation, but avoid it, all the sins of the Coptic people will be on your head.*

***Say: "O People of the Book! come to common terms as between us and you: That we worship none but Allah; that we associate no partners with him; that we erect not, from among ourselves, Lords and patrons other than Allah." If then they turn back, say ye: "Bear witness that we** (at least) **are Muslims** (bowing to Allah's Will)."*[526]

After Hatib bin Abi Beltaa had read the letter to the *Muqawqis* the latter said: *"You have been sent by one who has wisdom and you are one with wisdom"* and asked him to tell him about the Prophet (saw). He asked a number of questions, one of which was: *"If he is truly a prophet, then why does he not destroy his enemies with a curse?"*

Hatib answered as follows: *"Jesus was a prophet, but he suffered great torment and strife because his own tribe did not acknowledge him. Why did he not destroy them with a curse? Our invitation to the Qur'ân is like his invitation to the Jews to the Bible."*

After this conversation the *muqawqis* said: *"I knew that another prophet was to come. But I thought he would come from Damascus. The Copts... they*

---

526.  Surah Âl-i İmrân, 3: 64.

*will not listen to me on the matter of obeying the Prophet (saw)!..*" He placed the letter from Prophet Muhammad (saw) in an ivory box and gave it to a *jariya* (slave woman).

The *Muqawqis*, who had treated both the envoy and letter of the Prophet (saw) with respect, did not become Muslim in fear that he would lose his throne. Later, he called a scribe and wrote the following answer: "*I have read the text of your letter and I understand to what you are inviting me. I knew that another prophet would appear, but I thought that he would come from Damascus. I have honored your envoy. I send as a present to you two jariya which are respected among the Egyptian people, robes and a horse. My greetings to you...*"

The *Muqawqis* gave the letter to Hatib. Saying that the Egyptians were very devoted to their religion, and he presented the envoy with gifts and food, recommending that he keep what had happened in the palace secret from the other Egyptians.

While seeing off Hatib, he gave him Mariya (r.ah) and her sister Sirin to take to Prophet Muhammad (saw), and according to one report there were also two more *jariya*. He also gave him a slave called Mabur,[527] one thousand gold coins, a robe made from the soft textiles of Egypt, a horse and saddle, a mule[528], the famous honey *banha,* and a variety of incense.[529]


**Islam and the Journey to the Land of Islam**

The two sisters, as they were leaving their homeland bid a sorrowful fare-well, and with tears in their eyes took a last long look at the Nile and the land of their childhood, until it became lost to view.

In order to make them forget their sorrow, Hatib bin Abi Baltaa began with much enthusiasm to describe the new land they were going to, and the Prophet of Allah (saw). The two young girls were entranced by his descriptions of the religion and its lofty Prophet. Their hearts turned towards Islam and Allah's Prophet

---

527.   Celal Yeniçeri, Ibid., page: 118.
528.   This was the famous animal that carried Prophet Muhammad (saw), known as "Duldul".
529.   Ibn-i Abdi'l-Berr, el-Istiâb, IV, 397; Ibn-i Hacer, el-Isâbe, IV, 391; DIA, the article of "Mariye".

(saw). With a small invitation Hatib brought the two young sisters to belief on the road.[530] But the eunuch Mabur still clung to his former belief. However, later, this slave became Muslim in the presence of Prophet Muhammad (saw).

After a long journey this small caravan arrived in Medina, and this was in the seventh year of the Hijrah. Prophet Muhammad (saw) came out to meet them. He was given the letter and gifts from the *Muqawqis*. The Prophet (saw) accepted Mariya (r.ah) and was happy with her, and gave her sister Sirin to the poet Hassan bin Sabit (ra).[531]

After they had settled in Medina, this slave would often be in and out of Sayyidah Mariya's room, as he had of old, carrying wood for her. The hypocrites, not understanding the condition of this slave, started to spread gossip about him. The tricks of the hypocrites were once again foiled when it was understood that he was a eunuch, and there were no rumors left to be spread.

News of the young and beautiful *jariya* who came as a present from the land of the Nile and who was staying in the house of Harith bin Numan (ra), which was close to the masjid, reached the wives of Prophet Muhammad (saw).

Sayyidah Â'ishah (r.ah) did not give much importance to Sayyidah Mariya (r.ah) at first. However, later when she learned that Prophet Muhammad (saw) went to visit the young Egyptian *jariya* often and spend time there, she tried to find out more about her.

Sayyidah Â'ishah (r.ah) tells us of her feelings at that time as follows: "I was more jealous of Sayyidah Mariya than of any other woman. She was very beautiful, with a white skin and curly hair and she was very attractive."[532]

It was for this reason that Prophet Muhammad (saw) placed Sayyidah Mariya in one of the upper regions of Medina called Aliya.[533] The house in which she was placed was to become known as "Ibrahim's Mashraba" (High Villa), in connection of her being Ummu Ibrahim (mother of Ibrahim).[534]

---

530. DIA, the article of "Mariye".
531. DIA, the article of "Mariye".
532. Ayşe Abdurrahman, page: 139; narrated by Ziya Kazıcı, Ibid., page: 318.
533. DIA, the article of "Mariye".
534. Ibn-i Sa'd, et-Tabakât, VIII, 212; Ibn-i Hajar, el-Isabe, IV, 391.

## Being with Prophet Muhammad (saw)

Sayyidah Mariya was with Prophet Muhammad (saw) for a year. She was very happy in his presence because Prophet Muhammad (saw) did not treat her any differently from his other wives, but rather as if she was a free woman.

All her hopes and thoughts, her existence and her ego had melted when fate brought her face to face with this man of such lofty personality. From this aspect, Allah's Prophet (saw) was not only her master and owner, he was her family and her nation. Her only desire was to win his love and approval.

Our Mother Sayyidah Mariya (r.ah) carried the enchantment of the Nile, the fragrance with which the Nile was surrounded, and the intelligence of her ancestors. Whenever Prophet Muhammad (saw) came to her he would talk to her, listen to her, acting as her friend and confidante to help lessen the pain of her homesickness.

## To Be Like Hagar

Sayyidah Mariya (r.ah) resembled Hagar in her personality and in her fate; indeed, both came from Egypt. Both were presented to a prophet, and it was for this reason Sayyidah Mariya (r.ah) never tired of hearing the story of Hagar, the *jariya* of Prophet Abraham (as). Prophet Muhammad (saw) often told her the story about how Abraham (as) married Hagar, and for her each time was just like the first time.[535]

The land in which Sayyidah Mariya (r.ah) was now living was the land in which Prophet Abraham, Hagar and Ismail had lived. Her master, Prophet Muhammad (saw) was a descendant of the master of Hagar, Prophet Abraham (as).

---

535.   As we know, Abraham (as) had had no children with Sarah and they were both growing older. Sarah set her slave Hagar free and married her to Abraham (as). From this union Ismail was born and Prophet Muhammad (saw) was a descendant of Ismail. Sarah thought that the light of Muhammad (saw) would emanate from her and she was greatly saddened by the birth of Ismail; she told Abraham to take Hagar to live somewhere else. Abraham (as) took Hagar and her son Ismail, on the order of Allah, to the deserted location which was Mecca. They stayed there in that barren desert; then due to the patience and submission shown by Hagar and Ismail, drinking water (zam zam) flowed out from the middle of the desert and people (the Jurhumi) arrived, with whom they could form a society.

Would she be able to give Prophet Muhammad (saw) a child? If only!.. This did not seem very likely, or more truthfully, almost impossible. After the death of Sayyidah Khadîjah (r.ah), Prophet Muhammad (saw) had married ten women. Some were young and healthy, and some had children from earlier marriages, but not one of these women had borne Prophet Muhammad (saw) a child. And the Prophet (saw) was now nearly 60 years old.

But Sayyidah Mariya (r.ah) was not without hope. After being with the Prophet (saw) for two years, she suddenly became aware of the signs of pregnancy; however, she thought this was just her imagination, and she kept the situation secret. When the signs became more and more apparent, she told her sister Sirin, who responded that this was not just her imagination, what Sayyidah Mariya (r.ah) was feeling was real.

**The Mother of Abraham (as)**

Sayyidah Mariya (r.ah) was so happy to hear this that she nearly fainted. One day when Prophet Muhammad (saw) came by she told him this important secret. The Prophet (saw) of Allah remembered how Sayyidah Mariya (r.ah) had been upset and without appetite recently, the signs of her pregnancy were the same as those that had been displayed by Sayyidah Khadîjah (r.ah). Prophet Muhammad (saw) was overjoyed as this was the best comfort he had received since the loss of his daughter Zainab, and he gave thanks to Allah.

When Sayyidah Mariya (r.ah) told the Prophet (saw) that she had doubted her pregnancy in the first days, Prophet Muhammad (saw) recited the following verses from the Qur'ân:

*"Zakariyya said: O my lord! How shall I have a son seeing I am very old and my wife is barren?" "Thus" was the answer "doth Allah accomplish what He willeth."* (Surah Al-i Imran, 3: 40)

*"So (it will be) thy Lord saith, 'that is easy for Me: I did indeed create thee before, when thou hadst been nothing!'"* (Surah Maryam, 19: 9)

*"And We gave him the good news of Isaac[536] -a prophet- one of the Righteous. We blessed him and Isaac: but of their progeny are (some) that do right, and (some) that obviously do wrong, to their own souls."* (Surah Saffat, 37: 112-113)

While Sayyidah Mariya (r.ah) was listening to the Prophet (saw) reciting these verses she laughed, and this young woman, brimming over with life and health, said: *"But I am not an old woman Prophet!"*

The whole of Medina soon heard that Sayyidah Mariya was pregnant. There is no need to describe the depressing nature that this news had on the other wives of Prophet Muhammad (saw).

Prophet Muhammad (saw) then transferred Sayyidah Mariya (r.ah) to the lovely neighborhood of Medina known as "Aliya". This was a plateau, and Prophet Muhammad (saw) wanted to settle Sayyidah Mariya (r.ah) in a place that had fresh air before giving birth, much like the ancient Arabs used to send their new born babies to the desert to be suckled.[537]

Throughout her pregnancy Prophet Muhammad (saw) showed Sayyidah Mariya (r.ah) special attention. Whenever he had time, morning or night, he would be with her. Her sister Sirin also gave her special attention until it was time for the birth.

---

536. "Abraham (as) was 120 years old, while Sarah was either 90 or 99. According to Ibn-i Abbas, a group of angels, including Archangel Jibreel, came to give the glad tidings about the birth of Isaac to Abraham (as). They went from there to destroy the people of Lot.
The angels came to visit Prophet Abraham (as) disguised as human beings. Abraham (as) fried some meat for them and put it in front of them. But they did not eat of this meat. It was then that Prophet Abraham understood that these were angels. At first, not knowing that they had come to give him the glad tidings of the birth of Isaac, he was frightened and said: "Have I done something to anger Allah? Or have you come to destroy my people?" And he offered the meat to them, once again, so that he could determine whether or not they were angels. But the angels replied that they would not eat without payment. Then Abraham (as) uttered *Bismillah* and then *Alhamdullilah*. The angels said "It is true, Halil is Allah's friend..." Then they said to Abraham (as): "Fear not, Abraham. From here we are going to the people of Lot, to destroy them!.." Thus, the reason why they would not eat and the reason why they had come became clear. When Abraham had been reassured the angels gave him the glad tidings of the birth of Isaac. All the while Sarah had been listening from behind the curtain, and because Sarah was a woman of modesty she covered her face with her hands. She and her husband were shocked at these glad tidings considering their advanced years. The angels said: "Are you surprised by the order and appointments of Allah?" (Osman Nuri Topbaş, Nebiler Silsislesi, I, page: 364-366)
537. Ziya Kazıcı, Ibid., page: 322-323.

In the eighth year of the *Hijrah*, the time for the birth arrived suddenly in the night. Prophet Muhammad (saw) brought Salma, the wife of Abu Rafi, to act as midwife for Sayyidah Mariya. Then he retired to a corner to pray and supplicate.

According to information provided by Ibn-i Sa'd and other sources, after the birth Archangel Jibreel (as) arrived and said *"Assalamu alaikum, O Father of Ibrahim!"*[538]

The midwife Ummu Rafi (Salma) took the child. Her husband, Abu Rafi came and gave Prophet Muhammad (saw) the glad tidings. After receiving this news Prophet Muhammad (saw) gave a slave to him (as a gift for bringing the good news). The Prophet (saw) of Allah congratulated Sayyidah Mariya on the child that had set his mother free.[539]

The women of the Ansar competed for the honour of being wet nurse for Ibrahim. Prophet Muhammad (saw) hired a wet nurse, not only to maintain the traditions and customs of the day, but also to show that Sayyidah Mariya was now a free and noble woman.[540] The wet nurse hired was a woman called Ummu Saif who was in Medina.[541] She was given seven milking goats in return for her services.

Prophet Muhammad (saw) sacrificed a ram on the seventh day after his son's birth. After Abu Hind had shaved Ibrahim's head the Prophet (saw) distributed silver to the poor of Medina equel to the wieght of the hair. He then buried the hair in the ground and named his son.

---

538. Ibn-i Sa'd Tabakat, VIII, 214.

539. Prophet Muhammad (saw) had accepted Mariya as a present from the *muqawqis*, however, according to reports she continued to occupy the position of *jariya*. Islamic law allows a *jariya* who gives birth to the child of her master her freedom. Thus the child is born "free".

540. According to Islamic law, the *jariya* who gives birth to her master's child is considered to be *ummu walad* (mother of the child) and is free after the death of her master. Prophet Muhammad (saw) had the following to say about *ummu walad*: *"If a jariya gives birth to the child of her master, with the death of that master, even if he has not previously set her free, the woman will be free."* (Beyhaki, Sunen-i Kubra, X, sh: 342-343)

Another hadith states: *"Mariya's (ra) and the child have been set free."* In short, in order for us to understand the stipulations that had been described by Prophet Muhammad (saw) and for his Sunnah to be as complete as possible it was necessary for Allah's Prophet (saw) to be with such a *jariya*." (M. Hamidullah, Islam Peygamberi, II, 691)

541. Abdülmumin bin Halef, Nisâu Rasulillah, page.75; narrated by Ziya Kazıcı, Ibid., page: 323.

## Jealousy

Prophet Muhammad (saw) dearly loved his son, who was growing with every passing day, and demonstrated this love to all. One day, he took his son and went to Sayyidah Â'ishah (r.ah). *"Doesn't he look like me?"* he asked. Sayyidah Â'ishah (r.ah) replied in anger: *"I see no resemblance between you and he..."* Prophet Muhammad (saw) understood that he had offended Sayyidah Â'ishah and immediately left with his son.

Once there was a new opportunity for the flames of jealousy, which were never doused, to flare up once again among the Prophet's wives: when Prophet Muhammad (saw) was with Sayyidah Mariya (r.ah) in Sayyidah Hafsa's (r.ah) house whilst Sayyidah Hafsa (r.ah) was not around, the spark of the flames flared up once again and burned, so that Sayyidah Hafsa exclaimed: *"O Prophet of Allah!.. In my home and on my day?"* and began to cry.

Prophet Muhammad (saw), in order to comfort Sayyidah Hafsa (r.ah) told her that Sayyidah Mariya (r.ah) was now *haram* for him, but that she should not tell anyone of this. These words were not enough for her and she wanted him to swear to her that he would not touch Sayyidah Mariya (r.ah). Prophet Muhammad (saw) said: *"I swear to Allah, I will never touch her again."*[542]

Sayyidah Hafsa (r.ah) was very pleased by this. After the Prophet (saw) had left she told Sayyidah Â'ishah (r.ah) this secret, saying: "O, *Â'ishah, thanks be to Allah, we are saved from Mariya!.."* When Prophet Muhammad (saw) learned of the situation he swore that he would not go near any of his wives for the next month. It was after this event that the first verses of Surah Tahrim were revealed:

*"O Prophet! Why holdest thou to be forbidden that which Allah has made lawful to thee? Thou seekest to please thy consorts. But Allah is Oft-Forgiving, Most Merciful. Allah has already ordained for you, (O men), the dissolution of your oaths (in some cases): and Allah is your Protector, and He is Full of Knowledge and Wisdom. When the Prophet (saw) disclosed a matter in confidence to one of his consorts, and she then divulged it (to another), and Allah made it known to him, he confirmed part thereof and repudiated a part. Then when he told her thereof, she said, "Who told thee this? "He said, "He told me*

---

542.　Ibn-i Sa'd, Tabakât, VIII, 213; DIA, the article of "Mariye".

*Who knows and is well-acquainted (with all things)." If ye two[543] turn in repentance to Him, your hearts are indeed so inclined; But if ye back up each other against him, truly Allah is his Protector, and Jibreel, and (every) righteous one among those who believe,- and furthermore, the angels - will back (him) up."*
(Surah at-Tahrim, 66: 1-4)

There are other reports as to the reason for the revelation of these verses of Surah Tahrim.[544]

## The Death of Ibrahim

Despite all the jealousies, the joy of being given a child by Sayyidah Mariya (r.ah) to some extent quieted the pain the Prophet (saw) had experienced at losing his daughter.

However, this joy did not last long: Ibrahim became ill before he was two years old. His mother was worried and called Sirin. Both of them stayed by the child, nursing him night and day. However, the light in the child's eyes began to slowly fade. His father came and taking the boy on his lap looked on hopelessly and sadly. Tears dripped down his cheeks as he looked at his son and he said: *"My son, there is nothing we can do when Allah sends a thing to you."* He kissed the tiny body and then, trying to restrain himself, said:

*"O Ibrahim, if there was not a real order and a true promise and if those who came later were not to meet those who came before I would be much sadder now than I am. I am saddened at separating from you. The eyes cry and the*

---

543.   That means Sayyidah Âisha and Sayyidah Hafsa.
544.   The first of these is that the wives of Prophet Muhammad (saw) wanted better living conditions, and to live and eat like the wives of other believers. But Prophet Muhammad (saw), unable to meet their demands, freed them; that is, they were to choose Allah and His Prophet or this world, and it was at this time that he decided not to approach them.
According to the second report, Prophet Muhammad (saw) stayed too long in the house of one of his wives. This caused jealousy among his other wives, in particular, Â'isha. He had been given honey in this house which is why he stayed, but the other wives thought that he had been fed the liquid from the *urfut* tree (which is like glue and has a bad smell), because, they said, his mouth smelled like that. Then Prophet Muhammad (saw) swore never to eat honey again, and this caused the revelation of the verse. (See: The article of "Sayyidah Hafsa" in this book.)

*heart is mournful. However, I cannot say anything that will anger our Lord.*"[545]

Then he turned to Sayyidah Mariya (r.ah) and comforted her. Later he said:

*"Ibrahim was my son. He died before he finished breast-feeding. Two wet-nurses have been appointed to him to fulfill the time of breast-feeding in Heaven."*[546]

The wet-nurse washed his body, then the funeral procession took him from the house and placed him in his small coffin. The funeral prayer was led by the Prophet (saw). After the funeral they all walked to the Baqi Cemetery. They dug a grave for him next to that of Uthman bin Maz'un and Prophet Muhammad (saw) placed Ibrahim's body in the grave, then he ordered that the soil be spread soil over the grave and ordered that it be sprinkled with water.[547]

At this same time an eclipse of the sun occurred. Some of the Companions connected this to the death of Ibrahim, a custom dating from the Age of Ignorance. Prophet Muhammad (saw) prayed[548] two *rakah* during this event and informed the Companions that he did not approve of this belief: *"The sun and the moon are two of Allah's verses. They do not eclipse for the death or birth of any person. When you see an eclipse of the moon and sun praise Allah and pray!"*[549]

* * *

Anas bin Malik said: "I have never seen anyone as merciful to the children as Prophet Muhammad (saw). Ibrahim was given to a wet nurse on a plateau of Medina. We would go to that house with Prophet Muhammad (saw), İbrahim's milk-father was a blacksmith and the house was full of smoke. Prophet Muhammad (saw) would pick the child up, kiss him and then leave."

---

545. Ibn-i İshak, Sîre, page: 251-252.
546. Muslim, Fedâil, 15, Hadis no: 2316.
547. Abdülmu'min bin Halef, Ibid, page.75; narrated by Ziya Kazıcı, Ibid., page: 328-329.
548. Today in some regions we can see some superstitious practices like banging drums, or shooting guns rather than praying. These actions are nothing more than superstition and old wives' tales, based on folk belief and have nothing to do with Islam. Similarly, thinking that an owl hooting is bad luck and crying for this reason is based on the same incorrect concept belief from superstitious concepts of the ignorant!
549. Nesâî, Kusûf, 14.

## After Ibrahim's Death

Sayyidah Mariya (r.ah) displayed great patience after her son's death, retreating to her home and not making the wounds in her heart or that of the Prophet's bleed. One year later, in the first days of Rabiul Awwal Prophet Muhammad (saw) became ill and after a short time departed for the world of eternity.

Sayyidah Mariya (r.ah) lived another five years after the Prophet's death. She spent those years removed from other people, but she frequently visited the grave of her son and the Prophet (saw).

In keeping with the verse: *"Every soul shall have a taste of death"*[550] Sayyidah Mariya (r.ah) died in the 16th year of the Hijrah (637) during the month of Muharram; her funeral prayer was led by Umar (ra). After the funeral she was buried in the Baqi Cemetery.[551]

Sayyidah Mariya (r.ah) lived on the allowance that had been allocated to her from the Baytu'l Mal after the death of Prophet Muhammad (saw). In a hadith he said: *"Look after the former Egyptians and take them under your patronage, because we are related to them."* He recommended that people pray that Sayyidah Mariya's tribe be blessed.[552]

It is recorded that when the son of Ali (ra), Hasan (ra), was holding peace talks with Muawiya (ra) he asked that taxes not be imposed to the people of the Hafan village, where Ibrahim's uncles were residing.

According to another report, when Ubada bin Samit (ra) came to Egypt after the conquest he asked about this village, and he found Sayyidah Mariya's old house and had a masjid erected there.

For Sayyidah Mariya, the honor of being Muslim, being married to Prophet Muhammad (saw) and being the "mother of Ibrahim" were enough. May Allah be pleased with her.

---

550. Surah Al-i İmrân, 3: 185.
551. Ibn-i Sa'd, et-Tabakat, VIII, 216.
552. DIA, the article of "Mariye".

## Lessons We Can Learn From the Life of This Distinguished Mother

1-Fate sometimes leads people to adopt a great role in life, but this is not of their own will. Sayyidah Mariya (r.ah) was just a normal woman living in an Egyptian village. First she became a *jariya* in the palace and then was taken as a servant. From there, the Egyptian *Muqawqis* decided to send her to Prophet Muhammad (saw) in Medina. She must have had an inner beauty that was beyond her physical beauty which distinguished her from other women, so that she always achieved a higher position than the one she had previously at every stage in her life. This reality is clear in that she became honored with Islam before coming to Medina.

2-Of the Prophet's other wives, only Khadija (r.ah) gave birth to his children. Many years passed, and none of his wives, those that had never been married before, the widows and those who had already had children, were able to bear him a child. This blessing was to be that of Sayyidah Mariya (r.ah), from Egypt. Thus, she experienced a fate similar to that of Hagar (as). Hagar (as), too, had been presented to a prophet as a gift, she had had a child with that prophet, and also the other wife of that prophet had been jealous of her. However, this jealousy did not cause them to make actions in poor judgment, or to cause harm to those around them, and they were allowed to continue their lives in great peace and submission.

3-The birth of a child is less connected to the physical or spiritual characteristics of a person, but rather is more the predestination of Allah. Despite there being nothing physically wrong with them there are many people who are not able to have children. Allah grants boys to some, girls to others, and to some both boys and girls. Without a doubt, having children is a reason for test, and yet just having a child or not having a child is also a great test. One of the proofs of Allah's power and might is that there are men and women who have children in their advanced years (like Abraham (as) and Sarah). This and similar events show that people are being tested by every negative condition and by every blessing, and what the faithful and sincere servant should do is be aware of these tests and act accordingly.

4-Our mother Sayyidah Mariya (r.ah) did not see Ibrahim's (ra) birth as something she had accomplished and she did not protest when he died. This behavior is a good example for us women. We should not forget that our children have been granted to us as a trust and we should take care of this trust. If children are taken from us we must endure and not object.

5-Some ignorant or uneducated people offend women who have no children with unnecessary questions and words. For example, they might say: *"These are my children, where are yours? What's wrong with you, why can't you have kids!.."* These are great sins in the realm of *qul haq* (the rights of fellow servants). They should be aware that having children or not having children is not in our hands. Allah Almighty does not give children to some people, yet to others He gives girls, and to others boys, or perhaps boys and girls, testing everyone in a different way. The important thing is to come through this test in the best way according to one's own situation. Otherwise, *"having children or not"* or *"having boys or girls"* is neither a blessing nor an inadequacy on anyone's part. The important thing is to undergo this test with the principles of *taqwa* and submission. Women who cannot have children despite trying everything should, with the remembrance of the Ummul Mu'mineen, be content with what Allah has assigned to them. They should use this condition as an opportunity and apply themselves to their own religious knowledge and service.

6-The life of Sayyidah Mariya (r.ah) is also an example of a woman who was married in a foreign country. Prophet Muhammad (saw) showed great interest in Sayyidah Mariya (r.ah), telling her time and again about the story of Hagar, displaying a good example of how a husband should treat his wife from a foreign land, allowing her to shelter in safety. The husbands of women who come from a distant land without any family are not only their husband, but also their parent and their best friend.

7-Women go through a very sensitive time when they are pregnant and their emotions reach a peak. Thus, they expect interest, support and understanding from those around them, and especially their husbands. At that time Prophet Muhammad (saw) frequently visited Sayyidah Mariya (r.ah), and he moved her to a region where she could get plenty of fresh air, and he did not neglect to support her at the time of the birth.

# SAYYIDAH REYHANA BINT AMR (r.ah)

*"If you choose Allah and His Prophet
Allah's Prophet (saw) will choose you as his wife."*

(Hadith)

## The Battle of the Trenches and the Home of the Bani Qurayza

The Battle of the Trenches had been won and the enemy returned, defeated, to Mecca. Allah's Prophet (saw) returned to the homes of happiness, and in keeping with tradition took off his armour and washed himself. Archangel Jibreel (as) suddenly appeared, and said to Prophet Muhammad (saw): *"You have taken off your weapons? We have not yet abandoned the fight!"*

Allah's Prophet (saw) asked: *"There must be a campaign then, to where?"*

Archangel Jibreel (as) indicated the Bani Qurayza who had betrayed the Muslims in the time of war and said: *"There!"*[553]

This was because the Jews, like the Bani Qurayza, did not honour the promise they had made to Allah's Prophet (saw), and had betrayed him at a most vital moment. According to the covenant they had made they were to defend

---

553.   Bukhârî, Meghâzî, 30.

against the polytheists who were attacking Medina, but, on the contrary, they took advantage of the opportunity and committed a number of treasonable and abominable acts, thus dragging themselves towards destruction with their own hands.

Prophet Muhammad (saw), having received divine instructions immediately gathered together the Muslims and they marched against the Bani Qurayza. In fact, he said: "*Let all those who hear and obey not pray the afternoon prayer until we reach the land of the Bani Qurayza!*", thus going into action before the Jews had an opportunity to regroup.[554]

The Jews, seeing the advance guard under the command of Ali, instead of regretting what they had done, became angered and expressed offensive words about Prophet Muhammad (saw).[555] However, a little later, when they saw the three thousand strong army, headed up by the Prophet (saw) himself, they were struck dumb. They denied what they were saying when faced by the majesty of Allah's Prophet (saw).

Usaid bin Hudair (ra) said: "*O, enemies of Allah! We will continue to lay siege to your castle until you die of starvation! You are like foxes cornered in your den!*"

The Bani Qurayza Jews said in fear: "*O, Ibn Hudair! We are not allies of the Hazraj, but with you the Aws!*"

Usaid (ra) said: "*We have no promise and no treaty with you anymore!*"[556]

Prophet Muhammad (saw) approached as far as the foot of the castle before engaging the Jews and invited them to Islam. But the Jews did not accept.

When the siege became prolonged and the Jews began to feel the pressure, one of the leaders Ka'b bin Asad said: "*O, Jewish congregation! This disaster has fallen upon us. We suggest three things to you, choose which one you want and we will do it!*"

---

554. Bukhârî, Meghâzî, 30.
555. Vâkıdî, II, 499.
556. Vâkıdî, II, 499.

The Jews asked him what these three things were and Ka'b replied: *"The first is to affiliate with this man, to acknowledge the Prophet (saw)! I swear by God, this has come in a clear way, this is the man who has been sent to you as a Prophet and whose characteristics are written in your books. If you accept him and believe, your blood, goods, children and women will be safe!"*

*"We will never abandon the rulings of the Torah nor replace it with another book!"* they replied.

After this Ka'b suggested that they should kill the women and children, (so that they would not be captured or enslaved) and then enter into a battle with the Muslims on a Saturday night as that is a time that the Muslims would not expect to be attacked by them. They did not accept this either.[557] Allah had spread fear in their hearts.

Three youths called Sa'laba, Usaid and Asad, became Muslim seeing that Prophet Muhammad (saw) had the characteristics that their scholars described as the Final Prophet. They left the castle at night and came to Prophet Muhammad (saw).[558]

That day the Jews were forced to surrender unconditionally. The Bani Qurayza Jews were under the patronage of the Aws tribe, and the Prophet of Allah (saw) called the leader of that tribe Sa'd to act as judge. Even though Sa'd had been injured in the war he answered the request of the Prophet (saw) and came, in any case when he had been injured during the battle he had pleaded with Allah Almighty: *"O Lord! Do not seize my soul until I have revenge on the Bani Qurayza!"*

Sa'd (ra) delivered the Laws of Moses in the Torah[559], in keeping with the Jews own desires:

This ruling was approved of by Prophet Muhammad (saw) and he said: *"O, Sa'd! I swear that you have made a ruling that is in keeping with the rulings in Allah's seven skies!"*[560]

---

557. Ibn-i Hishâm, III, 254.
558. Ibn-i Hishâm, III, 256.
559. The punishment that they should receive for having acted in such a way was the killing of the men who had held weapons, the confiscation of their goods and the taking prisoner of their wives and children. (Torah, Deuteronomy, 20: 10-15)
560. Bukhârî, Meghâzî, 30; Ibn-i Sa'd, III, 426.

Sa'd's (ra) heartfelt prayer had been answered, and after giving the ruling about the treacherous Jews who had struck the Muslims from behind, his wound opened. A short time later this Companion of the Prophet (saw) released his soul and died a martyr.[561] *Innalillah wa inna ilayhir rajiun!* (We came from Allah and to Allah we will return!)

Despite the large body he had, when Sa'd (ra) died people noticed that his corpse was very light. Prophet Muhammad (saw) announced that the wisdom behind this was: *"Others are also carrying him! I swear to Allah, in Whose hands the power of existence is held, that the angels have pleased Sa'd's soul and that the throne of Mercy has shaken for him!"*[562]

## One of the Spoils of War

When it was time to divide up the spoils of war Rayhanah (r.ah), the daughter of Amr, fell to the share of Prophet Muhammad (saw). This noble woman was the wife a Qurayshi Jew called Hakem. After being taken prisoner she was appointed to stay in the house of a woman known as Ummu Munzir.

Prophet Muhammad (saw) went to the house of Sayyidah Rayhanah, who had fallen to the Prophet's share and who was considered to be a *jariya*, and called her to him, saying *"If you chose Allah and His Prophet, Allah's Prophet (saw) will choose you."*

That is, he said: *"If you accept Islam you will be my wedded wife."*[563]

However, this young woman, not understanding what Islam was all about, did not like Islam. *"I will remain a jariya; this is no burden for me nor for you."*

According to another report:

*"Rather than marraige, just keep me as your jariya... I would like to remain*

---

561.   Ibn-i Hishâm, III, 271.
562.   Ibn-i Hishâm, III, 271; Tirmîdhî, Menâkıb, 50/3848.
563.   Ayşe Abdurrahman, Ibid., page: 156.

*a jariya, because I do not want to cover my head or face like free Muslim[564] women."*[565]

From this meeting with Sayyidah Rayhanah (r.ah) it was clear that she would not abandon the religion of her tribe and accept Islam.

However a few days later Sayyidah Rayhanah (r.ah) became Muslim. Prophet Muhammad (saw) was very pleased by this. He kept his word to her and liberated her and married her. Thus, her life as a *jariya* did not last long.[566]

Another account from our Mother Rayhanah (r.ah) tells us: "I was very embarrassed when Prophet Muhammad (saw) came to me. He called me. He took me next to him and said "If you choose Allah and His Prophet, I will choose you." I chose Allah and His Prophet. When I became Muslim he set me free. Then he gave me 12 and a half *ukiyya*[567] mahr and we were married. We spent our wedding night in the home of Ummu Munzir. He gave one night to me as he did with his other wives. I covered (*hijab*) like his other wives."[568]

Prophet Muhammad (saw) married Sayyidah Rayhanah in the sixth year of the hijrah in the month of Muharram. Sayyidah Rayhanah died in the 10th year of the Hijrah, after Prophet Muhammad (saw) had returned from the Farewell Hajj. The Prophet (saw) had her buried in the Baki Cemetery.[569]

---

564. Covering is something that is more or less respected among all people, as nobody would go out in public with nothing on. However, Islam has a number of principles attached to covering and has detailed rules concerning how one should dress in certain situations, and depending on who you are with.

The most important of these principles is that a free Muslim woman who has reached puberty should cover every part of their body except their hands and face when they are with other people. The form of this covering is one of the most important indications that she is a free Muslim woman. Thus she is protected against the interference or denigration by any strange man.

On the other hand, there being a difference between being "free" and a "*jariya*", meant that there were some differences in the way the *jariya*s covered. The covering of a *jariya* was in general like the covering principles for a man, that is the mandatory areas were covered. Thus, even when walking on the street it was clear who was a *jariya* and who was a free woman. For more detailed information about this matter, see the books of *fiqh*.

565. Muhammed Hamidullah, İslâm Peygamberi, II, 690.

566. Muhammed Hamidullah, İslâm Peygamberi, II, 690.

567. an *ukkiya* was what 40 *dirham*. Half of this was called a *nashsh*. According to this calculation 12.5 *ukiyya* was about 500 *dirham*.

568. See: Ziya Kazıcı, Ibid., page: 355-356; Celal Yeniçeri, page: 117-118.

569. Ibn-i Sa'd, VIII, 129-130.

The wisdom behind the marriage of Prophet Muhammad (saw) and Sayyidah Rayhanah was to reduce the feelings of resentment and hatred felt by the Bani Qurayza tribe towards the Muslims, to establish ties of kinship with them and to give them an opportunity to experience Islam from up close.

As a result we can evaluate the marriage with Sayyidah Rayhanah as follows:

"-Our Mother Rayhanah (r.ah), originally a Jewess, was taken prisoner after the events of the Bani Quraytha and was the *jariya* of Prophet Muhammad (saw). Allah's Prophet (saw) liberated her, and she became free. Although she did not accept Islam at first, she subsequently became Muslim. After waiting for the period of *iddet* for her deceased husband to pass, she married the Prophet (saw). She died after the Farewell Hajj of Prophet Muhammad (saw). He led her funeral prayer and had her buried in the Baqi Cemetery. She had no child with the Prophet (saw). In addition to the above, there is also the opinion that she remained a jariya until the day she died."[570]

May Allah be pleased with her. Amen.

---

570.   Ziya Kazıcı, Ibid., page: 357.

# -II-

# APPENDIX

# MARRIAGE IN ISLAM

The religion of Islam encompasses every aspect of a person's life. Islam is a divine religion in that it offers a complete system in which all the stages of a person's life, from their birth to their death, from the time they get up until they go to bed: such that every aspect of daily life, all senses, thoughts and actions are appraised, directed and given form. There is no subject in Islam which allows for saying: *"This doesn't apply to me!"* or *"This thought or action has nothing to do with my religion...!"* Most certainly there is a relevant ruling for every type of misfortune, problem or situation that might arise in a person's life.

Thus, in light of this encompassing aspect of the religion, it is not possible that there would not be rulings concerning "Family Life", or more specifically "Marriage", an event that forms a turning point in a person's life. Here, without going into detail, we would like to examine one of the most important areas of *fiqh:* "Marriage and Divorce"; however, we will summarize the main outlines of how the "Institution of Marriage" is presented in Islam.

**Before Marriage**

In Islam, men and women are perceived as two different and separate sexes that were created to continue human life on earth. The protection and preservation of the different characteristics of these sexes has been given importance and it is forbidden for a man to act in an overly effeminate way or for a woman to be overly-masculine.

Those who possess these different natural characteristics and who have taken care to protect their purity until the day of their marriage (see: Nur, 24: 30-31) are brought together; their plan being to start a family in order to establish peace and tranquility in their souls and to raise faithful generations for the benefit of society. At this stage, there are certain protocols that have to be observed by both the man and the woman to maintain boundaries of purity. Before the marriage has been conducted neither party is *halal* to the other.

However, before taking a step towards marriage there is permission for both sides to meet and become acquainted, with certain conditions and limitations: in fact, Prophet Muhammad (saw) emphasised the importance of a bride seeing the groom and the groom seeing the bride before marriage.

In order for this marriage to be established on sound foundations, it is necessary that some aspects be treated with sensitivity so that peace and happiness can be spread throughout the family and society. For example, the enquiries concerning the other (*taharri*) made by the groom's side and the side of the bride must be equal. The prevention of any possible problems in the future can be ensured to the degree that fundamentals like this are respected, even if they are not "absolute conditions" of marriage.

One of the most important matters that must be paid attention to before marriage is that there are no impediments to the bride and groom getting married, (for example, they are not close relatives, such as blood or suckling siblings).

When a man asks for a woman's hand in marriage, and there are no such impediments, such as extended blood relationship or religious issues, Prophet Muhammad (saw) recommended that the families make the "marriage" easy. Even if one of the sides is poor, Allah Almighty will bless them with great wealth and plenty (see: Nur, 24:32)

**The Marriage and Wedding Ceremony**

In fact, in Islam, the "marriage" is to be made easy by both sides. One of the most important principles of the marriage is the "proposal and acceptance" and the "witnesses".

The "proposal" is the request by one of the parties for the marriage and the "acceptance" is the acceptance of this marriage proposal by the other party. If this proposal and acceptance is carried out in front of two male or one male and two female witnesses, then the marriage is accepted as having taken place. This proposal and acceptance can also be carried out via representatives.

On the other hand, the giving of *mahr*, which is considered to be a "loan given to the woman by the man", is not a precondition of marriage. More accurately, a marriage can take place without *mahr*, but it is not considered to be complete. For the marriage to be complete during the wedding or later, it is necessary for the *mahr*, which has been predetermined, to be paid. The *mahr* is not the same as a bridal payment, that is, it is not to be given to the parents or the family of the bride. It is the property of the bride and the amount is left up to the initiative of the woman. She can demand as high a *mahr* as she wishes, because this, in one sense, is her life insurance.

After agreeing on the amount of the *mahr*, the two parties express that they want to be united in front of witnesses, and the marriage is considered as having been completed. Now the wife is *halal* for the man and the man for the wife. Now with the marriage, the degrees of intimacy allowed between the other relatives take on new forms.

It is *Sunnah* to announce the marriage with a *walima* (wedding feast). Prophet Muhammad (saw) recommended that everyone, poor or rich, be invited to the wedding meal. However, it is *haram* to have a wedding that is extravagant and showy, as one that leads to waste.

**Within the Family Nest**

As we have stated before, Islam perceives the family to be the center of affection, peace in social relations and peace among spouses (see Rum, 30: 21). The family nest is not just somewhere to gratify pleasures, or a place that satisfies the desires of the carnal soul: there are limits that need to be observed by both the man and the woman (see, Rum, 33: 35). This is the nest of holy, divine, spiritual and heavenly values. Although a person's spiritual and physical needs are satisfied in the home, this is only possible within legitimate boundaries. Both men and women are responsible for fulfilling their rights and duties in a conscientious manner and for establishing and continuing the family according to these sensitivities.

With marriage a man takes on the responsibility of meeting all the material needs of his wife and children. If this fact needs to be stated more clearly: the man's responsibility is to meet the needs of the family, such as eating and drinking, clothing and shelter at equitable standards and to earn money in a *halal* fashion. The woman does not have to help the man, who has taken up this serious responsibility: that is, the woman is not held responsible for maintaining the household.

The responsibilities and duties of the woman consist of obeying her husband, within the bounds of what is legitimate in Islam. If the woman, of her own desires and within legitimate boundaries, wants to go into trade and earn some money, or if she has money left to her as an inheritance, or given to her as a donation, or from other means, she does not have to use this to help support the household. However, if with her own heart and will she wants to help her husband and children with what she has, then this is another matter!..

One of the aims of establishing a family, perhaps the most important, is to raise faithful Muslims and faithful future generations. This is the most important duty of mothers and fathers. As this aim is to increase the presence of a faithful generation, as well as the number of good people in society, abortion is forbidden if there is no physical cause such as illness or risk of death. According to Islam, to kill a fetus by aborting it is not very different from killing a child that has been born.

Spouses are friends, confidantes and helpmates to one another. This conjunction of the hearts brings them peace and tranquility in their own souls and their children are raised in homes of happiness and thus prepared for life.

### The End of Marriage with Death or Divorce

However, the situation may not always be so ideal: sometimes the confusion of daily life, the interference of those around them or their families, or different perspectives on the part of the couple can shake the home.

In Islam it is recommended that the family home be maintained, despite disturbances and upset. The following principles are put forward in the Qur'ân:

*"…If ye take a dislike to them it may be that ye dislike a thing, and Allah brings about through it a great deal of good.* (Nisa, 4:19) or *"Fighting is prescribed for you, and ye dislike it. But it is possible that ye dislike a thing which is good for you, and that ye love a thing which is bad for you. But Allah knoweth, and ye know not."* (see: Bakara, 2: 216).

Thus, *sabr* (patience) (see: Ahzab, 33: 37) and *sulh* (peace) (see: Nisa, 4: 128) are advised, while at other times it is suggested that *hakim* (judges) be appointed (see: Nisa, 4: 35) to help sort out problems between the two sides, thus preventing the destruction of the Family home.

However, if despite all these steps, one or both parties want to put an end to the marriage, then divorce has been made easy and there are no statements like: "Your marriage is sacred, you can never divorce." It is only indicated that divorce is an action that *"makes the heavens shake"* and which is "an unpleasant *halal* action" (Abu Dawood, Talaq, 3; Ibn-I Maja, Talaq, 1).

It is not desired that a gangrenous wound which is beyond treatment be endured with: if the spouses have tried every way possible, but still arrive at the decision to part ways, we are reminded that they should be able to move on with their lives, and that Allah Almighty has destined a different fate for them (see: Nisa, 4: 130).

Divorce in Islam takes place in three stages. The first two "divorces" (*ric'i talaq*) allows the possibility for changing one's mind. If the two parties (husband and wife) want to go through the third stage (*bain talaq*), then it is no longer possible for them to continue the marriage. Divorce is now compulsory!.. The woman can only marry her husband again if there has been no prior agreement and only after being married to another man in a legal way (*hulla*), having a family life with him and divorcing this second husband in the proper manner.

There are certain conditions and stipulations for a final divorce (*bain talaq*), which does not offer the possibility of changing one's mind. According to the

Sunnah, a woman cannot be divorced by her husband when she is menstruating or after childbirth. If she is not menstruating, there can be no sexual relations. However, if in contravention of this, words of divorce are uttered, these do have a legal value and are valid. The only thing lacking here is that the divorce has not been carried out according to the Sunnah. On the other hand, if the words of divorce are uttered in jest or when inebriated, these too are valid, and a person who uses these words three times has used up their right. It is necessary here to stress the significant aspects of this matter, because according to Islam, marriage and divorce are matters that are not to be jested about. Divorce that is uttered at times when a person is intoxicated is a shameful punishment for he who has uttered these words.

The right to divorce, in principle, has been given to the man in Islam. However, under certain conditions and situations, the woman has the right to divorce her husband via the courts (*tafviz-i talaq*).

Just as the expenses for the wife and children are the husband's responsibility during the marriage, after divorce, the husband must pay the *nafaka* (alimony) until her *iddet* is finished. If the husband dies, as the woman will be entitled to a certain percentage of the inheritance, there is no separate alimony. Moreover, if one of the spouses apostatizes, then the marriage is null and void.

* * *

These matters are incredibly complex, and we have tried to give a general overview in just a few pages. Those readers who want more information on this matter should turn to *fiqh* and *ilmihal* books. Our aim in writing the above, even if it is only just a beginning, is to remind the reader that in Islam there are such family laws.

# POLYGAMY

## What is Polygamy?

The word polygamy in fact refers to a man who has more than one wife (*taaddud-i zevjat*), but there is also a phrase for a woman who has more than one husband,polyandry, (*taaddud-i ezvaj*).[571] However, the word polygamy is much more familiar to people due to the fact that one woman marrying many men is something that does not happen very often, for reasons stemming from the nature of women, and from society and religion; even still these marriages are rare which consist of a man with many women.

## The History of Polygamy

Polygamy is a type of marriage that stretches back far in time. Eastern and Western people, like the ancient Babylonians, Egyptians, Athenians, Indians, Iranians, Turks, Slavs, Germanic tribes and Anglo-Saxons[572] practiced polygamy from time to time for a number of reasons, needs and under differing circumstances.

---

571.  DIA, article of "Çok Evlilik/Polygamy"; Kevser Kâmil Ali-Sâlim Öğüt, Ibid, VIII, page: 365,
572.  DIA, article of "Çok Evlilik/Polygamy".

## The Major Reasons for Polygamy

Among the most common reasons for polygamy are: the life style, traditions, and culture of society, the ratio of men to women, economic needs and possibilities, social status and regional conditions[573], as well as the spiritual and physical needs of human beings.

## Polygamy in Religions

Religions like Brahmanism[574] and Zoroastrianism see polygamy as being legitimate.

There is no law that forbids polygamy in Christianity or Judaism. The Holy Qur'ân informs us that Prophet Abraham (as)[575], Prophet Jacob (as)[576], Prophet David (as)[577], Prophet Solomon (as)[578] and other prophets[579] of the Children of Israel (Bani Israil) had more than one wife.

Polygamy continued among the Jews until the Middle Ages, but despite there being no ruling in the Bible or the Talmud, in the 11th century it was forbidden by Rabbi Gershom.[580]

There is no clear expression that forbids polygamy in the Bible. Luther, the founder of the Protestant movement, clearly stated that polygamy was legitimate.[581] Some other Christian sects give permission for multiple marriages. For example, the Anabaptists, who appeared in the 16th century in Germany and the Mormons, formed in the 19th century in America, who not only gave permission for polygamous marriages, they accepted it as a "holy and divine law."

Polygamy was allowed by the church in the Middle Ages, until the end of

---

573. DIA, article of "Çok Evlilik/Polygamy".
574. Afzalurrahman, Ibid., v: 2, page: 117.
575. Torah, Genesis 16/1-4.
576. Torah, Genesis 29/20-30; 30/3-6.
577. Torah, II. Samuel, 5/13-16.
578. Torah, I. Kings, 11/3; Psalm of Psalms, 6/8.
579. Torah, Exodus, 18/2-4; Numbers, 12/1.
580. DIA, article of "Çok Evlilik/Polygamy".
581. Muhammed Hamidullah, İslâm Peygamberi, v: II, page: 666.

the 17th century, and was accepted as an official form of marriage.[582] The fact that Judaism and Christianity are in general opposed to polygamy today is more a social phenomenon than a religious one.[583]

## Polygamy Among the Arabs in the Age of Ignorance

Before the advent of Islam polygamy was very widespread in the Arab peninsula.[584] Moreover, there was no limit to the number of women a man could marry. Polygamy was accepted as a natural way to increase the work force and power of the tribe and family; to maintain a large population; to form a dissuasive force in battles; and, to replenish the loss of life caused by the frequent wars. In fact, while polygamy was a symbol of fortune and power, a single marriage was seen to be a symbol of weakness and poverty. It was for this reason that polygamy was considered to be a matter of pride and respect.[585]

582. Ecyclopedia Britannica, London, 1900, XIII, page: 950; narrated by Afzalurrahman, Ibid., v: 2, page: 119.
583. DIA, article of "Çok Evlilik/Polygamy".
584. Rıza Savaş, Ibid., Asr-ı Saadette İslâm, v: I, page: 297.
585. DIA, article of "Çok Evlilik/Polygamy".

# POLYGAMY IN ISLAM

Before examining the matter of polygamy in Islam, I would like to examine the institution of marriage from the Islamic perspective in order to understand the subject better.

## Islam and Marriage

The first family was established in heaven and the first marriage was between Prophet Adam (as) and Eve (as), with the angels acting as witnesses.

As is known, Allah Almighty created Prophet Adam (as) from nothingness and then created a wife who would bring him peace of mind, in both a psychological and biological sense. In fact, one of the main purposes of marriage is this. That is, spouses find peace of mind with one another. The Qur'ân tells us:

*"And among His Signs is this, that He created for you mates from among yourselves, that ye may dwell in tranquility with them, and He has put love and mercy between your (hearts): verily in that are Signs for those who reflect."*
(Surah ar-Rum, 30: 21)

If we examine the contents of the above verse, the familiarity, love and tenderness that is bestowed by Allah on married spouses is so important that it can be considered to be one of the proofs of the existence of Allah. These expressions also indicate the great change that occurs in the life of the married person, because thanks to marriage, two strangers who did not know one another before, can become the closest beings to each other in this world.

One of the main purposes of marriage is the continuance of humankind. Allah Almighty, bestowing Adam and Eve with the duty of mother and father in order to populate the earth, has placed rights and qualities in keeping with the nature of men and the nature of women, and has ordered us to live in a way that is in keeping with these characteristics and aims. Allah has also demanded that all these natural characteristics, which differ between the two sexes, be preserved; that is, it is a principle that the man does not lose those characteristics that make him a man, nor the woman those that make her a woman.

According to Islam, the only way that men and women can carry out a legitimate life together is through marriage, and as we stated above, this means that two strangers of different sexes are joined together and they become the closest to each other in the world.

Islam has endowed marriage with a lofty meaning and responsibility. Through marriage, all the needs of the woman, that are eating, drinking, shelter and other needs, have now become the responsibility of the man. Thus, it bypasses the fact that women can have great difficulties and encounter abuse when trying to meet these needs herself in society. This situation, which is in keeping with the psychological and biological makeup of the woman, is not, as claimed, opposed to the woman's best interests. In fact, quite the contrary, marriage is an institution that is a graver responsibility for the man than for the woman.

In a home in which the principles set out by Islam are respected and maintained, if they are applied in a legitimate way, the woman is protected from a myriad of difficulties and she is presented with a variety of blessings. For example, she is under no financial obligation to look after herself or her family; and even if she is wealthy, she does not have to contribute to the sustenance of the family. She can own property, within legitimate boundaries, and even become involved in trade to increase her property; and also, she has the right to own wealth that is left to her through inheritance, or other means, and she has the right to accumulate wealth.

The husband, even if he is poor, must secure sustenance for his family by legitimate and *halal* means. The duty of meeting all the needs of the spouse and children is a duty placed only upon the man's shoulders.

Once again, according to Islam, with the death, divorce, imprisonment, etc. of the husband, or any other situation which means that the wife cannot be cared for, the responsibility for maintaining the family falls to the father, grandfather or older brother. If the members of the family are not around or they are in no position to secure her own sustenance, then the state must intervene and is compelled to care for women and children who are in need. As we have seen, such a system secures comfort for a woman in every aspect, and her every need can be met.

We should not allow this pure and encompassing concept of Islam to be corrupted by the ignorant, incorrect and unilateral approaches and behavior that some Muslims today demonstrate, from time to time.

Marriage in Islam was not established to attain personal advantage or pleasure: the home, established with understanding and maturity on both sides, founded on the basis of love and respect, brings to the fore the "human being", the most beloved being of society, and works to secure their needs and prepare their lofty qualities to benefit society. Thus, the smallest, but the most essential, foundation stone of society, the family, is formed. Every type of influence that can shake the family, such as adultery, slander, etc. is strictly forbidden in Islam and there are strict precautions in this matter.

In short, this "family home", the main outlines of which we have tried to depict here, has been given great importance by Islam, and the establishment, functioning and abolishment of the same is connected to permanent principles in the framework of "justice" and "fairness", with a completeness that takes into account the needs and characteristics of both sides. In this home, in which the rights and responsibilities of all have been clearly delineated, a number of ways to find solutions to the variety of needs and surprises that life throws up has been indicated. One of these solutions is "polygamy".

**The Method and Conditions for Polygamy in Islam**

**1-Polygamy was not begun by Islam; rather, the pre-existing order was limited.**

As expressed above, before the era of Prophet Muhammad (saw), in the time known as the Age of Ignorance, it was possible to marry a number of women at the same time, in Arabia and other countries. Some men, as everyone knows, were married to dozens of women or had slave women that they had purchased, or numerous illegitimate relationships with women (adultery). This situation not only upset those who had not been corrupted, but it was impossible for anyone to take a stance against this general movement. The Western society, which tends to protest against polygamy, does not have a life style that is very different than these pre-Islam conditions.

**2-To marry four women is not an "order" given to all believers, but it is a "right" and a "permission" given in some special circumstances.**

Islam, while encouraging single marriages, has not in principle forbidden polygamy. However, in addition to some stipulations and conditions, an upper limit has been imposed and a man has been given *ruhsat* (permission) to marry at most four women at one time.[586] There are thousands of experiences in the world. The man's "being" can be such that he needs more than one wife; and also sometimes it is difficult for a woman to continue the family life: such as a chronic illness. In such situations it would not be humane to destroy the family, pushing beloved spouses into loneliness or leaving children without parents. Also, there is the aspect of the level of intimacy between two people being made public or having to be explained to many people due to events like divorce, etc.

The principle of a man marrying at most four women was respected by Prophet Muhammad (saw) in daily life. For example, Nawfal bin Muawiya, who was married to five women when he came to Islam, was ordered to divorce one[587], while Qays bin Harith[588], who was married to eight women, and Gaylan bin Salama[589], who was married to ten, were ordered to divorce their wives, limiting themselves to four.

Islam, which limited the previously unlimited number of marriages to four, placed many stipulations concerned with the functions of establishing such

---

586. Afzalurrahman, Ibid., v: 2, page: 116.
587. Beyhakî, VII, 184.
588. Ibn-i Mâjah, Nikâh, 40.
589. Tirmîdhî, Nikâh, 33.

marriages. For example, it is forbidden to marry two women who are closely related, like two sisters, at the same time.

**3- The duty to "ensure justice" between the wives is imposed on any man who marries more than one woman (up to four). Otherwise he is warned that he will be exposed to Allah's wrath.**

In the Qur'ân it is stated: *"…marry women of your choice, Two or three or four; but if ye fear that ye shall not be able to deal justly (with them), then only one, or (a captive) that your right hands possess, that will be more suitable, to prevent you from doing injustice."* (Surah an-Nisa, 4: 3)

As we see in the verse above it is clearly stated that: *"if ye fear that ye shall not be able to deal justly (with them), then only one….will be more suitable."*[590] Thus, it is emphasized that for people who fear that they may not be able to treat their wives fairly, it is better for them not to marry more than one woman.

In another verse from the Qur'ân it is written: *"Ye are never able to be fair and just as between women, even if it is your ardent desire: But turn not away (from a woman) altogether, so as to leave her (as it were) hanging (in the air). If ye come to a friendly understanding, and practise self- restraint, Allah is Oft-forgiving, Most Merciful."* (Surah an-Nisa, 4: 129).

Prophet Muhammad (saw) said: *"If a man is married to two women and he does not observe justice between them, on the Day of Judgment he will resurrected with one side paralyzed"* (Ibn-i Maja, Nikah, 47). In this way Prophet Muhammad (saw) warned those who married one more woman that they would be subjected to Allah's wrath if they do not observe justice between them.

Although it is very difficult to treat two wives equally from an emotional aspect, it is a condition that equality be observed in material and physical treatment and in benevolence. This covers matters like devoting time to the wives, and meeting needs like accommodation, food and drink and clothing. If one of the wives feels that she is being neglected in one of these areas she can apply to the courts.[591] The judge can force the husband to treat the wife justly. If the

---

590.  Surah an-Nisa, 4: 3.
591.  Afzalurrahman, Ibid., v: 2, page: 116.

situation continues, according to the Maliki and Hanbali sects, the judge has the authority to divorce them with *talaq-i bain* and annul the marriage.

On the other hand, the fact that people cannot be fair in matters of the heart and affection has been affirmed by a Divine revelation: *"You are never able to be fair and just as between women, even if it is your ardent desire."*[592]

Prophet Muhammad (saw) tried to be just in the treatment of his wives and he pleaded with Allah Almighty: *"O Allah!.. The distribution that is within my power consists of this; do not punish me for that which remains beyond me and for matters that are only in your power!.."*[593]

Some scholars from recent periods have interpreted the verses: *"if you fear that ye shall not be able to deal justly (with them), then only one….will be more suitable"*[594] and *"Ye are never able to be fair and just as between women, even if it is your ardent desire"*[595] to mean that polygamy in Islam is very limited, that it is only for those who feel the need, and that it is only permissible as long as they feel confident that they can act with justice.[596]

However, it is not necessary to denigrate polygamy that is carried out in respect of these conditions, even though it has thus been limited; any home that has been established in this way is permissible and legitimate.

**4- The wife can limit the right of the man to marry more than one wife during the marriage.**

In Islam, it is a stipulation that a marriage be established in a contract that is agreed upon by both parties. In making the contract, if a woman makes the condition that "her husband remains married to her alone", and subsequently if the man ignores this condition and marries another woman, the wife can apply to the courts and ask for a divorce. Normally, Islam does not give the wife the

---

592. Surah an-Nisa, 4: 129.
593. Dârimî, Nikâh, 25; Abû Dâvud, Nikâh, 38; also see: Tirmîdhî, Nikâh, 1140; Ibn Mâjah, Nikâh, 47.
594. Surah an-Nisa, 4: 3.
595. Surah an-Nisa, 4: 129.
596. DIA, article of "Çok Evlilik/Polygamy".

right to divorce, but in such situations the judge can grant her the right to divorce her husband.

### Reasons for Polygamy

Islamic scholars have determined which conditions make polygamy permissible:

**1-An Imbalance in the Ratio of Men to Women** – After times of war, the ratio of men to women can sometimes change. Many men can die during a war, thus upsetting the ratio, bringing the number of healthy men to well below that of women.[597] In such situations how is a woman to meet her needs. Thus to increase the workforce, and so preventing hunger and disaster which could strike the society; and to prevent corruption and a collapse of morals: polygamy can be implemented. An example of this imbalance of numbers of men and women, was seen in the depressions that affected Europe after the First World War and again after the Second World War. In fact, this was so great that the matter of bringing "stud men" from other countries to Germany, which had lost 7 million people, was considered.

**2- Preventing the Collapse of Families without Children** - One of the main aims in getting married and setting up a home is to have children. If there are no children, due to the woman's health, in societies without polygamy such childless marriages can come to an end with the man marrying another woman. The religion of Islam offers the opportunity for the man not to divorce his first wife, but rather to make a second marriage. This situation is more moral and humane, not only for the first wife, but also for society.

**3-Maintaining Family Confidentiality** – Marriage is a sacred confidential institution in which the two sexes share the most intimate secrets and in which all forms of deficiencies and wants are kept under one roof. Illnesses, moments of power and weakness, sweet and painful memories, the past of the children

---

597. Afzalurrahman, Ibid., v: 2, page: 116.

and their future are all preserved here. However, the arrival of "another" woman on the scene can shake the family and make it vulnerable; such events possibly leading to the revelation of such secrets to a third party, such as in court or among relatives. This is one of the reasons why divorce is the "ugliest of that which is permitted."

**4-Not Allowing Illegitimate Affairs -** It is well recognized that in almost all societies a large number of men are involved in illegitimate affairs with women, without accepting any legal or moral responsibility. This type of relationship, an affair, takes place perhaps due to feelings of "love" that develop between the parties or due to the man undergoing temporary or long-lasting problems with his wife.[598] In either condition, the man whose eye and heart have wandered has started to take steps that will drag himself, his family, and society towards disaster. Islam, which aims to reduce to a minimum the harm caused to both the individual and the society by such a state of affairs, has made all forms of adultery *haram*. Adultery is to be punished in the most painful way (stoning). This situation is one of the factors that indicate to what degree Islam provides security for the family.

For any man who has difficulty in spending life with just one wife, polygamy is the only legitimate way out. Thus, polygamy is connected to legal and moral principles.

When one takes into consideration all of these conditions, it can be understood that Islam, a religion in which every situation and phase of life has been considered, would not allow adultery. It is a religion not only for the healthy, but for the old and weak as well. It is not just a religion of peace, but it is a religion that takes into account war and all the troubles that come with it. It is not just the religion of men, but it is the religion of women, protecting all their rights and needs. It is the sole religion that protects the chastity and dignity of humanity; it is the only religion which takes into consideration the needs of the individual and society to the extent that it prevents the needless destruction of the family home, and prevents families being brought to disaster and misery.

---

598.    Afzalurrahman, Ibid., v: 2, page: 117.

## Polygamy Today

In the twentieth century many countries in the Islamic World have debated arrangements for polygamy, some have taken limiting decisions on this matter and put it into practice. Let us briefly examine this subject.

In the last era of the Ottoman State, *Hukûk-ı Âile Karanâmesi* accepted that a woman could stipulate that her husband would take only one wife during the marriage ceremony, and the Ahvâl-i Şahsiye Commission, established in 1924 after the revocation of the law, stipulated that polygamy be subjected to permission from a judge.

Nowadays, in Islamic countries there are different legal arrangements and applications for the practice of polygamy. One of the countries to introduce it in its freest form is Saudi Arabia, while Jordan and Egypt have relatively more free frameworks for such practices. In most Islamic countries, including Syria, Iraq, Morocco, Yemen and Indonesia, polygamy is connected to permission from a judge, with a number of conditions: for example, the permission of the first wife and proof by the applicant that he is economically capable of supporting another wife, or that the first wife is ill or infertile. In Pakistan, although polygamy has not been completely abolished, the conditions for practicing it have been made very stringent. In Tunisia and Turkey polygamy is totally forbidden.

## Opposition to Polygamy

The matter of polygamy has been widely criticized in the West, with arguments that it destroys equality between men and women, that it is an obstacle to the woman's rights and freedom, that it destroys modern life, that it is regressive and a primitive practice; these same views have been repeated in some Islamic countries.

At this juncture, some Western thinkers have stated that, in contrast to the above, that polygamy should be legalized and that from a social, moral and economic aspect it is an exemplary system. They state that in the West many are not content with one marriage, but in reality carry out polygamy in an illegitimate manner; thus, the western system is criticized and this hypocritical attitude is denounced. In connection with this matter the German philosopher Schopenhauer and the French physician and psychologist Gustave Le Bon have interesting ideas.[599]

Furthermore Dr. Annie Besaht criticizes those in the West as follows:

*"While it is claimed that monogamous marriages are carried out in the West, there are actual cases of polygamy in which there is no responsibility. The man can discard his mistress when he tires of her and she gradually sinks to the level of a prostitute. The first wife carries no responsibility for the future of this woman who is in a position that is a hundred times worse than the wife and mother in a polygamous marriage. Seeing thousands of miserable women on the street at night in Western cities, we are aware of the hypocrisy of the West that finds fault with this Islamic ruling and forbids it. For a woman, for her happiness and esteem, to live in polygamy means being in a relationship with one man and having respect for the legitimate child on her lap; this is much better than being turned out onto the street, with her illegitimate child, without a home and with no one to care for her, better than being victim to those who come by, night after night, better than a motherhood with no legitimacy, one which is despised."*[600]

***

It can be understood that many of those who criticize Islam, which recommends monogamy in principle, for its support of polygamy are not sufficiently familiar with the related rulings and the stipulations connected to it; rather they interpret polygamy as an order and something compelled by the religion. The approach of the critics, who are tolerant of extra-marital affairs, in looking at the matter only from the aspect of the woman, is not correct. In fact, it cannot be said that the practice of polygamy is a situation that is opposed to the best interests of women, because when the matter is looked at from an individual aspect, although it may appear that the woman is harmed by polygamy, individuals, including the woman herself, and society benefit from this practice.

In the establishment of relationships with more than one woman, which is much more widespread in society than one would think, if the situation is not

---

599.   DIA, article of "Çok Evlilik/Polygamy".
600.   Afzalurrahman, Ibid., v: 2, page: 120.

given a legal status, the women will be deprived of a number of rights, and will be a victim of social pressure. The second wife will suffer many problems that are inherent in not being a legal wife. Moreover, a man who carries out this type of relationship, and the children that result from this relationship, in short the institution of the family, and society will all encounter a variety of problems.

Polygamy is an institution in Islam that can be accepted as a necessity when subjected to certain conditions and stipulations; it is a solution to solve some problems and to establish balance in society, and it is a form of "social security". Essentially, the fact that from time out of mind monogamous marriages have been the norm in Muslim societies, and the fact that no more than an estimated 10% of polygamous marriages include more than two wives supports this contention.

On the other hand, in Islamic countries where polygamy has been forbidden by law, the reality is that often the practice continues, and attempts have been made to protect those who are negatively affected by this de facto situation. Polygamy which is based on religious permission and the consent of both parties, rather than being limited by formal and legal regulations, should be taken within the conditions and stipulations set out by Islamic law itself and seen as something that is more suitable to Muslim social makeup and reality.

When one approaches the matter of polygamy from the stance of the equality of men and women, there are those who say that women are not granted the same rights as men. However, the practice of polyanthropy, which no one whose sublime human nature has not been severely corrupted could accept, is unthinkable from an Islamic point of view. Such an arrangement, which is not only unacceptable from the aspect of male-female relationship, but also from aspects of parentage, alimony, inheritance and other legal stipulations in family and social relations, has only been practiced in a very limited manner by some Eskimo, Indian and African tribes.[601]

**In Conclusion**

1- Throughout history polygamy is a reality that has been seen in almost all societies.

---

601. DIA, article of "Çok Evlilik/Polygamy".

2- Throughout history a variety of social, cultural and economic needs have made it necessary for men to marry more than one wife.

3- Many divine and human religions give permission for polygamy.

4- Islam is not a religion that introduced polygamy. On the contrary, Prophet Muhammad (saw) began to teach Islam in a period when polygamy was common and there were no limits applied to it. Rather, it was the religion that applied some rules and regulations to polygamy, which was previously practiced without limits and according to whim. An "upper limit" of four wives was placed with the imposition of the condition of "equality" among wives, something that is very hard to ensure.

5- In recent centuries as a part of modernization and industrialization, the defenders of individual freedom have concentrated on "human rights" and in particular "women's rights"; and for them, polygamy is seen to be in contravention of the equality of men and women. For this reason, a great propaganda program was begun against polygamy, or at least, those religions and systems that protect it. Unfortunately, one of the targets of this wholesale onslaught has been the noble religion of Islam. However, a matter that has been overlooked is that Islam does not encourage polygamy; it merely permits it in certain necessary situations with clear conditions and stipulations. When the situation is thus, this and other continuous attacks against Islam are clearly the result of ignorance, prejudice and ulterior motives.

6- According to Islam a stipulation placed during the marriage ceremony can make it a condition of the marriage that the husband is to take no other wife.[602]

If the husband does not respect this precondition, the wife can apply to the courts and request a divorce. Islam, which for a number of reasons does not normally give the woman the right to divorce, gives her the right to apply to a court and get a divorce in some situations, even if her husband is not willing. This shows to what extent the feelings and thoughts of the woman within the family are taken into account.

---

602.  Muhammed Hamidullah, İslâm Peygamberi, v: II, page: 667.

7- On the other hand, those who contend that polygamy nullifies the woman's rights and denigrates her before men, for some reason, fail to complain about the women who live as mistresses and the situation that society falls into: they also neglect the situation of children born as a result of illegitimate relationships.

8- Polygamy can at times be beneficial to women and the society at large, while at other times, it can cause harm. In fact, polygamy on its own is neither a vehicle that benefits nor harms. As with most other things, polygamy has different values according to the intention and the method in which it is implemented by the two parties, relative to the time, place and social conditions. Sometimes it can be something of great benefit when implemented well with good intentions, while at other times ulterior motives and bad implementation can cause everyone harm. Just as with monogamous relationships … For this reason, there is no point in making polygamy the scapegoat. What is necessary is to place regulations that will reduce harm to a minimum. This should be done according to the needs and structure of every society; and it is possible to do this in conjunction with religious, legal, moral and human regulations.

9- Islam is a religion that not only addresses the healthy, but also the old and weak. It is religion that can be applied not only in times of peace and security, but also during war, famine, drought and other similar extraordinary times. It is not a religion that takes into account only the needs of one nation, but rather it is a religion that considers all people in the world, on every continent, people of every race and every language. It is not a religion that protects only the rights of men; rather, it is a religion that protects all the rights and needs of women, giving them a lofty and virtuous position.

From this aspect, the fact that Islam shows the way to find legitimate and moral solutions that ease every stage of our life is not a deficiency of the religion, but rather is its virtue and superiority. However, it is not possible to explain anything to one who does not wish to see, hear or understand.


**The Instances of Wisdom in the Multiple Marriages of Prophet Muhammad (saw)**

Prophet Muhammad (saw) is a prophet who was sent by Allah Almighty as an example to the people. The Qur'ân tells us:

*"Ye have indeed in the Messenger of Allah a beautiful pattern (of conduct) for any one whose hope is in Allah and the Final Day, and who engages much in the Praise of Allah."* (Surah al-Ahzab, 33: 21)

As with all the other prophets, Prophet Muhammad (saw) was above all else a human being: not only did he need to eat, drink, sleep, rest and work to secure a living, he also experienced childhood, youth, maturity and old age, and in the end he died.

Allah's Prophet (saw), who left examples of many perfect modes of behavior at every stage and in every situation of his life, was also an example of "marriage and family life" for the ummah.

Prophet Muhammad (saw) lived in the best possible way with his wives, who were all raised in different environments, were of a variety of ages, and had different habits, morals and abilities; and without hurting them he helped them to fulfill their potential, raising them from being "women of the Age of Ignorance" to the position of "mothers of believers" (Surah al-Ahzab, 33:6).

In earlier sections of this book we discussed how Prophet Muhammad (saw) married these women and gave a detail account of what occurred during these marriages and for this reason here we will be content with reminding our readers of the wisdom behind the marriages. Without a doubt, the wisdom is much more than we can list here. There are works that have been written solely on this matter where one can find more instances of wisdom and advice described in detail: but so much more of the wisdom is beyond human perception and knowledge, and thus can only be known with divine power and understanding. However, we feel that it is appropriate to discuss the wisdom behind these marriages in this book.

**The Reasons and Instances of Wisdom in Prophet Muhammad's (saw) Marriages**

**Being an Example:** Islam is a universal and human religion that encompasses all the stages of human life. Allah Almighty sent Prophet Muhammad (saw) to the ummah as an example for all, and so his life was arranged to fulfill this divine wish. Believers are required to learn and understand all the different aspects of the lofty and exemplary Prophet and his life, because the Sunnah does not merely consist of Prophet Muhammad's (saw) words, but his actions, states and sometimes even his lack of action (when he saw something but did not interfere). For this reason, Prophet Muhammad's (saw) actions and states in his own home, within his own four walls, was not entrusted to just one pair of eyes, and his thoughts, words and actions were scrutinized, day and night, and transmitted to the ummah. He was not a person of legend or one whose private life is unknown. All his relationships with both men and women, in the street, at home, day and night, have been recorded. On the other hand the Prophet Muhammad's (saw) relationships with his wives of different ages, cultures and character, have provided examples for male believers, over the centuries, who have gotten married with many different kinds of women.

**Education and Training**: The details of the family life of Prophet Muhammad (saw), which was partially private, and the personal life of Prophet Muhammad (saw), have reached us today from the view of his wives, who were women of different ages, perceptions and who had different life styles. In this matter, the 2,210 hadiths reported by Sayyidah Â'ishah (r.ah) and the hadiths of the other women are enough for a general overview.

Moreover, at least half the Companions were women, and they had a need for women to teach them what had been ordered to do and what was forbidden in the religion. The large number of wives of Prophet Muhammad (saw) made it easy for the female Companions to learn the new religion directly. As each wife was from a different tribe and society they all had different relatives, friends and confidantes. Thus, the new information was able to be spread in a sound manner over a wide range of people in a very short time.[603]

This situation was faithfully followed while the Prophet was alive, and continued in the same way, and the mothers of believers continued to guide and instruct their own tribes and people.

Also, there are some situations that are unique to women, and it would not have been possible for some women to communicate with Prophet Muhammad (saw) comfortably about those matters and to attain his answers. Also, although

---

603.　Muhammed Hamidullah, İslâm Peygamberi, v: II, page: 670.

the women requested that the Prophet (saw) allocate them time for a special "lesson" every week, it would not have been possible for them to ask about all the matters in detail in the available time.

**Reduction of Enmity and Hate:** Prophet Muhammad (saw) was forced to fight with different countries and tribes, but even societies that had enough resentment and enmity to fight to the death with one another became peaceful relatives due to the Prophet's marriages. Thus, Prophet Muhammad (saw) realized this intention and was also the means for many people coming to Islam. The marriages with Sayyidah Safiyya (r.ah), Sayyidah Juwayriya (r.ah), Sayyidah Zainab bint Huzayma (r.ah), Sayyidah Maymunah (r.ah), Sayyidah Ummu Habiba (r.ah) were such marriages.

This method was not used only by Prophet Muhammad (saw), for many great emperors also married the daughters and sisters of the heads of states from whom they feared harm in order to reduce resentment and enmity.

**Strengthening Friendship:** The marriages to Sayyidah Â'ishah, the daughter of Sayyidina Abu Bakr, his closest friend and his "Friend in the Cave", and the marriage to Sayyidah Hafsa (r.ah), the daughter of Sayyidina Umar (ra), were this type of marriage. Also, the *jariya* sent by the Mukawqis of Egypt (Sayyidah Mariya Qibtiyya) was an indication of the friendship that this ruler had for Prophet Muhammad (saw).

**Obeying Allah's Order:** The marriage with his cousin Sayyidah Zainab bint Jahsh, and his accepting Sayyidah Hafsa back after they had gone through the first stage of divorce, were in accordance with a divine order. We can also add to this the marriage with Sayyidah Â'ishah in accordance with a *sadik* dream.

**Implementation of Religious Rulings:** The principles of Islam were being revealed. In order to realize some of these rulings Prophet Muhammad (saw) had to carry them out himself and be a pioneer in these matters. For example the abolition of adoption meant that he married Sayyidah Zainab bint Jahsh, the former wife of his formerly adopted son, Zaid bin Haritha (ra).

**As a Reward and Patronage:** One of the reasons for marriage was to reward and offer patronage to Muslim women who had suffered much for Islam, but despite all difficulties had remained faithful to the religion. Sayyidah Sawda (r.ah), Sayyidah Ummu Habiba (r.ah), Sayyidah Ummu Salama (r.ah), Sayyidah Zainab bint Huzayma (r.ah) and Sayyidah Maymunah (r.ah) are examples of these marriages.

**In order to Protect and Care for the Children**: Prophet Muhammad (saw) wanted to continue the care and raising of children without any interruption to raise people to be the best examples for the *Ummah*. The marriage with Sayyidah Sawda (r.ah) after the death of Sayyidah Khadîjah (r.ah) was such a marriage.

Under this heading, the marriages that he made with widows and women with children can be considered and most of the women Prophet Muhammad (saw) married (with the exception of Sayyidah Â'ishah) were widows, and many of these had children from earlier marriages. The care, protection, education and upbringing of these children were continued by Prophet Muhammad (saw) himself.

The Ansar of Medina opened not only their city, but their hearts to Prophet Muhammad (saw). At every opportunity they demonstrated that they were willing to sacrifice their own lives for his happiness and they wanted very much that he should be their relative. However, Prophet Muhammad (saw) did not choose any women from the Ansar. He chose the abandoned, stricken, women who were in need of protection, and these were mostly older women.

**To Save Them from Slavery**: Women who had fallen captive, for any number of reasons, were able to find freedom in their lives, and to abandon heresy for guidance due to marriage with the Prophet (saw). Examples of these women are Sayyidah Safiyya, Sayyidah Mariya, Sayyidah Rayhanah, and Sayyidah Juwayriya.

May Allah be pleased with them.

### How many Women did Prophet Muhammad (saw) Marry?

Prophet Muhammad (saw) married Sayyidah Khadîjah first, and he did not marry any other woman for 25 years. After her death, for the reasons given above, he married 10 more times. One of these wives, Sayyidah Zainab bint

Huzayma, died after being married for 2-3 months; thus Prophet Muhammad (saw) was married to nine women for a few years.

When Prophet Muhammad (saw) made these marriages the verse limiting men to 4 wives (Nisa, 4:3) had not yet been revealed. Prophet Muhammad (saw) married Sayyidah Maymunah in the seventh year of the Hijrah. The relevant verse was revealed in the 8th or 9th year.

However, after this verse had been revealed Prophet Muhammad (saw) gathered his wives together and told them he had thought of divorcing all but four of them, and said they should choose the four women themselves, but none of his wives wanted to divorce him. As the wives of Prophet Muhammad (saw) were considered to be mothers of believers, it would not be possible for them to divorce him and marry someone else. This matter is clearly stated in the Qur'ân: *Nor is it right for you that ye should annoy Allah's Messenger (saw), or that ye should marry his widows after him at any time. Truly such a thing is in Allah's sight an enormity.* (Surah al-Ahzab, 33:53)

As it was not possible for Prophet Muhammad's (saw) wives to marry another and as they did not want to divorce their husband, Prophet Muhammad (saw) limited himself to marital relations with only four, (Sayyidah Â'ishah, Sayyidah Ummu Salama, Sayyidah Zainab bint Jahsh and Sayyidah Hafsa), while continuing the marriage in name to the others.[604] This matter is recorded in the Qur'ân as follows: *"Thou mayest defer (the turn of) any of them that thou pleasest, and thou mayest receive any thou pleasest: and there is no blame on thee if thou invite one whose (turn) thou hadst set aside. This were nigher to the cooling of their eyes, the prevention of their grief, and their satisfaction - that of all of them - with that which thou hast to give them: and Allah knows (all) that is in your hearts: and Allah is All- Knowing, Most Forbearing."* (Surah al-Ahzab, 33: 51)

In some sources it is stated that Prophet Muhammad (saw) also continued to have marital relations with the other wives and that this situation was possible and probably due to the phrase in the verse: *Thou mayest defer (the turn of) any of them that thou pleasest, and thou mayest receive any thou pleasest: and there is no blame on thee if thou invite one whose (turn) thou hadst set aside.»* (Surah al-Ahzab- 33: 51)*[605]

604. Rıza Savaş, Ibid., Asr-ı Saadette İslâm, v: I, page: 310.
605. see: Rıza Savaş, op.cit., Asr-ı Saadette İslâm, vol. I, p. 310.

If in reality this was the situation, then it was carried out with divine permission given to Prophet Muhammad (saw). If it was not this way, then among the ones he no longer carried out marital relations were the youngest wives, Sayyidah Safiyyah and Sayyidah Juwayriya. This is evidence that Prophet Muhammad's (saw) marriages were not motivated for physical reasons.

In connection with Prophet Muhammad's (saw) family life, I would like to focus on another verse from Surah Ahzab: *It is not lawful for thee (to marry more) women after this, nor to change them for (other) wives, even though their beauty attract thee, except any thy right hand should possess (as handmaidens): and Allah doth watch over all things.* (Surah al-Ahzab, 33: 52)

In this verse Prophet Muhammad (saw) is being addressed and in it he is forbidden from marrying any other women than those to whom he was already married, even if they attracted him. This verse is evidence demonstrating the divine origin of the Qur'ân, because no one would want to place such a rule limiting themselves while they were alive. We do not know what will happen in our lives, and Prophet Muhammad (saw) could not know if one of his wives would die or leave him. Even if his wives were to die, he would never be able to marry another woman. It would not be possible for him to marry another woman that might attract him with her beauty. Even if one of his wives were to divorce him, or if one were to die, he would not be able to take another. And this ruling, as a revelation, took its place in a book that would be read until the Day of Judgment. No person would want to put forward something that touched on such a personal subject. In the same way, no person would want to be limited, to tie their hands in such a way while still alive.

This verse also brings up the point that Prophet Muhammad (saw) had carried out all his marriages under divine observation and with divine permission. If this verse had been revealed while Sayyidah Khadîjah was still alive Prophet Muhammad (saw) would have been limited to one wife. Thus this shows that all of Prophet Muhammad's (saw) marriages were approved of: they took place with divine approval.

If Prophet Muhammad (saw) had the ability to interfere with the Qur'ân, then it is certain he would have changed this and similar verses that were directed against him and which affected his life. However, his duty was to communicate that which was revealed to him without changing or altering it in any way. In the Qur'ân it is stated:

*"(This is) a Message sent down from the Lord of the Worlds. And if the apostle were to invent any sayings in Our name, We should certainly seize him by his right hand, And We should certainly then cut off the artery of his heart: Nor could any of you withhold him (from Our wrath)."* (Surah al-Hâkka, 69: 43-47)

In connection with this matter, Mahmud Akkad can complete our discussion with this evaluation:

"To those non-believers who state: "That Prophet Muhammad (saw) was married to nine women at the same time is evidence of his overly active sexual desire" we say that it is necessary that you do not qualify Prophet Muhammad (saw) as one of great lust because he was married to nine wives; you do not qualify Prophet Jesus (as), who never married, as one with no sexual desire. Before all else, we can see no objection in a great person loving and enjoying being with women. This is a natural need and is not something to be ashamed of. The most basic feeling of our natural disposition is to mate, male and female together. This feeling is something shared by all living beings.

However, love changes the flow and is a means for crossing the limits and taking a person away from their duty, suggesting a whole number of meaningless things; it is a means for a change in our nature. As all characteristic traits are considered to be shameful when indulged to an excess, an excess in this is also shameful.

Just as Prophet Muhammad (saw) was not overwhelmed by emotions as a child, in his youth - in the Age of Ignorance - he did not see everything as permissible and did not follow the other young men in their lusts. In fact, he was renowned for his cleanliness, reliability, seriousness and solemnity. After the advent of Islam, those who did not like him and were carrying out propaganda against him, searching for his weakness, never said anything or accused him in any way about this. They never said: "Oh people!.. Look at this young man; until yesterday he was intimate with women, doing such things….and today he invites you to cleanliness, chastity and asks you to abandon lust."

Although he had numerous enemies, no one ever said such a thing about him. If it had been true, then thousands would have spoken of it.

Those who slandered him, creating propaganda about him have forgotten all the truths of his married life that have been described to us in great detail. They have only one thing they can say, changing the meaning and intention, to slander him: "Why did he marry more than one woman?"

However, they forget that he was pure and chaste in his youth, that in the Age of Ignorance he did not approach the pleasures and lusts that were considered legitimate and normal for young men.

They forget that he did not want to carry out a legal marriage until he was twenty-five and that it would have been just as easy for him to marry as for any attractive youth from a noble family.

They ignored that when he was twenty-five and it was time for him to marry he married a woman in her forties and remained married to her until he was in his fifties: he was content with one wife while married to Sayyidah Khadîjah (r.ah).

They did not consider that he married some of his wives to make peace with other tribes or to take them under his protection: desire was not a consideration.

This holy person, whom they qualify as a victim of lust and physicality, would go hungry for days, eating only a little barley bread. It should be taken into account that even though it would have been easy to have many possessions and to please his wives, unless for a serious matter, he never went beyond economy or acceptance of what was available.

They did not remember that the facts about the number of his wives are a matter of historical record. These are all examples of such non-believers consciously trying to stain the character of the Prophet (saw), to slander him and to ignore the truth. However, if they really wanted to search for the truth and inform us of it, or to remind us of it, it would be easier for them to see this than it is for them to ignore it.[606]

---

606. Abbas Mahmud Akkad, Abkariyyetü Muhammed, sh: 98 vd, narrated by Sâliha Akgül, Ibid., page: 241-243.

# PROPHET MUHAMMAD (saw) AS THE HEAD OF A FAMILY

*"There are (two things) which Allah has made pleasurable to me:: women and beautiful scent. Although praying is the lights of my eyes."*

(Nesâî, 28/1, 36/1; Ahmed bin Hanbel, III, 128, 285)

**He met his wives' needs, both spiritual and material, that were the result of marriage.** Prophet Muhammad (saw) allocated each wife her own room, provided their *mahr* completely and in an equal manner, and did not differ between them on the matter of clothing or food. Although he preferred to live a modest, even poor life, he was very generous in helping his family with what he could attain.

**He tried to do his own tasks himself, as much as possible.** He would mend his own clothes, cobble his own shoes and from time to time do his own housework to help his families. Anas bin Malik (ra), who remained with him for many years has the following to say on this matter: *"He would look after the family affairs; he would sew and mend clothes, milk the sheep, repair shoes, and take care of himself, feed the camels, never stay anywhere but in his own homes and prepare his own mount himself. He ate with his servants and made dough with them. He himself would carry what he bought from the market."*[607]

---

607.    İbn Seyyidunnâs, es-Sîratu'n-Nebeviyye, c: II, sh: 426; narrated by Celâl Yeniçeri, Ibid., page: 462.

**He set time aside for his wives, talked with them and joked with them.** Despite the busy tempo of his life, Prophet Muhammad (saw) would visit each wife once a day, ask about their needs, learn what they wanted and their thoughts and would set time aside to talk to each one. That he spent the first night of his marriage to Sayyidah Safiyyah talking with her about her family and her close Jewish relatives, trying to reassure her worries and consoling her is recorded in all the sources. Sometimes he would make jokes during these conversations, allowing the other side to respond in jest, and approving of their activities that were carried out according to their hearts or upbringing. According to Sayyidah Â'ishah, he watched folk dancing in the *masjid* with her and participated in a footrace with her.

**He would consult with his wives on some critical matters.** During the first revelation Prophet Muhammad (saw) turned to Sayyidah Khadîjah, during the *ifq* (slander) event he turned to Sayyidah Zainab binti Jahsh and Sayyidah Â'ishah's *jariya* Barira; during the Hudaybiyah treaty he consulted with Sayyidah Ummu Salama and acted in accordance with what they advised.

**He approved of his wives for their virtues and morals.** Prophet Muhammad (saw) would comfort or approve of his wives for their spiritual states, and he would tell them that he loved them to their faces.

**He gave importance to the family and relatives of his wives.** For example, Prophet Muhammad (saw) continued to host and show respect to the closest relatives of Sayyidah Khadîjah after her death.

**He would take permission from his wives to perform supererogatory prayers.** Prophet Muhammad (saw) would visit his wives in turn and try to be fair to them. During some nights, he would sk for permission from his wife to get up and pray; and would then continue this worship until morning.

**He would become angry with them for the sake of Allah and again, for the sake of Allah, he would make peace with them.** Like all people, Prophet Muhammad (saw) and his wives would from time to time experience unpleasant events. For example, Sayyidah Hafsa revealed a secret and he divorced her (*ric'i talaq*), but on Allah's order he returned to her. Again, when his wives demanded luxuries and comfort, like their equals, he remained distant from them for a month[608], but during this time he did not do anything that would upset them or hurt them. In the slander campaign (*ifq*) against Sayyidah Â'ishah, who represented his own chastity and honor, he investigated the situation and did not say anything hurtful to Sayyidah Â'ishah. This situation continued for a month and was finally resolved through a revelation.[609]

**He endured their problems and mistakes.** Sometimes they would make mistakes from jealousy and were unable to get along, but he put up with this, merely indicating where they were wrong, or sometimes educating them in a gentle way, such as, by remaining distant for a while.

**He took close interest in their every situation and showed great care in teaching them.** He taught the revealed verses to his wives first, and showed great care that they carried out what had been revealed in these verses in their lives.[610]

**He set aside time for their children, and was concerned with their troubles and problems.** Prophet Muhammad (saw) took great interest in children, be they his own children, his grandchildren or even children he met on the street. He listened to their problems, embraced those who had no families, stroked their heads, gave presents, quieted them when they cried, let them sit on his lap and showed them great affection.

---

608. Surah al-Ahzâb, 33: 28-33.
609. Surah an-Nûr, 24: 11-20.
610. See: Hz. Peygamber ve ile Hayatı, İSAV, İstanbul, 1989, page: 285-343; Asr-ı Saadette İslâm, v: I, page: 306-310; Celal Yeniçeri, Ibid., page: 460-468; Muhammed Hamidullâh, İslâm Peygamberi, v: II, page: 663-676; Afzalurrahman, Ibid, v: II, 121-150.

# SLAVERY AND CONCUBINAGE IN ISLAM

## The Term 'Slave'

Words used in Turkish in the past to denote a slave include *köle*, as well as *kul*, *bende*, *halayık* and *esir*, while a concubine was simply referred to as a *jâriye* or *odalık*.

In Persian, the terms *ghulam* and *kaniz* were used to refer to a slave and concubine, respectively.

As for Arabic, words like *abd*, *raqiq*, *mamluk*, *qinn*, *ghulam*, *raqaba*, *wasif* and *milku'l-yamin* were used to denote slaves, while *mamluka*, *wasifa*, *jariya*, *ama* and *ghurra* to refer to concubines.[611]

The abundance of words used in relation highlight the long history of slavery, as well as the effects of the distinctive characteristics of slaves in their identification.

## The History of Slavery

Slavery has had a longstanding history. Well-known is the fact that slaves were in vast numbers in Ancient Egypt and Near East.

---

611.  DIA, article of "Köle", XXVI, page: 237-248.

A number of reasons may be enumerated to explain the existence of slavery during this long and dark epoch of history:

-Prisoners of war,

-Children born from concubines,

-People abducted from neighboring tribes,

-Children sold as slaves by their own fathers or immediate and distant relatives,

-People demoted to the status of a slave due to an outstanding debt or a committed crime. They were all bought and sold in like manner and were consigned to live an inhumane life.

Slavery was prevalent in both Ancient Greece and Rome. According to the dominant theme of the times, slavery was regarded as one of the most elementary institutions of society, like the family or the state. Aristotle, for instance, believed that many races lacked the supremacy of spirit necessary to lead a life of freedom.

The Roman Law (Ius Gentium) ascribed no value to slaves. In the beginning, it even prohibited their emancipation. As marriage between slaves was forbidden, their non-marital, promiscuous affairs were generally overlooked. The slave was at the disposal of his master's unconditional control and pleasure. Emancipated slaves were a given a different social status than those who were born free.

Slavery was equally widespread in the Arabian Peninsula. In the *Jahiliya* Society, slaves formed an inferior social class, separated from the free by a decisive line. The slave was under the full ownership of his master, at his unconditional disposal. There were even cases where the master would force his concubine to prostitution and earn money at her expense. This was a moral corruption that clearly stemmed from not recognizing slaves as human beings. Wars were the main reason behind slavery among Arabs. A child born from a concubine was equally considered a concubine or a slave. Mecca was home to slaves of various ethnic backgrounds (like Bilal Habashi, Suhayb Rumi and Salman Farisi, just to name a few).

## Slavery in the Old and New Testaments

By recalling a few examples from the Old Testament regarding the notion and practice of slavery at the time, we may arrive at a better understanding of the emergence of slavery and how this corrupt system was perpetuated in society.

As punishment for a sin committed by his father Ham, one of the three sons of Nuh (as), Kanan is handed over to his uncles Sam and Yafas as a slave. (Genesis, 9/20-29)

Elsewhere, it is mentioned that it is possible for a person to sell himself as slave to close an outstanding debt. (Leviticus, 25/39)

A creditor may also stake a claim on the children of a deceased debtor, if the debtor dies before restoring his debt and given he has left no wealth to cover it. (II. Kings, 4/1-7)

It is likewise possible for a father to sell his own daughter. (Exodus, 21/7)

As explained in the story of Joseph (upon him peace), a thief caught in the act was made the slave of the person from whom he had stolen. (Genesis, 44/10; The Qur'ân, Yusuf 12: 75)

The 'distorted' Old Testament, among the oldest of the Celestial Books, provides no ruling on the emancipation of slaves. Only in one place is there mention of a Jew, who sells himself for his debts and becomes free after serving six years. (Exodus, 21/2-6)

A slave is similarly set free, if his master blinds him or breaks his tooth. (Exodus, 21/26)

Neither does the New Testament contain anything with regard to the emancipation of slaves. The Catholic Church and other denominations alike have looked upon slavery as fact of life, seeing no scruple in Christians taking people from their own religion as slaves.[612]

---

612.   DIA, the article of "Köle".

## Examples of Cruelty Endured by Slaves

The lifestyle and cruel ways of the *Jahiliya* Arabs suffices to show how debased people had become and how enormous a lift Islam provided them with. To impart a better understanding, we will recount some of those historical examples below, although we ask for your forgiveness in advance, as they are sure to leave some bleeding hearts in their wake:

"Before the entrustment of Prophet Muhammad (saw) with the Divine call, bar from a few Jewish and Christian tribes, the Arabs were a bunch of crude idolaters, following brutal and barbaric practices since times immemorial. Common was the sacrifice of one human being for the comfort of the other, the burial of a female child by her very own father, fearing she might one day dishonor his name. The case was the same with taking women captive at will. Polygamy was unconstrained. Men bedded however many women they wanted do and so did women, often in an unabashed manner. Unabated feelings of vengeance and greed came with their disastrous consequences in ceaseless wars, which saw women become subject to never before seen assaults and violations. The powerful person was always in the right. The courtyard of the Kaabah, the exclusive center of worship in the land, stood witness to many a human sacrifice. Such was the plight of Arabia before Prophet Muhammad (saw)."

As for wars and their consequences during the period, the following can be said:

"**War and Plunder**: Plunder was the source of Arab life. Arabia was a desert incapable of growing the crops its dwellers could survive on. The Arab population was, moreover, ignorant. Life depended on flocks of sheep, goats and camels, and their ownership was limited to a fortunate few. War and plunder therefore provided the inevitable means of survival. Ignorance and corruption had the desire for spoils entrenched in the Arab character.

Blood feuds were also endemic. If one was killed, his family or clansmen would seek vengeance from the killer. And if they could not get their hands on the killer, they would not turn back from taking vengeance; they would murder someone from his family instead. Tribal enmity and warfare was thus ceaseless.

**Prisoners of War**: People fallen captive in battle were dragged with a rope around their necks and then executed. Their wives and children would also suffer the same fate, many a time in the form of being burnt to death.

**Raiding and Massacring the Sleeping Enemy**: It was common for Arabs to launch sudden raids on the enemy while they slept at night and to indiscriminately put every one of them to the sword. Warriors with expertise in this lauded method of attacking the enemy would rise to fame.

**Burning People Alive**: Many were burnt to death. When his brother was killed by the rival Banu Tamim Tribe, Amr ibn Hind, a notable Arab chieftain, vowed to put to the sword a hundred persons from the tribe for every person involved in the death of his brother. Yet, as Banu Tamim was able to flee his wrath, the only person Ibn Hind could lay his hands on was a woman from their tribe. She was viciously burnt to death. Noticing afterwards a man walking around the site of execution, Amr asked him as to why he was loitering in the area. "I have not eaten anything for days. And when I saw some smoke coming from this way, I thought maybe I could find something to eat here", said the man. Amr also ordered his execution. The man was likewise thrown into the raging fire.

**Children Used as Targets for Archers**: Children were used as shooting targets. Once, during a battle between two rival tribes, the children of one tribe were taken as hostage by the other. They were subsequently taken to a valley and arrowed to death. The few children who were able to survive were taken to the same place the next day and killed the same way, as a crowd looked on as if they were watching a spectacle.

**Torturing the Person on Death Row**: Arabs would first chop off the hands and feet of a person on death row and afterwards leave him in that state until he died. Many a prisoner would strangle themselves to death in order to avoid this horrible end.

**Taking Vengeance from Corpses**: They would sever the hands, feet, ears and nose of corpses and hollow out their eyes. After the Battle of Uhud, Abu Sufyan shouted, "Today, we have avenged our loss at Badr. Our men have severed the noses and ears of your dead (Muslim martyrs)." The women were the ones who had done this. They had mutilated the bodies of Muslim martyrs to avenge the losses of their relatives fallen at Badr. Abu Sufyan's wife Hind even made necklace from these severed organs. It was again the same Hind who had ripped out Hamza's (Allah be well-pleased with him) liver in an attempt to eat it; but she could not swallow it.

**Making Goblet's from the Enemy's Skull**: There was a common vow among Arabs that if they ever got their hands on the enemy, they would drink wine out of his skull. Numerous examples of this can be cited in *"Tabaqat Ibn Asad"*.[613]

Such atrocities were considered the norm of warfare. Here, we have only touched upon a few examples from the *Jahiliya* Arabs. Unfortunately, however, the entire world at the time was consumed in a war of attrition, resorting to unthinkable means to snuff out their inveterate feelings of hatred for one another; letting nothing stand in their way from taking vengeance. It was in such an uncompromising time and place, utterly remote from humaneness, that Islam brought a law that set limits even in the affairs of warfare. Islam's law of warfare seized people by their hands, just as they were brewing inside with cruel intentions, consoled their hearts and distanced them from any kind of behavior and habit unbefitting of human dignity.

## Concessions Introduced by Islam to Slavery

Islam did not seek to destroy slavery, which is a globally prevalent and accepted institution, in one single blow, since warfare and the taking of captives from the losing side, the underlying reasons of slavery, were still continuing. For Islam to one-sidedly announce that it would not take prisoners during war, would not have been realistic or deterring. Instead, Islam introduced unprecedented difficulties with regards enslaving others, at the same time eased the path of their freedom by encouraging their emancipation. We will now look into this matter in greater detail.

---

613.   See: **Prof. Dr. A. Reşid Turnagil**, İslâmiyet ve Milletler Hukuku, İstanbul, 1993.

**1-Islam limited the enslavement of free persons.**

Slavery, according to Islam, is relevant only for prisoners of war. Free persons cannot, in any way, be enslaved. Not only may a person be not enslaved owing to an outstanding debt or committed sin, a child born from a "slave", likewise, cannot be regarded a "slave".

*Then why did not Islam ban the practice of taking prisoners of war?*

In a setting where two sides are locked in a battle of life and death, the survivors of the losing side are either doomed to mass execution or given a lifeline. During the *Jahiliya* period, prisoners were always executed in order to inflict the enemy with the greatest harm. This method, with which the victorious side seeks to appease their feelings of vengeance, has been repeated in different places throughout history, assuming various forms to survive even to this day. Islam, in contrast, has categorically prohibited the killing of prisoners of war.

Captives who are given a lifeline are either to be sent back to their homeland, carelessly, without made to pay a price for their transgression, or released in return for ransom (*fidya-i najat*) or an exchange of prisoners, or be made to remain in the custody of the victor as slaves.

Releasing prisoners of war free of charge would not serve as a deterrent against war. But some of the practices of the Prophet (saw) has set standards for such trouble-free release. The release of each prisoner of Badr in return for teaching ten Muslims how to read and write, and the freedom granted to the prisoners of Banu Mustaliq upon the Prophet's marriage to Sayyidah Juwayriya (r.ah) are noteworthy examples.

Yet, in line with the rationale of warfare, we can also find instances in the life of the Prophet (saw) where prisoners of war are either enslaved or released in return for ransom.

Releasing prisoners of war in return for ransom is dependent upon them having the financial means to cover the relevant cost. But what is to be done with the captive given he has no financial means and there are no prisoners on the other side with whom an exchange may take place? Is he to be killed, released or enslaved?

Killing the prisoner would satisfy feelings of vengeance; yet it has been banned by Islam. Releasing the prisoner free of charge is tantamount to reinforcing the strength of the enemy and providing them with the opportunity to strike back.

Enslavement, on the other hand, is the best outcome given the circumstances, to the degree the prisoner's well-being is guaranteed. Death is, by far, the worst. Most would readily choose a life of slavery over death. Even today, when slavery is seemingly nonexistent, the usual fate awaiting unreleased prisoners of war are extermination camps; the collective death centers.

With that being said, in Islam, there is no categorical clause that demands prisoners of war be enslaved. Depending on the circumstances, they may be released, either in return for ransom or for free.[614] Islam holds freedom to be the essential factor of human existence, not captivity.[615]

On the other hand, soldiers who fight knowing that they may take prisoners from the other side as 'spoils' would not attempt to take more lives than necessary, as doing so would mean reducing the amount of spoils to be acquired in the form of prisoners of war. And this means fewer casualties for both sides.

On another note, how would it have reflected on the non-Muslims had it been known that Muslims could not, in any way, take prisoners from the enemy and had to release them regardless? The other side would have then enslaved or killed the Muslim prisoners they captured and watched while Muslims released their own prisoners. Would a one-sided goodwill be enough to abolish slavery?

Due to these and other reasons alike, Islam did not abolish slavery outright but prepared the groundwork that would clear the way for its eventual abolishment.

### 2-Owning a slave became difficult.

One of the main incentives as to why Islam did not abolish slavery was to give slaves, living under Muslim custodianship, the opportunity to gain a closer

---

614. "...and afterwards either set them free as a favor or let them ransom (themselves) until the war terminates." (Surah Muhammad, 47:4)
615. DIA, the article of "Köle".

acquaintance with the beauties of Islam, the religion they had hitherto opposed with blind enmity. Fed from what their masters ate, clothed from what their masters wore and never given tasks that exceeded their powers, many slaves[616] responded to this humane treatment by inclining towards Islam and becoming Muslim. History presents us with numerous examples of such cases. In fact, a majority of scholars in the first period of Islam, who ended up giving exceptional service to the world of knowledge, were children of slaves who had become Muslim in the said manner.

Muhammad Hamidullah, who we have already quoted with regard to the issue[617], assesses the matter from another perspective:

"Insofar as Islam is concerned, slavery is neither a means of punishment, nor a revenue acquired from the spoils of war that is utilized towards certain financial ends. The incentive behind slavery is rather for it to act as a rehabilitation center to treat captives and the weak and mend their ways"[618]

### 3-It became easier for a slave to gain freedom.

The compensation of many sins, in Islam, is through the emancipation of slaves.[619] Other means of compensation come into play, only if the person has no slave to emancipate.

A course of action peculiar only to Islamic law, a certain amount of the state's budget is set aside for the emancipation of slaves.[620]

Similarly encouraged is the willful emancipation of slaves.[621] The Prophet (SAW) has, for instance, said:

*"Whosoever sets a slave free, Allah will set free an organ from hell-fire in return for every organ of the freed slave".*[622]

---


616. Bukhârî, Iman, 22, Muslim, Eymân, 29-42; Musnad, I, 78; IV, 35-36.
617. See: the artichle "Sayyidah bint Cahsh" in this book; Muhammed Hamidullah, İslam Peygamberi, v: II, page: 683.
618. Muhammed Hamidullah, İslam Peygamberi, v: II, page:691-692
619. See: Surah al-Mâidah, 5: 89; Surah al-Mujadalah, 58: 3.
620. See: Surah at-Taubah, 9: 60.
621. See: Surah al-Bakara, 2/177; Surah al-Balad, 91/11-13
622. Bukhârî, Keffâret, 6; Muslim, Itk, 23, Abû Dâvud, Itâk, 13; Tirmîdhî, Nuzûr, 14.

The Prophet (saw) fully practiced the principle he preached throughout his life, setting free many number of slaves; such that at the time of his passing away, he did not have even a single slave in his custody. At the end of a given battle, he would release the prisoners, either free of charge or in return for ransom. Half of the prisoners captured from the Tamim Tribe, for example, were released without charge, while the other half were released in return for ransom.[623]

The Prophet (saw) would similarly advise and even command many slave owners from among his Companions to set their slaves free. According to records of *hadith* and history, through a letter he sent to the ruler of Yemen, the Prophet (saw) mediated the instant emancipation of 4,000 slaves.[624]

Also encouraged by Islam is the procedure where the slave and the master agree on the price of release, towards which the slave works to acquire his freedom (*mukataba*).[625]

The price is determined in line with the standard value of release at the given time and the slave either works for his master or for somebody else to cover the cost of his freedom. If the slave demanding this mutual contract of release is a Muslim, the master is given no choice but to accept it. The court determines the price, if they are unable to agree on a price between themselves. Once the agreement is instated, it is binding; the master cannot pull out from the agreement. The agreement may be terminated, however, if the master and the slave come to a mutual agreement.

Incidentally, Islam gave slaves a legal status, on level par in most cases with the free, the consistent application of which in social life provided the slaves with humane living conditions en route to their eventual freedom. Exemplifying this, among others, is the encouragement of marriage between slaves and concubines[626], as well as the prohibition of their mistreatment, making their well-being[627] a religious and legal responsibility upon their custodians.

---

623.   Muhammed Hamidullah, Ibid., v: I, page: 391
624.   DIA, the article of "Köle".
625.   See: Surah an-Nûr, 4: 33.
626.   See: Surah al-Bakara, 2/221; Surah an-Nisâ, 4/25.
627.   ...be good to the parents and to the near of kin and the orphans and the needy and the neighbor of (your) kin and the alien neighbor, and the companion in a journey and the wayfarer and those whom

As the core of this approach, it is fitting now to quote the 25th verse of Chapter Nisa:

**"If any of you have not the means wherewith to wed free believing women, they may wed believing girls from among those whom your right hands possess: And Allah has full knowledge about your faith. You are one from another: Wed them with the leave of their owners, and give them their dowers, according to what is reasonable: They should be chaste, not lustful, nor taking paramours: when they are taken in wedlock, if they fall into shame, their punishment is half that for free women. This permission is for those among you who fear sin; but it is better for you that you practice self-restraint. And Allah is Oft-forgiving, Most Merciful."**

The Prophet (saw) gave the following advice to his Companions, who had slaves and concubines under their command:

*"Do not call them 'slaves' instead address them as 'sons' and 'daughters'. As the children of Adam, slaves, too, are your brothers. It is Allah who made it possible for them to serve you. Remember that Allah could have easily put you at their service instead. Therefore, treat them well. And think that the right and power Allah exercises over you is much greater than that you exercise over your slaves."*[628]

In Islamic Law, the slave is subject to the same legal status of his/her mother. A child born from a free father and a slave mother, is a slave, whose custodian is the mother's master. An exception to this is the child of a concubine (*umm walad*), who is fathered by the master. In this case, the child is free. A concubine who gives birth following the death of the master automatically qualifies for freedom.

A child born from parents who are both slaves is considered a slave, too.

A child born from a free mother and a slave father is free, according to the general rule. This stems from the fact that Islam prioritizes freedom and not slavery. Apart from the already pointed facts of prisoners of war and slavery

---

your right hands possess; surely Allah does not love him who is proud, boastful." (Surah an-Nisa, 4: 36)

628. Miftâhu Kunûzi's-Sunne.

by birth, determined foremost by maternal lineage, there is no such thing as 'enslavement' in Islamic Law.[629]

## The Law of Slave and Concubinage in Islam

1-A Muslim slave is no different to a free Muslim, in terms of fulfilling non-financial deeds of worship and religious obligations. Since the slave has no financial means, however, he is exempt from alms and pilgrimage. The master likewise provides the slave's charity of *fitr*. In terms of his essential duties and status, the slave is also exempt from attending Friday and *eid* prayers and from taking part in *jihad*. The way concubines cover themselves differs from free women.

2-In terms of being subject to ownership and legal proceedings, the slave is considered a property. The slave may be bought, sold, leased, given or be inherited. He may be the subject matter of individual or common ownership. With regard to the slave's license (*ahliya*), or in other words what he is considered authorized to do, Muslim schools of jurisprudence (*madhhab*) are of a varied opinion. According to the conventional opinion, however, the slave has a deficiency of *wujub*. As he has no right of ownership, he may not work towards wealth; what he earns belongs to his master. Liability of compensation for a given indiscretion toward the slave is, therefore, also paid to the master. With that said, a slave may, however, come under debts of certain kinds.

3-From the perspective of family law, the slave exercises a partial license. A slave, male or female, may wed only with the permission of the master, as it is he who covers the financial burdens that come with the marriage. Yet, the slave exercises a full license of divorce; he may divorce his wife without seeking the permission of his master.

4-The general principle concerning certain crimes that require official retribution (*hadd*) is for the slave to receive half the punishment a free person would receive in the same situation.[630]

---

629. DIA, the article of "Köle".
630. DIA, the article of "Köle".

5-The Holy Qur'ân recognizes slaves as human beings, enjoining their kind treatment.[631] The slave's cost of living is for the master to cover. Many *ahadith* advise against discriminating slaves from family members in this matter. Offenses against slaves, including rape, are categorically punished. A master, who has no intention of entering a marital relationship with a concubine (*istifrash*), must have her wed to a free man or a slave.[632] Marriage between free people and slaves or concubines has also been encouraged.[633]

"Insofar as Islam is concerned, the difference between the free and the slave is merely nominal, an upshot of a social condition. Indeed, when the dwellers of a town, besieged by the Muslim forces during the caliphate of Sayyidina Umar (ra), informed the soldiers that they had been given 'amnesty' right before they surrendered, it soon transpired that the 'amnesty' was given to them by a slave; yet it did not make a difference"[634]

### Concubinage in Islamic Law

In terms of legal content, there is no difference between a slave and a concubine; the difference is merely of gender. Both words are used to denote 'slavery' (*riqqiyya*).

Pejoratively taken, concubinage is understood as "a means of pleasure, whose sole duty consists in satisfying, on demand, the sexual appetite of her master." Let it be known straight off, that this is entirely incompatible with the definition of a concubine set forth by Islamic Law.

To elaborate, concubines, who are likewise prisoners of war, are classified under two groups:

**The First Group**: These are concubines who are under their masters' command, solely for the purpose of seeing to their daily chores. This is also referred

---

631. Surah an-Nisa, 4: 36. (See: Miftâhu Künûzi's-Sünne, the articles of "abîd" and "ıtk")
632. Surah an-Nûr, 24: 32.
633. Surah al-Baqarah, 2: 221; Surah an-Nisâ, 4: 25.
634. Mevlânâ Shiblî (Trs: Ömer Rıza Doğrul)- İslâm Tarihi, c: VII, İstanbul, 1928, page: 192; See: Kadir Mısıroğlu, İslâm Dünya Görüşü, 2008, page: 198.

to as ownership of interest (*mulk-u manfaa'*) or of slavery (*mulk-u raqaba*). The master may not engage in a sexual relationship with the concubine. Such concubines are no different from today's housekeepers; their relationship with their masters is strictly that of employer-employee. Despite being a concubine, she is sexually impermissible to her master. Besides, concubines of this sort are mostly married to men, who are slaves just like them. They come in the morning for work and return home in the evening.

**The Second Group**: These are concubines with whom their masters enter a marital relationship. The marital right between the master and the concubine, in Islamic Law, is called the right of *istifrash* or *tasarri*. Within legal guidelines and regulations, there are concubines classified under this title. In a sense, they are like legally wedded wives. A concubine of this sort is sexually impermissible to any other person than her partner. The male partner is obliged to treat her like a wife. The only difference between a marital relationship of this kind and a legal marriage is that the master may marry more than four concubines, given he does not legally marry the concubine. By contracting a legal marriage with the concubine, it is possible to promote her to the legal status of a wife. But marrying her before granting her freedom is not allowed.

The entire living expenses of a concubine of the said kind are for the master to cover. Such concubines are, therefore, a financial burden on the household; and only the rich can provide them with this means. A concubine under this status thus leads her life in a wealthy environment. Her obligation consists of not refusing her partner regarding a sexual need.

An emphasis needs to be made here; namely that both biologically and psychologically, men are different from women. For men, sexual relations are part of their essential needs (*hawaij-u asliya*), while it is not the same case with women.

A female prisoner of war may tend to resort to prostitution, if she has to, in order to cover her essential needs like food and shelter in the land in which she has fallen captive. This effectively means her becoming the part and parcel of all, damaging the integrity of both herself and of society. Yet, it is unthinkable for a woman, who obtains her essential needs like food and shelter by living with a wealthy family, to resort to prostitution to satisfy her unessential needs.

A woman, who, like in this case, remains in the safekeeping of a wealthy family, not only stands in no need of any other than the man she is with, she moreover leads a clean and virtuous life remote from their violations. Indeed, concubines considered living under such conditions a golden opportunity, as most of them could not find conditions of this sort even in their native lands. Now, what is to be preferred: a life of captivity open to all forms of cruel oppression and violation or a life of integrity in the midst of a virtuous family? There is no need to even answer this question.

There are thus certain principles that regulate entering a marital relationship with concubines. A man, for instance, cannot be in a relationship with two sisters at one time. Similarly, if a concubine in a marital relation sleeps with someone else, she is considered to have committed adultery and is punished accordingly. Should a concubine be sold to some other man, the man must wait a period of two menstruation cycles in order to acquire the right of *istifrash* and enter a marital relation with her. This is to make sure she is not pregnant with the child of her former partner.

If it turns out that the concubine is pregnant, the *umm walad* regulations come into effect. She will have acquired half her freedom once she gives birth to her master's child and her full freedom, once her master passes away. If she is not pregnant, however, she can then enter a marital relationship with the new man, after her waiting time is finished.

According to Hanafi jurists, a man cannot enter a marital relationship with a concubine with whom he has made a pact of *mukataba;* that is of emancipation. If he seeks *istifrash*, he must pay the required *mahr*, or dower.

## The Abolishment of Slavery

Slavery was headed towards abolishment by the end of the 18th century, in large part due to promising improvements in human rights and the establishment of the notion of ceaseless peace in international law. Also playing a significant hand in this development was the utilization of slaves as 'high-priced workforce' in the agricultural, industrial and social sectors following the Industrial Revolution.

Slavery was abolished in France with the French Revolution of 1789, with Great Britain following suit in 1807. It would be towards the latter stages of the 19th century, however, before it was brought to a complete end throughout Europe.

In the United States, slavery was abolished after the Civil War (1861-1864) with the victory of the Northern States. The right of freedom is included among the rights guaranteed by the Human Rights Treaties and the complementary protocols signed in 1950.

The earliest attempt towards abolishing slavery in the Ottoman State was in 1847, with the prohibition of slave markets in Istanbul. The Ottoman State was among the powers that signed the Brussels Conference Act of 1890 that put an end to black slave trade. The banning of white slave trade, on the other hand, that was taking place mainly through Caucasia, came in 1909.

In Iran, slavery was abolished with the constitution of 1906. Slavery was completely abolished in other Muslim countries by the first half of the 20th century.

It must finally be stated that Western orientalists, who condemn 'the reformed institution of slavery and concubinage in Islam', somehow find no trouble in persisting with the privileges of birth sustained in their own domain. Titles of 'nobility' like 'Lord' in England or 'Duke' 'Duchess' and 'Marquis' in France are acquired through birth, as is the case with the German title 'Von'. In similar vein, the caste system still persisting in today's India, whose population is now well in excess of a billion, continues to keep a firm grip on privileges of nobility acquired through birth.

Islam considers such privileges unacceptable. Just as a person of the highest social rank has stood shoulder to shoulder, for 1400 years, with the weakest in the presence of the Almighty during prayer, another falls prostrate behind the feet of another.

It was perhaps due to this that Bernard Shaw felt obliged to admit:

*"My nation is well ahead in democracy. Should it go any further, I fear it may become Muslim"*.[635]

---

635.   Kadir Mısıroğlu, İslam Dunya Görüşü, page: 200.

## Conclusion

As is evident, Islam uplifted slavery, a practice persisting due to a necessity entailed by the human condition, to a level befitting of human dignity, entrusting slaves to the custodianship of their masters. Responsible with seeing to all the requirements and living expenses of the slave, the master is obliged to look upon him as one of his own and cover what needs he may have.

Accommodated in a warm and tender home after an uncompromising war, slaves are thereby given the chance of gaining firsthand knowledge of Islam, the object of their hitherto prejudiced enmity. And impressed by the humane and just treatment they receive and the exemplary lifestyle they witness, they, more often than not, end up becoming Muslim. Thus through a blessing in disguise, they are saved from a life of waste, as they enter the climes of inner peace. What other aim could there be in life anyway?

Those who, scrolling through the painful and evocative pages of history, express their dismay at how human beings were once enslaved, have unfortunately accepted and have even become inured to the modern system of slavery. How can the living standards of laborers working under horrid conditions for a mere morsel to eat or women who sell their souls to prostitution just to stay alive be compared to slaves living under the hospitable shade of Islam? Let's assume for one moment that slavery, then, was the inevitable upshot of never-ending wars, in which the strong always crushed the weak. But what kind of war is being waged today that millions of people work for the comfort of a handful of magnates? Which is more benign: the slavery of yesteryears or the modern system of slavery today? We leave that answer to you.

| Name | Age at Marriage | Year | Age at Death | Year | Recited Hadith | Age of the Prophet at Marraige | Time Together years |
|---|---|---|---|---|---|---|---|
| 1-Khadijah bintü Huwaylid (widow) | 40 | 15 years before Prophethood | 65 | 10th year of Prophethood | - | 25 | 25 |
| 2-Sauda bintü Zem'a (widow) | 55 | 10th year of Prophethood | 72 | 22 years after Hijra | 5 | 50 | 14 |
| 3-Aisha bintü Abu bakr (virgin) | 9 | 1st year after Hijra | 66-67 | 57-58 years after Hijra | 2210 | 54 | 9 |
| 4-Hafsa bintü Umar (widow) | 21 | 3rd year after Hijra | 63 | 45 years after Hijra | 60 | 56 | 8 |
| 5-Zaynab bintü Hüzeyma (widow) | 30 | 4th year after Hijra | 30 | 4th year after Hijra | - | 56 | 3 months |
| 6-Ümmü Salama bintü Huzeyfa (widow) | 29 | 4th year after Hijra | 84 | 61 years after Hijra | 378 | 57 | 7 |
| 7-Zaynab bintü Cahsh (divorced) | 36 | 5th year after Hijra | 53 | 20 years after Hijra | 11 | 58 | 6 |
| 8-Juwariya bintü Hâris (widow, war captive) | 25 | 5th year after Hijra | 70 | 56 years after Hijra | 7 | 58 | 6 |
| 9-Safiyah bintü Huyey (widow, war captive) | 27 | 7th year after Hijra | 70 | 50 years after Hijra | 10 | 60 | 45 months |
| 10- Ümmü Habibah bintü Abu Süfyan (widow) | 33 | 7th year after Hijra | 70 | 44 years after Hijra | 65 | 60 | 4 |
| 11-Maymune bintü Hâris (widow) | 36 | 7th year after Hijra | 80 | 51 years after Hijra | 76 | 60 | 39 months |
| 12-Egyptian Maria (virgin, slave) | 20 | 7th year after Hijra | 30 | 16 years after Hijra | - | 60 | 4 |
| 13- Rayhan bintü Amr (slave) | - | 6th year after Hijra | - | 10 years after Hijra | - | 58 | 4 |

# REFERENCES

*"Kur'ân-ı Kerîm ve Açıklamalı Meali"*; **Heyet**, T. Diyânet V. Yayınları, Ankara, 2000.

**Afzalurrahman;** *"Hazret-i Muhammed (sav) Sîret Ansiklopedisi"*, İstanbul, 1996.

**Âyşe Abdurrahman;** *"Terâcimu Seyyidâti Beyti'n-Nübüvve"*, Kahire, tarihsiz.

**Âyşe Abdurrahman;** *"Hazret-i Muhammed'in Mübârek Zevceleri"*, Tercüme: Selâmi Münir Yurdatap, İstanbul, 1970.

**Akgül, Sâlihâ;** *"Saâdet Hânesinin Bahtiyar Gülleri Ezvâc-ı Tâhirât"*, İzmir, 2007.

**Akyüz, Vecdi;** (Editör) *"Asr-ı Saâdette İslâm"*, İstanbul, 1995.

**Atasoy, İhsan;** *"Rasûlullâh'ın Âile Hayatı, Neden Çok Evlendi?"*, İstanbul, 2007, 7. Baskı.

**Balcı, Ramazan;** *"En Sevgilinin Sevgilisi: Hazret-i Âişe Hayatı ve Şahsiyeti"*, İstanbul, 2005.

**DİA (Diyanet İslâm Ansiklopedisi);** Ankara, I-XXXII. ciltler.

**Cerrahoğlu, İsmail;** *"Tefsir Usûlü"*, Ankara, 1979, s: 71.

**Ergin, H. Kübra;** *"Hazret-i Muhammed'de Aşk"*, İstanbul, 2005.

**Erul, Bünyamin;** *"Hazret-i Âişe'nin Sahabe'ye Yönelttiği Eleştiriler"*, Kitabiyât, Ankara, 2002.

**Hâkim;** *"Müstedrek ale's-Sahihayn"*, Haydarâbâd, 1334-1342.

**Işık, Havva Ergene;** *"Hanım Sahabiler"*, İzmir, 2006, 5. Baskı.

**İbn-i Abdi'l-Ber;** *"el-İstiâb fî Esmâi'l-Ashâb"*, Mısır, 1939.

**İbn-i Esîr;** *"Usdu'l-Gâbe fî Mârifeti's-Sahabe"*, Mısır, 1280.

**İbn-i Hacer el-Askalânî;** *"el-İsâbe fî Temyizi's-Sahâbe"*, Mısır, 1939.

**İbn-i Hacer el-Askalânî;** *"Tehzîbu't-Tehzîb"*, Beyrut, Tarihsiz.

**İbn-i Hişam;** *"es-Sîretü'n-Nebeviyye"*, Kahire, Tarihsiz.

**İbn-i İshak;** *"Sîretu İbn-i İshak"*, Tahkîk: Muhammed Hamidullah, Konya, 1981.

**İbn-i Kesir;** *"el-Bidaye ve'n-Nihâye"*, Beyrut, 1985.

**İbn-i Sa'd;** *"et-Tabakâtu'l-Kübrâ"*, Beyrut, 1960.

**Kara, Hilâl-Kara, Abdullah;** *"Cennetle Müjdelenen Hanımlar"*, İstanbul, 2007.

**Kazıcı, Ziya;** *"Hazret-i Muhammed'in Âile Hayatı ve Eşleri"*, İstanbul, 2003, 4. Basım.

**Kazıcı, Ziya;** *"İslâm Müesseseleri Tarihi"*, İstanbul, 1991.

**Konrapa, M. Zekâî;** *"Peygamberimiz"*, İstanbul, 1987.

**Madni Abbâsî;** *"Hazret-i Peygamber'in (sav) Âile Hayatı"*, Tercüme: Ali Zengin, İstanbul, 2000.

**Mevlânâ Şiblî;** (Terc: Ömer Rıza Doğrul)- *İslâm Tarihi*, İstanbul, 1928.

**Mısıroğlu, Kadir;** *İslâm Dünya Görüşü*, 2008.

**Muhammed Hamidullah;** *"İslâm Peygamberi"*, Tercüme: Prof. Dr. Salih Tuğ, İstanbul, 1993.

**Savaş, Rıza;** *"Hazret-i Peygamber'in Âile Hayatı ve Evlilikleri"* adlı makale, *"Asr-ı Saâdette İslâm"*, İstanbul, 1995.

**Topbaş, O. Nûri;** *"Kur'ân-ı Kerîm Işığında Nebîler Silsilesi"*, (I-IV), İstanbul, 2004.

**Topbaş, O. Nûri;** *"Kur'ân-ı Kerîm Işığında Nebîler Silsilesi"*, (I-III), Genişletilmiş Baskı, İstanbul, 2006.

**Topbaş, O. Nûri;** *"Hazret-i Muhammed Mustafa (Mekke Devri)"*, İstanbul, 2005.

**Topbaş, O. Nûri;** *Hazret-i Muhammed Mustafa (Medîne Devri)"*, İstanbul, 2005.

**Turnagil, A. Reşid;** *İslâmiyet ve Milletler Hukuku*, İstanbul, 1993.

**Uraler, Aynur;** *"Peygamberimizin Hanımı Ümmü Habîbe ve Rivâyetleri"*, İstanbul, 1995.

**Vâkıdî;** *"Megâzî"*, Beyrut, 1989.

**Yazır, Elmalılı Muhammed Hamdi;** *"Hak Dini Kur'ân Dili"*, Eser Neşriyat, 1979.

**Yeniçeri, Celal;** *"Peygamber, Devlet Başkanı, Âile Reisi Hazret-i Muhammed ve Yaşadığı Hayat"*, İstanbul, 2000.

**Zehebî;** *"Siyeru A'lâmi'n-Nübelâ"*, Beyrut, 1985.

# CONTENTS



## -I-

## THE MOTHERS OF THE BELİEVERS

## -II-

### APPENDİX